Inside Notting Hill

Published in May 2001 by Portobello Publishing,
in association with Pallas Athene,
13 Blenheim Crescent, London W11 2EE

Editorial

Supplementary listings and boxes by Jessica Morris and Annabel Hendry

Further supplementary listings by Caroline Bretherton, Andrew Baldwin,
Annabel Hendry and Fernanda Hanson (Restaurants); Leigh Diamond (Fashion);
Katrina Phillips (Antiques); Peter Ridley (Music); Polly Thomas (Clubbing)

Pictures

Inside: 1 from Old and New London; 2, 3, 4, 5 & 6 illustrations and photos courtesy of Royal Borough Kensington & Chelsea; 7, 8, 9, 11 & 12 photos © Charlie Phillips; 10 photo courtesy of Notting Hill Methodist Church; 13, 21, 25, 26, 27 photos © Chris Wade-Evans; 14 photo by Keith Morris © Redferns; 15 & 19 photos courtesy of Wilf Walker; 16, 17, 18 & 22 photos © Michael Woods; 20 & 24 photos © Peter Ridley; 23 photo © Charlie Murphy; 28 photo © Joelle Pineau

Cover photo: Sarah Anderson, from an original idea by Joelle Pineau

Back cover photos: Sarah Anderson: Travel Bookshop
and the Coronet; Michael Reed: Carnival

Production

Production managed by Sandie Steward

Copy editing by Sophie Pither

Cover design by Jamie Keenan

Design and typesetting by positivesite.com

Printed in the UK by Mackays of Chatham

Distributed by Portfolio

Available from www.umbrellabooks.com

A catalogue record for this book is available from the British Library.

ISBN 1 873429 41 X

Inside

Notting Hill

Richard
Enjoy the book
you were bamboozled
into buying me a
pub lunch! Love

Miranda Davies and Sarah Anderson
with Annabel Hendry

Sarah
12.05.01

Portobello Publishing
London
2001

Contents

Part 2
HISTORY

Part 3
WRITINGS 1767–2000

Acknowledgements

The making of this book has relied on the good will and support of many different people. Among those who so kindly shared their knowledge, contacts and Notting Hill stories, special thanks go to: Eddie Adams, Richard Adams, Elisabeth Anderson, James Anderson, Clarice Armatrading, Hilary Arnold, Liz Bartlett, Philip Black, Roddy Bloomfield, Roifield Brown, Kevin Brownlow, Henry Clive, Mark Ellingham, Andrew Fergusson-Cuninghame, Iain Finlayson, Paul Fogelman, Marinella Franks, Alexander Fyjis-Walker, Mary Gaine, Simon Gaul, Mark Girouard, Gertrude Goode, Marianne Harper, Andrew and Margaret Hewson, Roy Holland, Roger Hudson, Angus Hyland, Natania Jansz, Marie Jelley, Jane John, Anthony Juckes, Carol Kane, Linda Kelly, Isabel Kenrick, Father Mark Langham, Clare Manassei, John Michell, Michael Moorcock, Colin Prescod, Michael Reed, Jean Ross-Russell, Julian Rothenstein, David Salisbury, Lyndy Saville, John Scott, Shaila Shah, Glynn Snow, David Solomon, David Stern, Susie Symes, Henry Vivian-Neal, Wilf Walker and Robert Winder.

Further thanks are due to Bridget Davies, for sharing her long experience of local community politics and applying her meticulous eye to the manuscript in progress; and to Tom Vague who commented on each chapter, as well as generously contributing his remarkably detailed knowledge of the area. (His own witty and original commentaries on Notting Hill's history are strongly recommended.) Thanks also as always to the Travel Bookshop and to the helpful staff of the London Library and Kensington & Chelsea Libraries, especially Richard Marshall in the Kensington Local Studies section and those working at the Ladbroke Grove and Pembridge Road branches.

Compiling and writing listings was an enormous task. Among those credited, particular thanks are due to Jessica Morris for her energy and willingness to take on more and more as the deadline approached and gaps still needed to be filled. Both Jessica and Katrina Phillips drew on their family experiences of the local antiques trade. Listings were further enhanced by the personal enthusiasms of Caroline Bretherton, a committed foodie responsible for some of our most evocative restaurant reviews, and musician Peter Ridley who spent hours visiting every music shop, as well as taking pictures and supporting the book in many other ways.

Finally, a huge thank you to Annabel Hendry who has not only contributed an excellent history and written with equal authority on several of Notting Hill's churches, but also provided support, humour and a much needed critical eye all along the way; and a big hug to Ella and Lucia who suffered their mother's obsession with this project over many months. We hope it was worth it.

About the authors

Miranda Davies is an editor, writer and author of many anthologies including three volumes of *Women Travel* for the Rough Guides (with Natania Jansz). She has lived in Notting Hill since 1973.

Sarah Anderson is the founder of the Travel Bookshop which she started in 1979 and moved to Notting Hill in 1981. She has lived and worked in the area ever since.

Foreword

Notting Hill is a special place, both to those lucky enough to live here and to the thousands of visitors who flock to the market or Carnival, or who come simply to hang out in one of the many bars and restaurants that have multiplied in recent years.

Much of the neighbourhood's attraction lies in its bohemian past, from the Fifties' era of steamy coffee bars and clubs, through to the crazy, creative spirit and energy of the Sixties and Seventies when many writers, musicians and artists made this their home. But it has taken the extraordinary success of the film *Notting Hill* to launch the area onto the world stage. It is almost two years since the film made local history by being shown simultaneously at two neighbouring independent cinemas. Today there are few shopkeepers, market stallholders or even residents who haven't been asked at one time or another for the location of the Blue Door.

A guide was clearly needed – a practical yet evocative book as much about people as places. The result is a detailed tour of Notting Hill, a fusion of history and writings, supported by practical information, that delves beneath the hype to reveal the extraordinarily rich diversity of our 'elusive district'. In many ways this has been dream project, close to our hearts and endlessly illuminating. We hope you enjoy it too.

Miranda Davies and **Sarah Anderson**
March 2001

St John's Church, Stephen Wiltshire

Part 1

THE GUIDE

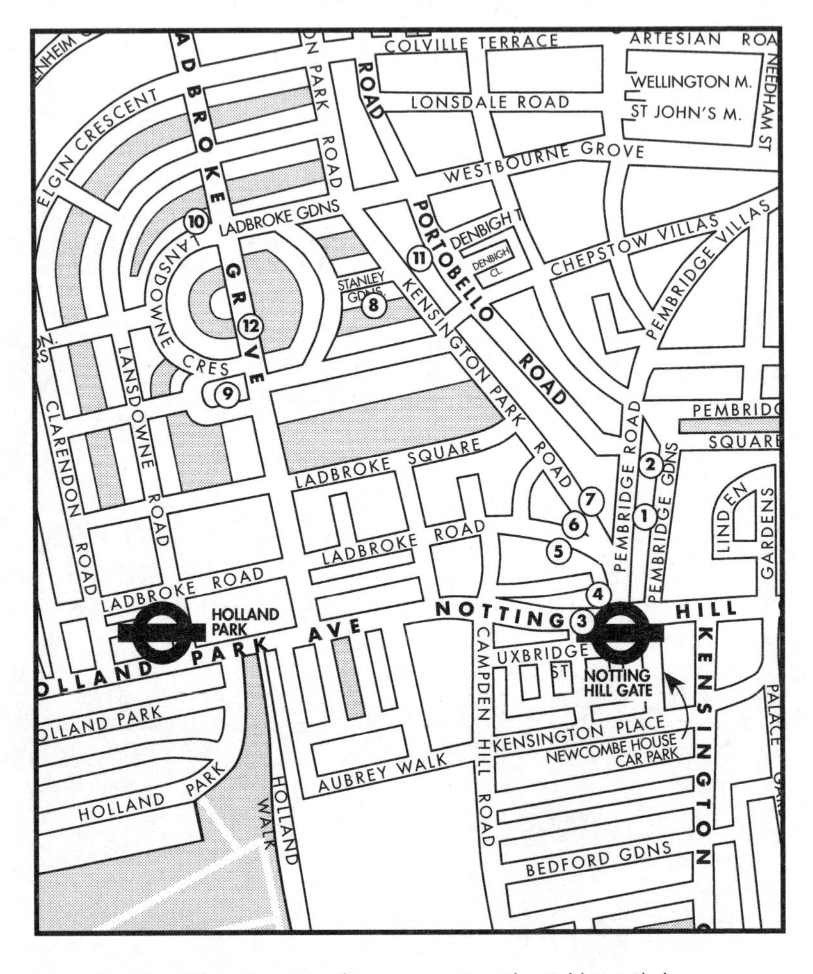

1 The Abbey Court Hotel
2 The Pembridge Court Hotel
3 The Coronet Cinema
4 The Gate Theatre
5 The Mercury Theatre
6 Kensington Temple
7 The Cabbies' Shelter
8 The Portobello Hotel
9 St John's Church
10 The Samarkand Hotel
11 St Peter's Church
12 The Pushkin Club

1. Notting Hill Gate

The appeal of Notting Hill Gate is not immediately obvious. Much of this once quaint Victorian high street was destroyed and redeveloped in the late 1950s to early 60s and, despite a few recent improvements, the immediate impression remains that of a busy thoroughfare, choked with traffic and bordered by featureless concrete. Apart from a couple of independent cinemas and the seemingly enduring curiosity of the Pharmacy Bar & Restaurant, most of the attractions lie in the streets on either side – to the south, among the small, multi-coloured houses of Hillgate Village, bordered by Kensington Church Street and Campden Hill Road, and north along Pembridge and Kensington Park Roads, two of the main routes into the heart of Notting Hill.

Origins of Notting Hill Gate

'The Gate' has long been an important thoroughfare, from Roman times when it formed part of the Great West Road running from London to Silchester (near Basingstoke in Hampshire), through to the eighteenth century when the allure of its proximity to Kensington Palace was boosted by the spread of roadside inns. Even in these early days, the tone of the area was not all gentility and the road was a notorious target for aggressive highway robberies, as well as thefts from the gardens, orchards and poultry-yards of the still rural Notting Hill.

It was attempts to control highway theft through the Turnpike Acts of 1769 that gave the Gate its name. The idea was for tolls to be issued to road users, controlled by tollgates, with the funds vested in trustees made responsible for lighting, protection and upkeep. One of three such gates was located at the junction that now marks the exit from the underground station. The tollgates were never popular, provoking decades of public protest and campaigns that finally put an end to the system in 1864 – a foretaste of the kind of hard-fought community action for which the area is still renowned.

In and around Hillgate Village

Hillgate Village has two pretty pubs, both miraculously festooned with flowers all year round, and some good, reasonably priced restaurants. Otherwise, apart from the odd media office and a French boutique, Antoine et Lili, this network of pretty flat-fronted terraced houses is strictly residential. Teresa Waugh supplies a good description in her novel, *The Gossips:*

> *Annie's house, tucked away in Hillgate Village, behind Notting Hill tube station, was in a quiet street of brightly painted, early*

nineteenth-century workmen's cottages, a bit jerry-built, but somehow resistant to the passage of time despite insidious rising damp and somewhat insecure foundations. Sometimes, when she walked down her street, it reminded her of nothing so much as the set for a musical comedy. Whenever a house changed hands, it was always a matter of concern what colour the newcomers would paint it. There were a few nasty years when number fourteen, on which Annie looked out, was painted a hideous shade of purple, but it had lately been changed to a more tasteful mushroom with an olive-green door. Annie's house was always painted grey and her door was always white, but, whilst never wishing to choose them herself, she rejoiced in the cheerful blues and pinks and yellows of her neighbours.

Hillgate Village is also the home of Fox, one of the best and certainly the grooviest primary school in West London. If you're around on the third Saturday in June, it's worth visiting Fox for its annual summer fair where, in recent years, games stalls, bric à brac and a superior auction have been joined by a mouth-watering barbecue by local chefs Alastair Little and Rowley Leigh. Leigh's inspired dishes lie behind the long-lasting success of Kensington Place, just around the corner in Kensington Church Street. Leading out of Notting Hill, the top end of Church Street has more recommended restaurants, plus a scattering of specialist antique shops, a few of which, like the art nouveau dealer John Jesse, have been here since the Sixties. In Newcombe House car park, at the back of Kensington Place restaurant, there is also a Saturday market where farmers from various parts of the country sell an impressive range of produce at very reasonable prices.

Along the Gate

Facing west outside the underground station, two very different cinemas, The Gate and the Notting Hill Coronet, offer a choice between arthouse films and more mainstream productions. Only once have their programmes coincided – in May 1999 – when both featured *Notting Hill*. Being the location where Hugh Grant gazes wistfully at Julia Roberts on screen, the Coronet clearly won hands down. With its silver dome and wedding-cake façade, this former music hall theatre stands as a delightfully frivolous antidote to the unremarkable buildings all around. It also has an intriguing history (see p 3).

Between the cinemas, in among the rash of estate agents, the window of No.99, a shop front, gallery and information point dedicated to the activities of the Notting Hill Improvements Group (NHIG), commands increasing attention. Not everyone supports the Group's current aim to raise more than £3 million for a wackily ambitious public arts project to improve the dreariness of the Gate.

Many locals feel the money would be better spent on more socially useful schemes, but the planting of trees and central reservation flowerbeds, widespread repaving and the installation of benches and cycle racks in the last decade have all been well received. So too has the recent transformation of a dingy office block on the south side through the inspired addition of two strips of brightly painted panels. It really works. Barney McMahon's Technicolor mural over the road, alongside the alley just east of Pharmacy, was also commissioned and funded by the NHIG.

Notting Hill Coronet

A Grade II-listed building, the Coronet was originally built as an opera house in 1898 to a design by WGR Sprague for the theatre impresario Edward George Sanders. Inside, the theatre boasted six gilt boxes upholstered in red plush, seating for 1,100 and a 'crush bar' where the foyer is today. Of its initial splendour only the distinctive dome and the ornate auditorium of Screen One, with its huge proscenium arch, curved balcony and red velvet seats, remain. During the 18 years or so before it was converted into a cinema, many stars graced the stage, among them Henry Irving, Sarah Bernhardt, Lily Langtry and Mrs Patrick Campbell.

Less well known from that time is the theatre's resident ghost, as described in Richard Jones' *Walking Haunted London:*

> *One Christmas in the early 1900s a cashier was caught stealing from the till and, confronted by the manager, ran up to the Gods and threw herself from the balcony. Thereafter, when staff meetings were held in the upper section of the cinema her ghost caused so much disturbance that such meetings were transferred to offices lower down in the building. Footsteps have often been heard climbing the stairs that lead to the Gods, and on one occasion pots of paint were moved by an unseen hand from a room that was awaiting decoration. Staff have more or less come to accept the inconvenience that their resident spectre causes. The ghost is most active in Christmas week, the anniversary of the cashier's suicide.*

The cinema has come under threat from far more powerful sources on several occasions, including an ominous bid from McDonald's, but happily its future now seems secure.

The Notting Hill Improvements Group

For the last eight years the Notting Hill Improvements Group, formed by the sponsors of the award-winning 'Turquoise Island' (see p 103), has been campaigning to 'Green the Gate'. Numerous improvements, from new litter bins and pedestrian railings to tree planting and the building of a 'Haiku' sculpture garden (on the corner of the Czech Embassy at No.25 Kensington Palace Gardens), have already been achieved but there are far more adventurous schemes afoot. Dedicated as much to public art as to greening the environment, the NHIG is currently working with an international team of artists and designers on a series of constructions which, if approved, will dramatically transform the urban landscape of the Gate. Among the proposals so far are a clock tower, a series of giant skyline sculptures, two solar-powered neon haloes (at the intersections of Pembridge Road and Kensington Park Road) and further colour schemes for the drab Sixties' façades, one of which (above Boots) will become the capital's first hairy building, accomplished by planting the walls with thousands of fibre optic cables, which will glow and quiver like a 'vertical meadow'. Backed by, among others, the Arts Council of England and the Royal Borough of Kensington & Chelsea, all these plans are at the consultation stage only and local opinion, and of course support, is always welcome. For up-to-date information, visit the project's website at www.nhig.co.uk

Directly facing Pharmacy is the junction with Campden Hill Road, popular with drivers for its quick access to Kensington High Street. It's hard to imagine, but Campden Hill was once the site of a reservoir, as well as the grey brick water tower famously championed by the writer GK Chesterton in *The Napoleon of Notting Hill* (see p 186). The reservoir was covered over to become tennis courts, still very much in use, but to the anguish of conservationists obsolescence led to the tower's demolition in 1970. Thirty years on, the Campden Hill Residents' Association has recently lost another battle, this time against the proposed building of 19 houses and 48 apartments by property company St James Homes. In addition to the loss of trees and open space, this has entailed the destruction of the Victorian pumping station, the Water Tower House and part of the old tennis club. After a five-year dispute the development started in 2001.

Heading back east, the opposite north side of Notting Hill Gate takes you past the concrete high-rise of Campden Hill Towers (soon due for redecoration) and across Pembridge Road to Pembridge Gardens, home of two good hotels. The next block is the only terrace to have escaped Sixties' redevelopment and leads to the entrance into Linden Gardens, once protected from the unruly high street by ornamental gates. Known in Victorian times as Linden Grove, this oval-shaped cul-de-sac stands on one of the first of James Ladbroke's plots ever to be built upon (see History, pp 166–68). The largest of these early two-storey houses was Linden Lodge, designed in 1826 by Thomas Allason who also lived there for a time. Contemporary records describe the house as having two acres of gardens, including a lake, stables and a gardener's cottage, all of which were demolished within less than 50 years for the making of the railway. Other prominent residents of Linden Gardens were the artist Thomas Creswick and William Mulready, who designed the first penny postage envelope depicting Britannia, and Ossie Clark, one of the most influential fashion designers of the 1960s and 70s.

After the turning into Linden Gardens, the old high street quickly becomes the Bayswater Road, leaving Notting Hill to skirt Kensington Gardens and its latest children's attraction – the Princess of Wales Memorial Playground (see Listings, p 19).

The Gate Theatre

As you climb the narrow stairs up to the box office you could be forgiven for thinking that the Gate Theatre is just another down-at-heel fringe venue, like so many in London, but this chamber theatre has become a springboard for many talented actors, writers and directors. Since starting up in 1979, it has managed to achieve widespread artistic recognition (winning a sheaf of industry awards along the way) and a growing, loyal audience for its productions of classical and contemporary work from abroad. It has helped to discover or revive interest in many major foreign dramatists, including Botho Strauss, Euripides, Goldoni and Strindberg, and 35 of the 50 new translations commissioned since 1990 have been published by Absolute Classics and Methuen. With little or no public funding (for a donation of £20 you can join the Gate 2000 scheme, and have your photograph in their hall of fame), the theatre is run by a tiny permanent staff on nominal wages, plus a team of volunteers, all of whom are young, friendly and full of enthusiasm for their work. Often they'll stay on to help facilitate post-show discussions where members of the audience can meet the artists, either in the auditorium or the Prince Albert pub downstairs. In London, where you can easily pay a small fortune to see mediocre productions (despite sometimes global acclaim), the Gate is a gem.

Kensington Park Road

Back at the underground station, turning north, near the site of the old tollgate and the courageously innovative Gate Theatre, Pembridge Road forks, offering alternative paths into the hub of Notting Hill. Tourists tend to be drawn to the right, down the cramped commercial strip of Pembridge Road which leads directly to the top of Portobello. Since the market doesn't start till further down (near the crossroads with Chepstow Villas) it pays to follow the wide and far more peaceful Kensington Park Road, with its two immediate landmarks: Kensington Temple and the green cabbies' shelter. A more distinguished site is the Mercury Theatre, just around the corner in Ladbroke Road. Having started life in 1851 as a Congregational Sunday School, the building was transformed into a theatre in 1931 by the playwright Ashley Dukes, husband of Marie Rambert. Within five years Dukes had gained national recognition for the Mercury by staging the first ever production of TS Eliot's *Murder in the Cathedral*. Around this time it also became the headquarters of Marie Rambert's School of Russian Dancing, precursor to the world famous Ballet Rambert. It was here that Madame Rambert ran her Ballet Club company, showcased in a series of Sunday evening performances that featured such budding stars as Robert Helpmann and Frederick Ashton. No longer a theatre, the building retains a ballet connection as the premises used by the West London School of Dance.

Kensington Temple

This hugely popular evangelical church on the corner of Kensington Park Road was built in 1846 as an Independent Presbyterian Chapel with an adjoining Sunday School, which later became the Mercury Theatre. Originally Horbury Chapel, it was renamed the Kensington Temple (KT to its contemporary followers) in 1935 when it was used by George Jeffreys, founder of the Elim Pentecostal movement, which now boasts 400 churches throughout the UK. The current minister, Colin Dye, draws a packed international congregation every Sunday, with a live TV link nearby to cater for the overflow at the 11 o'clock service. In an era when less than nine per cent of London's six million population attends church of any kind this has to be quite an achievement.

The Cabbies' Shelter

In the middle of Kensington Park Road, level with the Temple, stands a bright green hut serving tea and sandwiches to taxi drivers from the adjoining rank. This is one of London's last remaining 'cabbies' shelters' still in use. As described in Andrew Duncan's *Walking London*, the origin of these 'refreshment rooms' for cab drivers dates back to 1874 when Captain George Armstrong, Managing Editor of the *Globe* newspaper, was looking for a hansom cab in bad weather. On reaching the stand, he found plenty of vehicles but not a driver in sight. He was determined to get a ride and eventually tracked the men down in a nearby pub where they were enjoying a drink out of the way of the weather. Convinced that they'd be better off hiding from the elements in a less tempting environment – many cabbies were notorious drunkards – Armstrong came up with the idea of building special shelters, complete with tables, benches and cooking facilities, so that they could take a break and enjoy reasonably priced refreshment protected from the influences of alcohol. By the following year, the Cabmen's Shelter Fund had been formed and, by 1914, 61 shelters had been built. The hut in the middle of Kensington Park Road is one of only 13 left, five of which can be found in Kensington and Chelsea. It was restored in 1988.

Running parallel to Portobello (which you can join at several points), Kensington Park Road soon takes you alongside Ladbroke Square. Covering seven acres, this is the largest of Notting Hill's communal gardens and, like all of them, officially open only to resident key-holders who pay an annual fee for the privilege.

After crossing Chepstow Villas the road slopes downhill, past St Peter's Church which stands opposite the turning for Stanley Gardens. White and cream stucco mansions line this elegant street which has the added cachet of housing the Portobello Hotel, discreetly situated halfway down on the left. The hotel has always been associated with musicians, models and film stars, from Mick Jagger to Kate Moss and Johnny Depp. Less is known about its appeal to literary figures, such as the late Jean Rhys who enjoyed several winter holidays here towards the end of her life. Diana Athill, her editor and friend, recalls visiting Rhys at the Portobello which, she soon realised, provided a lively antidote to the writer's bungalow home in a sleepy West Country village:

> *The first time I visited Jean there I was greeted at the reception desk by a faun-like being in a pink T-shirt trimmed with swansdown which had little zipped slits over each breast, both of them unzipped so that his nipples peeped out. This seemed such a far cry from Cheriton Fitzpaine that I wondered whether Jean, much as she longed for a change, would find it upsetting; but she loved it, was fussed over charmingly by both the manageress and the saucy faun, and would have been happy to spend the rest of her days at the Portobello.* (Diana Athill, *Stet*)

Continuing downhill, Kensington Park Road leads to the intersection with Westbourne Grove. Even if you can't afford the prices – or if you miss the raucous cry of parrots outside L'Artiste Assoiffé, the charmingly eccentric restaurant which occupied this site for nearly 30 years – it's worth entering Paul Smith's corner emporium for the impeccable style of everything, from natty tailored suits to clockwork toys and other hand-picked curios, not to mention the beautifully restored interior. Further on down, past a line of elegant villas painted various shades of murky green, and you arrive at the nucleus of restaurants and shops which, along with greedy landlords and the rise of Westbourne Grove, have been a key factor in Notting Hill's recent history.

If eating and shopping aren't immediate priorities, instead of heading down to the crossing with Westbourne Grove, a left turn at Chepstow Villas will take you along the lofty residential splendour of Kensington Park Gardens. The scientist Sir William Crookes (1832–1919) lived at No.7, which may be why it was the first London house ever to receive electricity. Around the same period, the real-life 'Darling' family, immortalised in JM Barrie's *Peter Pan*, occupied No.31. They were actually Arthur and Sylvia Llewelyn Davies, and their five sons, Sylvia's brother being Gerald du Maurier, the original Captain Hook and father of writer Daphne.

Ladbroke Grove south

Kensington Park Gardens leads to the upmarket end of Ladbroke Grove and St John's Church on the brow of the hill. Erected in 1845, on a site which once offered a grandstand view of the Hippodrome Racecourse, this was the first Kensington church to be built north of Holland Park Avenue, and now shares its parish with the less gloomy looking St Peter's in Kensington Park Road.

The Hippodrome Racecourse

During the building slump of the late 1820s and 30s (see History, p 168) a developer by the name of John Whyte attempted to establish a huge Hippodrome racecourse on the crown of Notting Hill. Reminiscent of this century's Millennium Dome at Greenwich, the project stands out as one of the most spectacular failures in the history of development in Notting Hill. It also provides an early example of just how effective community action can be.

Bounded by Portobello Lane to the east and on the west side by the 'public way' from Notting Barns, the racecourse covered nearly 200 acres with an entrance at Notting Hill Gate. As well as three courses, this vast racing emporium was to provide all manner of recreational activities: a saddling paddock for 75 horses; training and riding facilities; ponies and donkeys for the use of children and invalids; and provisions for 'revels and amusements', including archery and cricket on non-racing days. There was local opposition to the enterprise from the start. The opening of the Hippodrome in 1837 was marred by a huge invasion of protesting locals, boosted by a healthy injection of spirited support from the Potteries.

Local feeling ran very high because the racecourse closed off a footpath which crossed the hill from north to south. For decades this path had been used by local inhabitants anxious to bypass Pottery Lane (long nicknamed 'cut-throat lane'), which intersected the Potteries of Notting Dale. The racecourse was replanned and the contentious footpath reopened, but to no avail: the track was on heavy clay and the jockeys hated it. Riff-raff continued to lower the tone; as Barbara Denny puts it in her excellent study, *Notting Hill and Holland Park Past*, 'a growth of sleazy betting booths and gin shops added to the deterioration'. The course never caught the imagination of the racing public. It failed, and closed in 1842.

The Church of St John the Evangelist

St John's was the first church to be built north of the Uxbridge (now Bayswater) Road and remains a centrepiece of the Ladbroke Estate. Constructed of ragstone in the 'Early English Gothic' style, it is a typical example of Anglican architecture of the latter half of the nineteenth century. Its grand scale attracted criticism and even *The Ecclesiologist* thought it looked too much like a cathedral. The architects John Hargrave Stevens and George Alexander designed a basic cruciform shape with a central tower and broach spire, the top 26 feet of which was rebuilt in 1957 after damage during the Second World War. No interesting stained glass remains apart from Kempe windows at the east end, and a little rose window in the west gable and small panel in the south aisle, both by Warrington. Added in 1890, the panelling, reredos and sedillia are of terracotta in a hard, neo-Perpendicular style. Art-nouveau influenced sculptures of the Crucifixion are by Emmeline Halse as, possibly, are standing angels on either side of the reredos.

St John's has an active congregation that organises several popular events, among them a delightful carol service for children just before Christmas, and the May Fayre, a fundraising event that draws people from all over the area.

The Church of St Peter

St Peter's shares a parish with St John's. It was designed by Thomas Allom, the architect responsible for many of Notting Hill's large Italianate houses, and is notable as one of very few Church of England churches to be built in the classical style in London after 1837. St Peter's is the focal point for the view looking east down Stanley Gardens, and the classical design is in harmony with Allom's overall scheme for the estate. The stucco façade has a pediment and entablature on six Corinthian columns, and the central square clock-tower is topped by an octagonal copper-roofed belfry. In a description of 1872 the interior was said to have been 'worked out in Pompeian red', which might have infused some life into what is now a rather leaden picture. The only decorative elements to relieve your eye from the stern classicism are the gallery fronts with their floral swags, winged putti and panels containing the Keys of St Peter. There are also decorative rosettes on the plaster ceilings which were rebuilt in a series of framed panels in 1951. Still on the Italianate theme, the apse has a rather crude mosaic version of Leonardo da Vinci's Last Supper executed in 1880. The marble altar in the sixteenth-century Florentine manner and the marble dado behind it were carved in Italy. The 1889 pulpit is of alabaster and marble, and the font has bronze acanthus-leaf rings.

St Peter's was consecrated on 7 January 1857 and assigned a district chapelry in the same year, but its most interesting history is far more recent. The merger with St John's didn't take place until 1983, by which time St Peter's – always something of a 'poor relation' of the 'higher' church – had been virtually abandoned by its congregation and the building left to deteriorate. It took the inspiration of one curate, Bruce Collins, to rescue it from ruin. Collins came to the parish in 1984 with a vision of St Peter's once again filled with worshippers. His vision was so powerful that ten members of the congregation of St John's came over and every Wednesday night for nine months prayed on their knees for the revival of this crumbling church. Their numbers gradually increased and on Whit Sunday 1986 the doors were finally reopened to a congregation of 30, all aged under 35. With its emphasis on charismatic, evangelical worship, St Peter's has since grown into a thriving Christian community. In addition to regular services, the main building, now substantially restored, is used as a venue for concerts and plays, as well as a crèche, while the adjoining church hall houses the nursery school next to the popular Mannacafé. For more information about the activities of both St John's and St Peter's, telephone 020 7792 8227.

Two less salubrious landmarks lie a three-minute walk from St John's in either direction. To the south, at No.7 Ladbroke Grove, stood the house where the distinguished biographer James Pope-Hennessy was murdered on 25 January 1974. He was working at the time on a biography of Oscar Wilde. Apparently, the house was already haunted by two ghosts. According to Pope-Hennessy 'a little man who was always smiling and friendly' used to hang about on the stairs where a local ostler who looked after horses for a nearby inn had been stabbed; while a second more evil presence roamed the upper floors. Pope-Hennessy even called in a Catholic priest to exorcise them. The house was subsequently demolished and replaced by a mock-Georgian building which is occupied today by a charity, the Tudor Trust. One can't help wondering if the biographer now haunts the site on which he was choked with his own hairnet by an 'associate' of the dodgy young men with whom he liked to mix.

Back up the hill is the location of another untimely death. Bear right past the front of St John's into Lansdowne Crescent and you come to Nos.21–22, the Samarkand Hotel, where, on 17 September 1970, electric guitar virtuoso Jimi Hendrix died from a drug misadventure in the basement rented by his girlfriend, Monika Danneneden. American writer and agony aunt Irma Kurtz was living next door at the time, where she once sheltered two of the era's leading young revolutionaries in her attic. She describes their brief stay in *Dear London:*

> *Hans Werner Henze, the German composer whom I had interviewed in Italy, came over for tea when he was visiting London, and he left behind two handsome young protégés who needed a place to stay for a while. One of them was Dani Cohn-Bendit who I hear is a plump green politico in Germany these days. At the time 'Dani the Red' was admired everywhere in the world where young people were planning revolution; he was not all that well known in London. The other boy was the German firebrand, Rudi Dutschke. Rudi was intelligent and fierce, and apparently he meant every word he said for he did not make old bones. My goodness, could those boys talk! With the volume of Paris in the old days, though what they had to say was more cynical than our arty palaver, and they were much more apprised of evil than café philosophers at the end of the Fifties and into the early Sixties. While the boys talked and talked, and ate, smoked, drank and talked, and slept in my upstairs study, men in raincoats watched the house from the front seats of a series of cars that would have looked ordinary enough except they had too many aerials. The presence of 'fuzz' didn't suit Lansdowne Crescent, especially when they got out to stretch their legs and marched around like extras on the set of Oliver.*

> *From my window I watched one of them grind a cigarette out on his gloved hand, rather than drop it on the pavement. Policemen were a lot more ill at ease in the crescent than the revolutionaries who seemed perfectly at home and were in no great hurry to leave.*

Across Lansdowne Crescent, on the opposite side of Ladbroke Grove, you'll notice several large Victorian houses set back from the road. One of these, No.46, has a strong Russian connection and provides the meeting place for the Pushkin Club. The rest are owned mainly by private landlords who long ago converted them into flats.

Carrying on north along Ladbroke Grove, a few minutes' walk down the hill, leads you past the junctions with Lansdowne Road (which runs all the way back to Holland Park Avenue) and Elgin and Blenheim Crescents with their rows of pretty coloured houses backing onto communal gardens. Several well-known figures have lived in Elgin Crescent, including the artist Osbert Lancaster at No.79 (see 'All Done from Memory', pp 187–89), the actor Laurence Olivier at No.86, the writer Katherine Mansfield at No.95 and Jawaharlal Nehru, the first prime minister of India, at No.60.

After these turnings the buildings in Ladbroke Grove become noticeably shabbier and the atmosphere distinctly less rarefied. For many it is only here, in and around the streets close to Portobello Road, that you can still detect the true beating pulse of Notting Hill.

The Pushkin Club

Founded in 1955 by eminent Russian émigrés, the Pushkin Club meets every other Tuesday evening at 7.30pm in the front room of 46 Ladbroke Grove, a house rented to Russian students and members of the Russian Orthodox Church and administered by the charity Forum House. The Club presents a programme of readings and lectures in both Russian and English, concentrating on Russian poetry from Pushkin's time to the present. Previous highlights have included reminiscences of the childhood of film director Andrei Tarkovsky by his sister, and readings by one of the Club's organisers, Richard McKane, of his own translations of Gumilyov's *The Pillar of Fire* published in conjunction with Survivor's Poetry Press. The season runs from October to June and visitors are always welcomed with a mug of lemon tea and a muffin. Enquiries about membership should be addressed to Lucy Daniels on 020 7221 1981. Admission is free to members and £3.50 to visitors (£2 concessions).

ACCOMMODATION

HOTELS

The Abbey Court
20 Pembridge Gardens W2
020 7221 7518/Fax 020 7792 0858
info@abbeycourthotel.co.uk
www.abbeycourthotel.co.uk
Comfortable Victorian townhouse hotel, conveniently placed in a quiet street midway between Notting Hill Gate and the top of Portobello Road. Each of the 22 rooms is individually designed using antique furniture to create a traditional, cosy feel. Rates from £99 for a standard single to £195 for a deluxe double; continental breakfast included.

The Pembridge Court
34 Pembridge Gardens W2
020 7229 9977/Fax 020 7727 4982
reservations@pemct.co.uk
www.pemct.co.uk
Another comfortable townhouse hotel, but livelier than the Abbey Court with a notably relaxed and friendly atmosphere, enhanced by the presence of two large ginger cats. 'The Pem' attracts a similarly laid-back clientele, including quite a few music and media people seeking a cheaper, less fashionable alternative to the Portobello. Twenty rooms, from £120 for a small single to £190 for a deluxe double (with CD & cassette player); English breakfast included.

The Portobello Hotel
22 Stanley Gardens W11
020 7727 2777/Fax 020 7792 9641
info@portobello-hotel.co.uk
www.portobello-hotel.co.uk
Discreetly situated in an elegant white Victorian terrace, the Portobello's interior is serene yet delightfully eccentric. Potted palms, travellers' curios and squishy sofas scattered with richly embroidered cushions set the scene downstairs, while each of the 24 rooms has its own style, from colonial to Japanese or Moroccan. Facilities include a restaurant and 24-hour bar where, in 1990, you might have been served by Damon Albarn before Blur hit the big time and he could afford to buy his own house around the corner. During its 30 years, the Portobello has also attracted an impressive list of music celebrities among its guests, plus actors and writers such as the late Jean Rhys (see p 7). A single will set you back £140, a double £185 but this can rise to more than £300 for a 'Special Room', all with 'complimentary' continental breakfast.

EATING AND DRINKING

CAFÉS, SNACKS AND TAKEAWAYS

Food on the Hill
1 Hillgate Street W8
020 7792 5226
Mon–Fri 7.30am–5pm
Delicious, freshly prepared food using high-quality ingredients to eat in or take away. Mainstays range from traditional English breakfasts at around £3 to imaginative salads, soups and a truly wicked chocolate mousse. You can also order dinner party food to eat at home or rent this small cosy space for a private evening with friends.

The Organic Café Cookshop
101 Notting Hill Gate W11
020 7243 6232
info@organic-cafe.co.uk
Mon–Fri 8am–9pm; Sat 8.30am–9pm; Sun 9am–9pm
This latest venture from the Organic Café Group extends its commitment to

sustainable living by combining the scrumptious wholesome food served in the downstairs café with two floors of organic household goods (see p 24).

Sarnie Asylum

10 Notting Hill Gate W11
020 7243 5744
Mon–Fri 7.30am–5pm; Sat 9am–5pm
Home-made soups, juices and smoothies are among the specialities of this friendly, oddly named outfit which also does a great toasted baguette. Stews, notably Irish, feature on the menu too. Prices range from around £2 for a sandwich to £2.35 and £3.95 for soups and stews; £2.75 for a large fruit smoothie.

RESTAURANTS AND BARS

English

The Twelfth House

35 Pembridge Road W11
020 7727 9620
www.twelfth-house.co.uk
Mon–Fri 8am–6pm; Sat 8am–10.30pm; Sun 9am–9.30pm; brunch served daily 10am–4pm
This recently opened astrology café offers everything from a cup of coffee to a three-course meal, plus a 15-minute chart reading for £5. The food is traditional English, with starters such as ham hock terrine with piccalilli (£5.50), followed by smoked haddock, colcannon potatoes and poached egg (£12), plus quite a few vegetarian options. Staff wear T-shirts bearing their star sign, also on sale for £15 so you too may advertise your compatibility (or not) to fellow diners. In these modern baroque surroundings – the colour scheme is copper, green, burgundy and gold – linking up with your cosmic 'other half' is all part of the package.

Fish

Costas Fish Restaurant

18 Hillgate Street W8
020 7727 4310
Tues–Sat 12 noon–2.30pm & 5.30–10.30pm
This much lauded takeaway has been serving consistently high-quality fish and chips for longer than this writer can remember. The small licensed restaurant at the back offers a slightly extended menu including kalamari, Greek salads, houmous, pastries and retsina, very reasonably priced at £7.50. Take-away fish and chips cost around £5; two courses in the restaurant from £8.

Geales

2 Farmer Street W8
020 7727 7969
Mon–Sat 12 noon–3pm & 6–11pm; Sun evenings only 6–10.30pm
Opened in 1939, this must surely be the oldest restaurant in Notting Hill. It's certainly one of the most popular. Traditional fish and chips are the mainstay but a growing list of less English dishes such as *moules marinières*, deep-fried king prawn rolls and grilled goat's cheese have crept onto the menu. There's also a good choice of wine.

These developments undoubtedly reflect the change of ownership in 1999 (after 60 years in the Geales family), also evident in the clean, modern décor, but the food remains generally good if not cheap. Average price for starters is £4.50; main dishes £8.50; desserts, including old school favourites like treacle tart and sticky toffee pudding, £3.75.

French

Rotisserie Jules

133 Notting Hill Gate W11
020 7221 3331
Mon–Sat 12 noon–11.30pm;

Sun 12 noon–10.30pm. Delivery hours Mon–Sat 12.30–3pm; 6–10.30pm; all day Sunday. Average delivery time 30 minutes
Jules specialises in free-range chicken, flame-roasted at the entrance of this plain modern restaurant, even more popular as a takeaway. A whole chicken costs around £10, with a limited choice of side dishes – ratatouille, *gratin dauphinois*, fries and salads – for up to £2.50 per person. At £1.25, the mouth-watering chicken baguette is especially good value.

Greek

Costas Grill

12–14 Hillgate Street W8
020 7229 3794
Mon–Sat 12 noon–2.30pm & 5.30–10.30pm
Like its better known partner above, Costas hasn't changed for years. Typical Greek staples such as moussaka, meatballs and lamb on the spit are dished up in cosy surroundings totally untouched by the relentlessly commercial advance of Notting Hill. Starters from £1.50; main courses from £5 to £7.50 for charcoal-grilled fish.

Indian

Malabar

27 Uxbridge Street W8
020 7727 8800
Mon–Sat lunch 12 noon–2.30pm; dinner daily 6.30–11pm (Sun 10.30pm)
A sophisticated but friendly Indian restaurant that never lets you down – except when you can't get a table. Sizzling hot and well-spiced food. Average main course around £7.

Italian

The Ark

122 Palace Gardens Terrace W8
020 7229 4024
Mon 6–11.30pm; Tues–Thurs 12 noon–3.30pm & 6–11pm; Fri & Sat 12 noon–3.30pm & 6pm–midnight
The Ark has come a long way since its 30 years or so as a ramshackle French bistro. After a brief spell under former super-chef Jean Christophe Novelli, the latest owners have turned this odd, shack-like restaurant into an upmarket modern Italian. Both food and wine are deliciously authentic but with first courses at around £6 and main courses starting at £14.50, it's a far cry from the cheap and cheerful place it used to be.

Calzone

2a/2b Kensington Park Road W11
020 7243 2003
Daily 10am–11pm
The Notting Hill branch of this small chain occupies a prime people-watching site at the fork of Pembridge and Kensington Park Road. Pizzas are available as *calzone*, folded over with the topping steamed inside, or flat with all the familiar variations. The space is cramped but the food is reasonable and, if you can stand the traffic, there are a few tables outside. Eat in or take away for around £7 per person.

Pizza Express

137 Notting Hill Gate W11
020 7229 6000
Daily 11.30am–midnight
A friendly, reliable restaurant in arguably London's best pizza chain, this outlet achieves the difficult feat of appealing to children *and* parents. Last year's addition of rocket and goat's cheese toppings to the menu was clearly aimed to keep the latter happy. Eat in or take away from around £5.

Modern European

Kensington Place

201–05 Kensington Church Street W8
020 7727 3184
Mon–Sat 12 noon–3pm & 6.30–11.45pm; Sun 12 noon–3pm & 6.30–10.15pm; breakfast daily 7.30–10.30am

You'll almost certainly need to book for a table at this hugely successful, glass-fronted emporium renowned for its din, for people spotting and, above all, for excellent food. Usually described as 'eclectic', head chef Rowley Leigh's cooking has maintained a consistently high standard over more than ten years, with the accent on Mediterranean dishes such as fish soup and bruschetta (£6), as well as original combinations like roast squab pigeon with chickpeas and chorizo, turbot with borlotti beans and lobster sauce (both around £16). There's also a set lunch for £16 – not much more than a full English breakfast which at £14.50 has not surprisingly failed to pull in much custom.

The latest addition to Kensington Place is a **Fish Shop** next door at No.201 which sells a combination of high-quality fresh fish and cooked delights such as octopus stew and Thai fish cakes, including home delivery. *Open Tues–Fri 10am–7pm; Sat 9am–4pm* (020 7243 6626)

Pharmacy Bar & Restaurant

150 Notting Hill Gate W11
020 7221 2442
pharmacy@aol.com
Bar Mon–Thurs 12 noon–3pm; 5.30pm–1am; Fri 12 noon–3pm & 5.30pm–2am; Sat 12 noon–2am; Sun 12 noon–midnight. Restaurant daily 12.30–2.45pm & 7–10.45pm (Sun 10pm)

Pharmacy opened in 1998 and became instantly famous as a showpiece for the marriage between Damien Hirst's pharmaceutical installations and the gastronomy of Marco Pierre White. The marriage ended and each went their separate way but the installations remain and the food is still good if pricey.

The restaurant is entered via the downstairs bar where prescriptions are dispensed in the form of alluring cocktails. Choose from 'strong prescriptions' to 'one shot "jabs"', such as a 'detox' or the irresistible 'drugged frog' (all £7), plus various non-alcoholic concoctions like 'safe sex on the beach', a delicious mix of peach, raspberry, cranberry and pineapple juice at £3.50 – cheaper than an NHS prescription. The doses are generous and somehow in this relentlessly themed space wackiness wins over antiseptic cool. Perching on aspirin-topped stools or sitting around aspirin tables, no one seems fazed by the walls of glass cases, stacked with the neatly arranged contents of a chemist's shop. Snacks are provided, some of them substantial, including steak and fries at £8.50. Expensive (expect a service charge of 12.5%) but highly recommended, with the added advantage of late-night hours.

Upstairs, the pharmaceutical theme is more subdued. Hirst's elegant series of encased butterflies are spaced around walls lined with discreet pill-patterned wallpaper, with Danny Chadwick's giant molecule providing an arresting focal point. The effect is tasteful, serious and airy – designed to please rather than shock. This is reflected in the menu. No pharmaceutical puns here, but careful descriptions of ingredients. Adorned with various coulis, purées and braised veg, the food looks pretty on the plate, but is sometimes a bit too easy on the taste buds. Starters and side dishes, notably some excellent baby squid, perfectly textured gnocchi and a green salad dressed with just the right balance of oil and lemon, have been the most memorable. The service is professional and friendly (anyone expecting nurses' uniforms will be disappointed). The extensive international wine list is biased towards European selections and contains the odd hair-raising entry: 82 Chateau Pétrus weighs in at a cool £1,650. Fine, if you can put your meal on to an expense account, and here might lie the rub. Pharmacy's success inevitably rides partly upon a cloud of fame and hype. The dinner crowd upstairs tends to include quite a few tourist groups and businessmen, which together with the unchallenging food, can lend an oddly corporate air to eating here.

Asian

The Churchill Arms

119 Kensington Church Street W8
020 7792 1246
Mon–Sat 12.30–2.30pm & 6–9.30pm; Sun 12 noon–2.30pm
The Thai food served in the conservatory of this popular pub is way above average and reasonably priced, with main dishes for around £6. It's become even more crowded since winning the *Evening Standard* Pub of the Year award in 1999, so avoid peak times such as Friday and Saturday nights if you can.

New Culture Revolution

157–59 Notting Hill Gate W11
020 7313 9688
12 noon–11pm daily
The home cooking of northern China provides the inspiration for this canteen-style restaurant, serving lightly cooked food, with an emphasis on dumplings and noodles and plenty of choice for vegetarians. The prices, £5–8 for a main course, make it good value and you leave feeling healthy too. It feels a bit stranded on the end of the Gate, but this is the longest surviving restaurant on this site so the formula must be working.

PUBS

The Champion

1 Bayswater Road W2
020 7243 9531
Mon–Sat 12 noon–11pm; Sun 12 noon–10.30pm
Notting Hill's only overtly gay venue – pretty much men only – has always had a mixed reputation (see Duncan Fallowell, pp 229–31).

The Ladbroke Arms

54 Ladbroke Road W11
020 7727 6648
Summer Mon–Sat 11am–11pm; Sun 12 noon–10.30pm. Winter Mon–Fri 11am–3pm & 5–11pm; Sat 11am–11pm; Sun 11am–10.30pm
Excellent owner-managed pub conveniently situated opposite the police station should any customers get out of order. Outside, there's a pleasant seating area while inside is reminiscent of a lounge bar in a country hotel, but without the piped music. The owner is keen to reflect his own taste rather than that of any hired designer and the result is uncontrived and relaxed. A short menu of the day offers straightforward, well-prepared dishes for lunch and dinner at prices you might well pay for the pre-packaged fare in many pubs. Very good puddings. Eat well and enjoy yourself here, with wine, for under £30 a head. It gets busy in the evenings and tables can only be reserved up to 7.30pm. Well worth booking or trying your luck for a good meal in a friendly, down-to-earth setting.

Uxbridge Arms

13 Uxbridge Street W8
020 7727 7326
Mon–Sat 11am–11pm; Sun 12 noon–10.30pm
Unlike the Ladbroke Arms above, this

traditional English pub has changed very little over the years. Real ales, a cosy ambience, no music and a prime position behind the Gate draw a mixed crowd of cinema-goers and regular locals, some of whom feel clearly at home from home. Standard pub fare is served at lunchtime; only snacks in the evening.

The Windsor Castle

114 Campden Hill Road W8
020 7243 9551
Mon–Sat 12 noon–11.30pm;
Sun 12 noon–11pm
Close your eyes and ears to the traffic outside and this could be a cosy old pub in the country. Don't be surprised to find a few hunting and fishing types here too. Standard pub food is supplemented by treats such as oysters in season, and there's a pretty back garden for summer drinking. Look out for the resident tortoise.

ENTERTAINMENT

FILM AND THEATRE

The Gate Cinema

87 Notting Hill Gate W8
0207 727 4043
Box office opens half an hour before first performance
This small independent cinema started life as the Electric Palace and was converted from a restaurant in 1911. Nothing much to look at on the outside, you'll be surprised by the fabulous plasterwork walls and ceiling which helped establish architect William Hancock as an early cinema specialist. Nowadays The Gate shows some of the more arty or cultish current releases in rapid turnover, as well as Sunday afternoon one-off screenings of classics such as *A Bout de Souffle*, *Casablanca* and *Performance*, chosen in conjunction with Video City (see p 19).

The Notting Hill Coronet

103 Notting Hill Gate W8
020 7792 2020
Box office opens half an hour before first performance
Recently boosted by the addition of a second screen, the Coronet shows popular current releases in an irreverent atmosphere encouraged by its status as the last smoking cinema in London.

The Gate Theatre

Above the Prince Albert
11 Pembridge Road W11
Box office 020 7229 5387/
Disabled access and administration
020 7229 5387
www.gatetheatre@freeserve.co.uk
Office Mon–Sat 10am–6pm;
shows start 7.30pm. No matinees
Over the 22 years since its inception at this same tiny premises above the Prince Albert pub, the Gate Theatre has built up a strong reputation for staging high-quality innovative productions, mainly from abroad (see p 5). The front door, to the left of the pub, is easily spotted by the noticeboard with posters for the current season of plays. On Monday nights you pay whatever you can afford, otherwise tickets cost up to £12. Book early to avoid disappointment.

MUSIC AND CLUBBING

The Notting Hill Arts Club

21 Notting Hill Gate W11
020 7460 4459
Mon–Sat 7pm–2am; Sun 7pm–midnight
Expect to find a good range of ages and people at this basement club which, though undoubtedly trendy, somehow manages to represent the more genuine aspects of Notting Hill. The music varies

from live jazz to Brazilian funk and French disco – the small dance floor soon fills up, whatever the style – and comfortable leather armchairs and sofas are provided for the less actively inclined. Arrive early, especially on Friday and Saturday when the queues extend quite a way along the Gate. Entrance fee around £5.

STAYING IN

Video City

117 Notting Hill Gate W11
020 7221 7029
Mon–Thurs 9am–10pm; Fri & Sat 9am–10.30pm; Sun 11am–10pm
With its huge selection, including hundreds of foreign and arthouse films, managed by unfailingly friendly, efficient and knowledgeable staff, Video City easily lives up to the claim of being the best small video shop in London. Prices – to rent or buy – are reasonable too.

CHILDREN

The Princess of Wales Memorial Playground

Kensington Gardens W2
020 7298 2000
Daily summer 10am–6.45pm; winter 10am–3.45pm. Children must be accompanied by an adult (one adult per five children) and adults can only enter in the company of a child
A lot of thought went into the planning of this enclosed play area and it shows. Conceived as a lasting tribute to Princess Diana, it was built on the site of an existing playground just north of her home in Kensington Palace. The designers have used the park's long association with another local resident, JM Barrie, author of *Peter Pan* (see p 8), to link different areas of play. These include a beach cove complete with a magnificently rigged pirate ship, a tree house encampment and a movement and musical garden where children can create melodic tunes on various interactive instruments, from wooden xylophones to metal dance chimes, or swivel and spin on turning discs and saucers. Near the cove there's even a ticking crocodile half submerged in a rivulet of water. Care has been taken to appeal to a range of ages up to 12, with special attention to the needs of children with disabilities. Extensive planting and landscaping using only natural materials ensure that the playground blends harmoniously into the surrounding park land.

A more energetic antidote to the consumer pressures of Notting Hill is the circular Memorial Walk which can be picked up from here. This second tribute to Diana covers seven miles across Kensington Gardens and three more parks – Hyde Park, Green Park and St James'. The way is charted by 90 plaques by sculptor Alec Peever, set in the ground.

SHOPPING

ANTIQUES

John Jesse

160 Kensington Church Street W8
020 7229 0312
Mon–Fri 10am–5.30pm; 11am–4pm
One of the old established antique dealers on this street, John Jesse specialises in highly collectable art nouveau and art deco ceramics and furniture, plus arts and crafts pieces, including some exquisite jewellery. Prices reflect the quality and rarity value of the items on offer.

Mercury Antiques

1 Ladbroke Road W11
020 7727 5106
Mon–Fri 10am–5.30pm; Sat 10am–12.30pm

Mrs Richards has owned this shop since 1963 and specialises in eighteenth- and early nineteenth-century English porcelain, potteries and Delft. She sells almost exclusively to collectors, many of whom flock every June to her exhibition of recent acquisitions at London's International Ceramics Fair. An unexpected bastion of old-fashioned taste, it may well be the last such business to survive so close to the Gate.

Dyala Salam

174a Kensington Mall W8
020 7229 4045
Tues–Fri 10.30am–6pm; Sat by appointment
This dark Aladdin's cave of a shop specialises in antiques from the Ottoman Empire. In fact, the Lebanese owner, Dyala Salam, who single-handedly buys and sells the sumptuous collection of decorative furniture, embroidery, rugs, ceramics and other treasures, modelled it on the harem quarters of the Topkapi Palace in Istanbul.

ART SUPPLIES

The Print Gallery

22 Pembridge Road W11
020 7221 8885
Mon–Fri 9am-6pm; Sat 10am–7pm
All you need in the way of photocopying, laminating, binding and offset printing services is combined with a reliable selection of graphic and fine art supplies. Staff are friendly, helpful and admirably unflustered in the face of a seemingly constant demand for instant photocopying.

BOOKS

Notting Hill Books

132 Palace Gardens Terrace W8
020 7727 5988
Mon–Sat 10.30am–6pm; early closing Thurs 1pm
Sheila Ramage fulfilled her dream of starting a bookshop in 1969, making this now the oldest bookshop in the area. She sells good-quality remainders and review copies with the emphasis on art, literature and history. There's also a table of reduced price paperbacks by the bus stop outside.

Waterstones

39 Notting Hill Gate W11
020 7229 9444
www.waterstones.co.uk
Daily 9am–10pm
After the sad demise of Elgin Books, one of the many resourceful local businesses to be forced out by wildly exorbitant rent increases (see p 30), this branch of the Waterstones chain is a welcome resource, offering a wide selection of books sold by helpful, well-informed staff.

CHARITY SHOPS

The Charity Shop

Notting Hill Housing Trust
59 Notting Hill Gate W11
020 7229 1476
Mon–Sat 10am–7pm; Sun 1–6pm
Like some of the Oxfam shops, Notting Hill Housing Trust has developed its own range of household goods – mainly cushions, bed covers, candles and ceramics – to sell alongside the usual second-hand clothes, books and bric à brac. Prices are very reasonable and some of the special items such as animal print cushion covers and spotty china are as stylish as you'll find in many of the popular high-street stores.

Trinity Hospice

20a Notting Hill Gate W11

020 7792 2582
Mon & Thurs–Sun 10.30am–8pm; Tues & Wed 10.30am–7pm
This rather shabby establishment has had none of the style-conscious treatment bestowed on some of the other charity shops. The result is lower prices and an even better chance of finding a good bargain.

FASHION

The Dispensary
25 Pembridge Road W11
020 7221 929
Mon–Sat 10am–6.30pm
An increasingly popular place for offbeat streetwear, trainers (including Campers) and accessories for men, women and children, the Dispensary has a large cult following among Japanese tourists and media/advertising types. Its own label consists of denim, unusual T-shirts, bags, belts and a good collection of leather jackets and trousers. (Also at 200 Kensington Park Road, just off Portobello Road.)

Jane Kahn
4 Pembridge Road W11
020 7792 2616
Mon–Sat 9.30am–6pm; Sun 12.30–6.30pm
Apart from its prime position on Notting Hill Gate, a secret of this shop's success has been to change with the times – moving from an emphasis on clothes (often designed by Jane herself) into the ubiquitous lifestyle slot, but with more than a hint of originality. The result is a quirky mix of up-to-the minute shoes, tops, bags and jewellery mixed in with stationery, shower curtains, hot-water bottles, clocks and other household items. Favourites include glass cutting-boards in different designs (£14.95), stamp watches (£9.99) and leopard-print crockery. Unusual cards and wrapping-paper help make this one of the best places for presents in the neighbourhood.

The London Hat House
7 Kensington Mall W8
020 7727 3859
Tues–Fri 10am–5pm; Sat 1–5pm
Upmarket custom-made hats and bags to match any outfit. In two to six weeks, partners Sharon Williams and Ellen Bonner will create your own unique head gear, from extravagant head-dresses to a simple pillbox in just the right colour. Prices start at £290 for hats; £75 for a head-dress.

Natural Selection
57 Pembridge Road W11
020 7792 2717
Mon–Fri 11am–6.30pm; Sat 9.30am–6pm
A team of London-based designers supplies this pleasingly low-key shop with dresses, skirts and tops, mainly in cotton and hemp, plus sweaters made from recycled cashmere. Best-sellers are the cotton-linen knitted cardigans with rose fastenings (£68) in luscious shades of pink, purple and blue. Lampshades, jewellery and hand-made notebooks mingle with children's clothes in the bright back room.

Paul Smith
Westbourne House
122 Kensington Park Road W11
020 7727 3553
www.paulsmith.co.uk
Mon–Thurs 10.30am–6.30pm; Fri & Sat 10am–6.30pm
Paul Smith has sympathetically renovated a large Victorian house to create probably the most elegant retail space in Notting Hill. A beautiful glass staircase connects three floors on which you will find his complete ready-to-wear and made-to-measure lines for men, women and children, as well as a tasteful range of

'lifestyle' objects, from the more usual cushions and vases to genuine posters from the Sixties. The clothing is smart and sophisticated and if you find nothing to your liking on the shop floor, a bespoke suit can be ordered from a master tailor upstairs. Most of the clothes are made in Italy, all with the finest fabrics and craftsmanship. Well worth a visit even if you can't afford to buy.

Tease

47 Pembridge Road W11
020 7727 8358
Mon–Sat 10.30am–6.30; Sun 12noon–5pm
Especially suitable for shoppers in the 15–25 age group, Tease offers affordable T-shirts sporting just about every trendy, ironic or controversial logo or slogan. Worth looking out for is the cute and sexy Ava Maria lingerie with a Jesus/Mary theme. The shop also stocks a large selection of Paul Frank bags and wallets. Clear displays make it easy to find what you're looking for.

Vintage and second-hand

Dolly Diamond

51 Pembridge Road W11
020 7727 2479
vintaged@globalnet.co.uk
Mon–Fri 10.30am–6.30pm; Sat 9.30am–6.30pm; Sun 12 noon–6pm
No credit cards
Dolly Diamond has trawled high and low, including the West Coast of America, for the rich combination of Twenties' to Eighties' clothes that make up her unique collection. Depending on your style everything is wearable, making this a popular hunting ground with designers, among them Galliano who eulogised an exquisite black top edged with layers of petals, in a recent book. Dolly also sells shoes, bags and jewellery and will hunt out special items if needed.

Retro Man and Retro Woman

4 & 32 Pembridge Road W11
020 7792 1715/4805
www.buy-sell-trade.co.uk
Daily 10am–8pm
These two out of 13 General Trading Stores scattered around the Gate concentrate on second-hand clothes, shoes and accessories, from designer wear by the likes of Prada, Katherine Hamnett and Dolce and Gabbana, to Gucci watches and special-edition T-shirts. Plenty of bargains to be found, though prices sometimes belie the rather grotty surroundings. Other shops specialise in jewellery, film and music memorabilia, computers, kitsch household goods, book & comic and record & tape exchange – all on a buy, sell and trade basis.

Sebastiano Barbagallo

15a Pembridge Road W11
020 7792 3320
Mon–Fri 10.30am–6.30; Sat 9am–7pm; Sun 10.30am–6pm
Heading along the well-beaten tourist path to Portobello Road, you might easily miss this treasure trove of South East Asian, Tibetan and Chinese clothing, artefacts, furniture and textiles. In fact it's a favourite well-kept secret of both textile and fashion designers who come here looking for inspiration, be it from pre-revolutionary Chinese garments or new cheong sams and cute pyjamas for children. Some of the most interesting garments are simply hung haphazardly in wooden cupboards.

FOOD AND WINE

Chalmers & Gray

67 Notting Hill Gate W11
020 7221 6177
Mon–Fri 8am–6pm; Sat 8am–5pm
The smell of this upmarket fish shop announces its presence almost as soon as you emerge from the south side of the underground. Swordfish, salmon, squid, cod, halibut, clams and succulent looking tiger prawns are just some of the fish laid out on the marble slab which dominates Chalmers & Gray. Prices are generally steep while service tends towards offhand.

Clarkes

124 Kensington Church Street W8
020 7221 9225
Mon–Fri 8am–8pm; Sat 9am–4pm
Next door to Sally Clarke's excellent restaurant, this tiny rustic-looking shop sells a mouth-watering selection of cheeses, home-made preserves, cakes and pastries, but it's mainly the freshly-baked breads that have earned it such a high reputation. These range from familiar continental loaves such as ciabatta and baguettes to bread made with walnuts, spinach, fennel, raisins and all manner of different dough. There are also a few tables where you can sit and drink excellent coffee while you sample whatever you fancy.

The Farmer's Market

Newcombe House car park
Kensington Place W8
www.londonfarmersmarkets.com
Saturdays only 9am–2pm
Who says organic produce has to be expensive? This enticing market sells not only fresh-looking fruit and vegetables, but meat, cheese, fish, flowers and a dazzling array of home-baked bread and cakes – all direct from the producer, hence very reasonable prices. Stallholders include Rookery Farm from Sussex, for organic free-range eggs; the Garlic Farm, based in the Isle of Wight; and Grasmere Farm in Lincolnshire, specialising in organic pork, sausages and traditionally cured bacon and hams. This is a largely residential area and the long-term survival of the market is dependent on neighbourhood goodwill. With its future uncertain, it needs all the support it can get.

HOME

Frontiers

37–39 Pembridge Road W11
020 7727 6132
Mon–Sat 11am–6.30pm;
Sun 12 noon–4pm
This attractive shop sells a combination of jewellery, furniture and pottery, with a special line in Lloyd Loom chairs, mostly displayed in the basement. Pots and jewellery, mainly from Asia and North Africa, include both new and ancient pieces with some wonderful amber necklaces. Prices are fair, large terra cotta pots from China at £34 seeming especially good value.

The Futon Company

138 Notting Hill Gate W11
020 7221 2032
www.futoncompany.co.uk
Mon–Wed & Sat 10am–6pm; Thurs & Fri 10am–7pm; Sun 11am–5pm
The success of this chain lies in its narrow focus on simple, inexpensive and practical furniture and furnishings, from beds, sofa beds, tables and wardrobes to cushions, bedspreads and ready-made curtains in strong plain colours. Futons have always been the mainstay, but a team of young designers ensures that innovative items are constantly introduced. Some of the best are 'beds in a hurry', a selection of roll-up and zip-up mattresses, from £29 for a basic 'roly-poly' to £99 for a 'bed in

a bag'. Another plus is the company's policy that all timber used must come from sustainable sources.

John Oliver

33 Pembridge Road W11
020 7221 6466
Mon–Sat 9am–5.30pm
One of several long-established shops in this road, John Oliver specialises in high-quality paints in a range of beautiful shades of his own invention. He also stocks a huge selection of wallpapers and will give advice on mixing and matching colours, patterns and textures. Expensive but worth it.

The Natural Homestore

The Organic Café
101 Notting Hill Gate W11
020 7243 6232
info@organic-cafe.co.uk
Daily 10am–7pm except Sun
The Natural Homestore sells clothes, bedding, recycled stationery, paint, soaps and skincare lotions from a wide variety of sources: woollen blankets from Scotland, French Savon de Marseille soapflakes (£8 a bag), hemp socks from Germany (£6) and English children's furniture, such as a beautiful wicker crib for £130 – all guaranteed to be chemical free.

Vessel

114 Kensington Park Road W11
020 7727 8001
Mon–Fri 10am–6pm; Sat 10am–6.30pm
Among the many newcomers to Notting Hill, this international temple of good design is definitely one worth visiting. Upstairs houses a range of beautiful yet functional glass and ceramic tableware, while the downstairs gallery showcases more experimental work by the likes of Tom Dixon, Tord Boontje, Nigel Coates and Anish Kapoor. Nothing is cheap, but several smaller items such as bottle openers, bowls and coffee cups are affordable for anyone prepared to invest in lasting quality and style.

MIND AND BODY

BEAUTY THERAPY

Joy Weston

142 Notting Hill Gate W11
020 7229 4141/4111
Mon–Wed 10am–7pm; Thurs–Fri 10am–8pm; Sat 9am–6pm; Sun 11am–5pm
With the emphasis on Joy, this salon uses a variety of beauty treatments, from waxing, pedicures and facials to lymphatic drainage massage, aimed at soothing away the stresses and problems of everyday life and thereby benefiting body and soul. This kind of pampering never comes cheap, but you're in expert hands and £38 for an hour's top-to-toe intense massage seems pretty good value.

HAIRDRESSERS

Bladerunners

158 Notting Hill Gate W11
020 7229 2255
Mon, Tues & Fri 10am–7pm; Wed & Thurs 10am–8.30pm; Sat 10am-6pm; Sun 10am–5pm
Bladerunners specialises in extensions and treatments for African-type hair, but caters for everyone with a range of treatments such as 'glossing', 'body boosting' and 'deluxe reconstruction' (for limp hair), as well as the usual cut & blow dry (from £35 for women). Conditioning treatments are £10–£35 while extensions start at £200.

Le Léon

2a Ladbroke Grove W11
020 7792 9122
Mon–Sat 9am–6pm
Not surprisingly, this French-owned salon has successfully captured a loyal clièntele from among the growing number of French who have made their home in Notting Hill. Competent cutting and good value – a cut & blow dry costs £30 for women, £20 for men, highlights £50 – keep plenty of others coming too.

Sala Nova

3 Ladbroke Road W11
020 7229 6318/3976
www.sala-nova.co.uk
Tues–Thurs 10am–6pm; Fri 9am–7pm; Sat 9am–4pm
In addition to English, Spanish is the language spoken here and there are definite echoes of Gaudi in the colourful décor. Sala Nova is a friendly, unpretentious place, rightfully proud to display its three stars from the *Good Salon Guide*. Prices start at £27 for a cut & blow dry and around £60 for full colour.

HEALTH AND FITNESS

The Life Centre

15 Edge Street W8
020 7221 4602
www.thelifecentre.org
Mon–Fri 8am–10pm; Sat 8.30am–7.30pm; Sun 9am–7pm
Dedicated to natural health and fitness, the Life Centre offers a variety of alternative therapies and exercise, the latter with an emphasis on 'dynamic yoga'. Other classes include tai chi and pilates, and all take place in the building's main space – a large, airy studio with a glass roof through which you can watch the clouds scudding by from your relaxation mat. Prices range from £5 to £9.50 for exercise classes (depending on length), while natural therapies and treatments start at £20 for a half-hour Indian head massage and go up to £80 or so for healing and homeopathy.

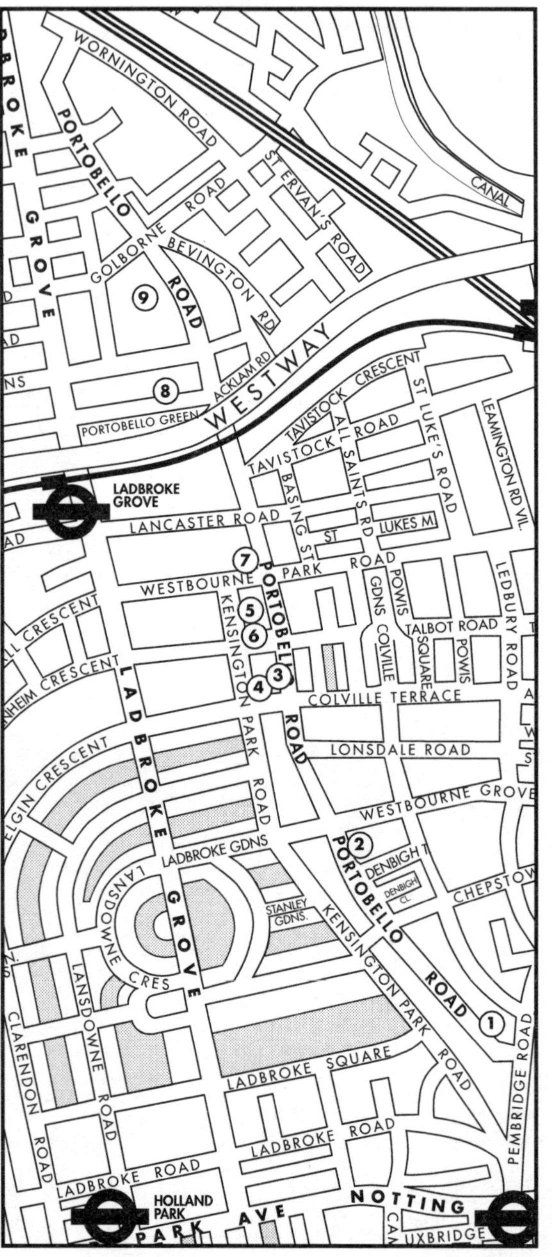

1. The Gate Hotel
2. The Portobello Gold Hotel
3. The Electric Cinema
4. The Peniel Chapel
5. The Notting Hill Synagogue
6. The Travel Bookshop
7. The Blue Door
8. Canopy under the Westway and Portobello Green
9. Colegio Español

2. Portobello Road

Notting Hill's popularity has always owed a lot to Portobello, from the road's eighteenth-century beginnings as a pleasant green lane winding north from what is now Notting Hill Gate (once Kensington Gravel Pits) towards the village of Kensal Green, to its development as a thriving commercial centre. By 1880 the Lane, as it was known then, was already lined with shops, augmented by regular fruit and vegetable stalls. After the Second World War the market's status was enhanced by people's growing interest in the bric à brac that had long been sold on Saturdays, later joined by antiques. Novelist Monica Dickens, who grew up around the corner at 52 Chepstow Villas (also once home to a cousin of Napoleon Bonaparte), recalls visiting the market as a child in the 1920s:

> *Ever since memory the Portobello Road market has happened on Saturday mornings. In those early days when we ran down for a packet of sherbet, or walked in kilts and tams to the grocers with Fanny, it was still literally a flea market. All along the gutter rickety stalls and barrows were piled high with rags, torn jerseys, mismatched shoes, chipped china, bent tin trays, three-legged furniture and unfunctioning appliances from the early days of electricity.* (Monica Dickens, *An Open Book*)

Now, of course, thousands of visitors flock here every Saturday in search of antiques and collectibles. Yet despite its international reputation as a number-one tourist attraction, Portobello Road, inseparable from the market, still retains its own very special character.

Origins of Portobello Road

Portobello Road was named after Portobello Farm, itself named after Admiral Sir Edward Vernon's capture of Puerto Bello from the Spanish in the Gulf of Mexico. The battle took place in November 1739 at a time when the farm – all of 170 acres – was owned by a builder called Adams. When news of the victory finally reached England the following March, there was widespread rejoicing with many streets and even a town in Scotland named after the event. Vernon's triumph is also commemorated in Vernon Mews, off Portobello, as well as at Admiral Vernon's Antiques Market at Nos.139–51.

The top end

Starting from Pembridge Road, the first landmark on Portobello Road is the Sun in Splendour, Notting Hill's oldest surviving pub, built in 1850 and still serving traditional ale and basic pub food in rather spartan surroundings. Walk on between a small cluster of shops and the Gate Hotel, with its disgruntled parrot in the basement, and you soon come to a long terrace of two-storey Victorian cottages much in the style of Hillgate Village, though with tiny gardens at the front. At least two writers are known to have lived here: novelist and political essayist George Orwell at No.22 and contemporary poet Roger McGough a little further down. On the other side of the road, it's worth stopping at the Mannacafé, both for its peaceful courtyard setting and the food, which manages to be wholesome, delicious and cheap. This was once the premises of Petersberg Press, fine art printers whose regular clients included David Hockney, Jim Dine and Henry Moore. Owner, Caroline Bretherton, now rents the galleried space from St Peter's Church on Kensington Park Road. She took it over in 1991 when the press went into liquidation. St Peter's also has the nursery school next door. The building beyond, now occupied by one of two local branches of David Wainwright's global style emporium, has a less illustrious claim to fame as the premises where Richard Branson set up the Virgin record label.

Across Chepstow Villas, the first mansion on the right was a location for some of the filming of Hanif Kureishi's disastrous *London Kills Me* (1991). Kureishi's first foray into directing was intended as an authentic look at the seedy underbelly of Notting Hill. To this end, he employed the services of various dubious characters who smartly repaid him by genuinely squatting the building as soon as filming was over. It took a while to get them out, after which the building spent months boarded up and the film was panned by the critics. Although films of Kureishi's work have often been a success, he has yet to have another go at directing.

Market days

Many visitors head for the market on weekdays and especially Sundays, only to feel let down by the dormant antiques arcades and slightly tatty air of Portobello without the crowds. To avoid disappointment it's important to know that the market divides into three main sections, each with its own location, trade and approximate opening hours:

- The antiques market, mainly between Chepstow Villas and Elgin Crescent, is Saturdays only – approx. 6am–5pm.

- The fruit and vegetable market, which occupies the middle blocks of Portobello up to the junction with Lancaster Road, is open daily except Sundays – around 9.30am–6pm, closing 1pm Thurs. There is also an organic market on Thursday, 9.30am–6pm, under the canopy beneath the Westway.

- The flea market, starting from this same spot under the Westway, is most extensive on Saturdays but in many ways is best on Fridays around 8am–5pm. It's also becoming increasingly active under the flyover on Sundays – starting a little later.

The next section of Portobello marks the beginning of the antique shops, many of which, including Alice's on the corner of Denbigh Close, have been here since the 1960s. Poet and writer Christopher Logue lived in the Close in those days and refers to this corner in his memoir, *Prince Charming*:

> *By 1965, the stall holders of Denbigh Close had begun to arrive each Saturday morning at 5am, for the Portobello Road street market was becoming the rage it remains. The bargain hunters of old were replaced by Italian dealers. Furniture conversion became antique restoration. Mad John was dead. Harry Dust had a council flat. Middle-class people had bought the cottages that they had lived in. Having introduced decorative mirrors, Kenny put a number of art-school students to work paining furniture, turning out pictures to resemble naive art. HMS Victorys and Battles of Portobello sold well. I borrowed money to raise the roof of No.18.*
>
> *Living at the blind end of the mews was Mr Eric Jones. Since 1934 he and his mother had occupied a cottage with a third floor the height of my planned extension. Eric was a cross-dresser with dyed, orange-blond hair. On summer Saturdays before the road boomed, he would tie on an apron over his pink dress and sweep the mews from end to end when the marketeers had left.*

Denbigh Terrace, the next turning on the right, has been home to two more colourful characters, each of whom – comedian Peter Cook and tycoon Richard Branson – resided at different times at No.19. The other side of the terrace suffered badly from wartime bombing, to be replaced by council flats such as Longlands Court, opposite the Portobello Gold pub and hotel, and Portobello Court, which borders the right-hand side of the next block down from the junction with Westbourne Grove. Various antique shops and arcades continue down to the crossroads with Elgin Crescent and Colville Terrace, but most are open only on Saturdays when they're joined by a medley of stalls set up on either side of the road. No.142, Nicholls Arcade next to the butcher's, provided the location for the Travel Bookshop scenes in the film *Notting Hill*. (The real bookshop on which it was modelled is in Blenheim Crescent, just a few minutes' walk away, see p 35.)

Elgin Crescent to the Westway

Elgin Crescent, with its upmarket paint shop, juice bar and local branch of Neal's Yard Remedies represents something of a battleground as a cluster of old businesses struggles to keep up with escalating rents.

First of the 'old school' to arrive was Mr Christian's delicatessen, opened in 1974 and still much loved by locals for its affable staff and delicious home-made food. After Mr Christian's came Graham & Green, which quickly established a successful business selling attractive household goods and ethnic items such as baskets, kelims, beaded curtains and pottery from Morocco. Today, Antonia Graham has three shops and, though she still imports from India and the East, her skilled eye is turned more towards designer objects such as lighting and kitchenware, as well as the exquisite clothes sold in No.10, apparently the most lucrative wing of her little empire.

Last of that era of newcomers was Tom the florist, who pioneered the trend for creating unusual flower combinations wrapped in string and brown paper. Like the much lauded Elgin Books, which tragically closed early last year, Tom was forced out of his shop premises by rent increases and now just has a stall on the corner with Kensington Park Road, with a tiny shop on Clarendon Road (see p 156).

A fierce critic of the changes caused by rent increases is writer and musician Michael Moorcock, who lived around here in the 1970s. His latest rollercoaster of a novel, *King of the City*, includes a reference to the time when Annie Lennox, later of Eurythmics fame, served behind the counter at Mr Christian's. Moorcock, a respected cultural figure and early proponent of 'sex and drugs and rock'n'roll', goes on to launch into a typically wild tirade about the neighbourhood's decline:

> *I loved and admired Annie Lennox. She was a pro, like Rosie. She didn't mind working. I'd known her when she was with the Tourists, grafting days behind the counter at Mr Christian's the grocer in 1977 when I lived in Colville Terrace, off Portobello Road, married to Barbican's alleged half-sister Julie May.*
>
> *By then the area was getting iffy. The Grove was filling up with liberal professionals – writers, TV producers, models, literary agents, bohemian aristos, film directors, lefty columnists, barristers – the entire fucking fancy. So many wankers that if you went out to the pub your feet stuck to the pavement. The pubs remained, in the main, our own. Speed in the Alex. Dope in the Blenheim. Junk in Finch's. They kept tarting up Finch's and Heneky's and we kept tarting them down again. As my friend DikMik put it late one evening: you could*

take the needles out of the toilets but you couldn't take the toilets out of the needles.

Drugs are still an indelible part of Notting Hill but most of the pubs have been more or less straightened out, with the introduction of better amenities, fancy food and a ubiquitous change of name: Finch's on Elgin Crescent is now the Duke of Wellington, the Alex, a former bikers' hangout, became the Portobello Gold and Heneky's the Earl of Lonsdale.

There are still a few relatively old businesses in Kensington Park Road, among them Barnett's toyshop and the launderette (owned by the same family), the Special Photographers Company and Crystal Cleaners, which took over from the dolls' hospital that occupied this site until 1977. Otherwise the street is now almost entirely given over to clothes shops and restaurants among which the Peniel Chapel, an example of Victorian Gothic revival, squats rather awkwardly, as if half waiting to be put to similar use. The recently renovated Chapel in fact has had an active congregation since 1923 and holds Brazilian services three times a week. It is the Notting Hill Synagogue at Nos. 206–208 that stands silent. In its heyday early last century, the synagogue was a dynamic focus for the hundreds of Jewish families who settled here after fleeing to the West from Eastern Europe and Russia. But its life was comparatively short-lived: by the 1960s the numbers attending Saturday worship had seriously dwindled and the synagogue finally closed last year.

The Notting Hill Synagogue

From the 1880s until the beginning of the twentieth century, pogroms drove thousands of Jewish people from their homes in Russia and Poland. Of the many who fled to England, some settled in and around Portobello Road. By 1883 there was already a synagogue in St Petersburg Place, Bayswater, and by the turn of the century enough Jewish people lived in Notting Hill to merit the opening of another. Most of these immigrants were poor, hard-working Yiddish-speakers – tailors, dealers, stallholders and small shopkeepers – who wanted a small intimate place of worship. Meetings had been conducted in various people's houses from 1897 but soon Moses David, a wealthy businessman who lived at 40 Ladbroke Grove, realised that a synagogue would provide a much needed focal point for this expanding community. He eventually found a suitable site in a former church hall in Kensington Park Road, and on 27 May 1900 Notting Hill Synagogue was consecrated.

The synagogue was given a Sefer Torah from Moscow and also had silver ornaments donated. It had many generous local supporters including Morris Poresky whose house in Tavistock Crescent became an unofficial reception centre for immigrants from Poland and Russia. In 1904 a Jewish Lads' Club was opened next to the synagogue, followed by a club for Jewish girls which later moved to near Westbourne Park. The numbers of Jewish people increased dramatically during the First World War as the area was considered safe, being away from the Zeppelin air raids that harassed the East End. In the early 1920s there were well over 600 Jewish families living in Notting Hill, and Convent Gardens with its 28 houses was known as Jews Alley. Sarah Soremekun recalls the extent of the community in *Portobello: Its people, its past, its present:*

> *Portobello Road was our family's shopping street. There were lots of kosher butchers, eight or nine quite close, and Jewish delicatessens where you could get lovely bagels and kosher bread . . . We attended Saturday worship at the synagogue in Kensington Park Road. It was nothing to go there in the Twenties and Thirties and have to stand, there were so many people.*

The Notting Hill Synagogue was one of the first to be affiliated to the Zionist Federation and over the years it attracted several famous cantors and scholars. Rabbi Judah Newman, appointed in 1922, symbolised the Jewish concept of learning; among his pupils was Abe Herman who went on to become Israeli Ambassador to the US. Also in the 1920s, a group of local Yiddish writers – Leo Koenig, Shlomo Goldenberg, AM Kaizer, L Credito, Asher Balin, Shamai Pinaky and Alexander Myerovitz – met frequently in the area. Barnetts Printing Works (the same family who runs the toyshop and launderette in Elgin Crescent) was the printer to the synagogue. Ten years on, the community was dwindling and by the end of the Second World War the vitality had disappeared as people moved out of the area, often to North London. On 8 June 1997 there was a service of commemoration to mark the centenary of the first Notting Hill service, after which a dedicated few kept the synagogue going until its final closure in September 2000. The building is still owned by the local Jewish community who are now considering what to do with it.

Of the restaurants in Kensington Park Road, 192 was the trendsetter in the early 1980s. Before then several establishments came and went, most notably on the site of Osteria Basilico which, after nearly ten years, seems set to stay. The most successful previous occupant was Monsieur Thompsons, much frequented by Notting Hill's literati. They included Emma Tennant, a prolific writer and founder of the ground-breaking literary magazine, *Bananas*. Edited by Tennant and designed by Julian Rothenstein (who went on to form Redstone Press), the magazine attracted some of the most talented creative figures of the 1970s, among them Angela Carter, Bruce Chatwin, Alberto Moravia, Ted Hughes and Yevgeny Yevtushenko. Tennant would quite often lunch or dine with authors at Monsieur Thompsons, referred to in the Summer 1976 entry of her *Burnt Diaries* as the 'Ruff Tuff Saloon':

> *Someone waved a wand over the dreary dog-dinner-on-tin-plate restaurant round the corner from the* Bananas *office and it has become Monsieur Thompsons, le patron mange ici joint with a palm tree, a feeling of authentic French provençal, with faded ochre walls and pine tables where you can sit as long as you like. 'Shall we share a starter?' says Ian Hamilton, poet and editor of the New Review, who has become a friend despite his kick-off review of Bananas' first issue as 'a literary magazine like any other, but raunchy'. Dominique Rocher, proprietor and maître d' of Thompsons – as this modest establishment on the corner of Portobello Mews and next to a new dry-cleaner's soon becomes known – doesn't mind if all you do share is a starter. The food is on the whole excellent, however, even if some of the dishes, like 'skirt of beef' are weirdly translated, or have clearly been stewing in translation for some time. The waiters are so French it's impossible to imagine them even knowing where England is – and indeed this corner of Notting Hill would be hard to define in a travel guide. It's possible to think of it as Albion, when Michael Horovitz walks past, or as Boadicea's city, when John Michell, decoder of ancient runes and druidic circles, breezes along the pavement outside.*

Back along Portobello Road, the fruit and vegetable stalls begin at the corner with Colville Terrace – how many traders depends on the day of the week. Fridays and Saturdays always find the first pitch occupied by the Caines selling fruit, not the cheapest but always high quality. A few stalls along, next to the flowers, Lynne and Alan Wakeling have been selling vegetables on various sites on Portobello since 1983, with six stalls currently in the family. Like every trader they lament changes: the lack of weekday trade since the rise of supermarkets, the dwindling numbers of family customers, the unwillingness of youngsters to carry on the trade and the rise of stalls selling anything but food have radically altered the nature of the market in the last 15 years. But the

Wakelings are survivors. From selling only basic English vegetables, they soon picked up on people's growing taste for Mediterranean food and now sell some of the best aubergines, rocket and baby plum tomatoes to be found. They also enjoy the 'chattiness of foreigners, especially the ones new to the area who don't know many people and treat us like family'.

Opposite the Electric Cinema, two foodshops on this block, the Breadstall and the Tea & Coffee Plant next door, started life as market stalls. They've now made way for relatively new arrivals, such as the excellent French cheese stall (Fri & Sat) and Dodie's Cool Chile Co. further down (Saturdays only). The Caines have another fruit stall on the corner of Talbot Road, sadly depleted last year by the death of Nelly Caine. Although she never seemed old she must have been at least 70 when she stood out in all weathers, her immaculate blond hair tucked under a beret against the cold. In keeping with market tradition, Nelly's flower-covered funeral cortège passed along Portobello Road as stallholders ceased trading to pay their respects.

The Electric Cinema

> *We understand and respect the special place that the Electric has in the hearts of many, both locally and nationally. We intend to build upon these associations to create something of unique and lasting value, both for ourselves, the Borough, and the industry at large.* (Gebler Tooth Architects, Restoration Proposal for the Electric Cinema, 2000)

A Grade II*-listed building, the Electric has strong claims to be the oldest surviving purpose-built cinema in England, substantially unchanged since its construction in 1910. (A purpose-built cinema in Colne, Lancashire is older, but no longer in use.) An extremely fine example of movie-house design of the period, the façade is covered in cream faience tiles and swags of fruit and flowers. The interior is also festooned with swags of fruit (and a globe above the screen) in gilded plasterwork, plaster panels, and gas secondary lighting with pink art deco glass lightshades. A free-standing screen now rises from the stage in front of the original, too narrow for modern film format, thereby leaving the original design uncompromised.

Throughout most of its history the Electric has been used as a cinema, apart from a short spell as a music hall under the name Imperial Playhouse. In recent times, after a period of steady decline, the Electric stood empty until it was bought by Peter Simon, the founder of the Monsoon Group, who started his fashion empire from a stall outside and still has his headquarters further down the Portobello Road. It reopened in February 2001 with a repertoire that includes arthouse, independent and foreign-language films, as compiled by City Screen, programmers for the Curzon Group. The huge restaurant next door is annexed to the building and still awaiting completion.

The next turning on the left is Blenheim Crescent, known mostly for its trio of impressive specialist bookshops, Books for Cooks, Garden Books and especially of course the Travel Bookshop. But for the presence of Minus Zero Records, with its devotion to psychedelia, it's difficult to imagine this patch dominated as it was by the 'alternative' culture of the Sixties: Marc Bolan lived at No.57 in 1967 when he was forming his band T Rex, while Minus Zero used to be the Dog Shop, selling hippy paraphernalia with Aquarius Waterbeds above, later to become the premises of the Frestonian Embassy (see pp 133 & 211–14). Even harder to picture is the time, only a few years earlier, when Totobags, according to Tom Vague in *Psychogeography,* the 'most important West Indian café' in the neighbourhood, occupied No.9. While, for the mostly Jamaican regulars 'dominoes, cards and smoking were the order of the day', writer Colin MacInnes and wealthy aristocrats like Sarah Churchill, used to come here regularly to savour a bit of 'low life'.

The Travel Bookshop

The Travel Bookshop, which was founded in 1979 by Sarah Anderson, was devised on the revolutionary concept of transcending the division between guides and other forms of writing by including every kind of book about a country on the same shelf. The premise is that the more widely you read about a country, the more you will gain from your travels. Books are therefore arranged geographically but with fiction, history, biography, natural history and out-of-print books alongside the more obvious maps and guides. Second-hand bookshops throughout the UK are constantly trawled for new stock, and the shop, with its knowledgeable staff, offers a service for tracking down elusive titles.

Over the past 22 years the Travel Bookshop has developed an enthusiastic following among travellers, writers and dreamers alike, but no one could have predicted the extraordinary flood of interest sparked by the film *Notting Hill.* In the mid-Nineties, Richard Curtis, a neighbour, asked if he could sit in the shop and take notes as he was thinking of writing a film set in a bookshop. This was followed up a few years later by a photographer taking stills which were used to help build the film set of both the interior and the exterior of the shop (see p 29). Filming then began; the area buzzed with camera crews and stars, and both Julia Roberts and Hugh Grant visited the Travel Bookshop as part of their research. Since the film opened in 1999, the shop has become a 'must-see' for the film's aficionados. Meanwhile it continues to sell travel books to locals as well as to visitors from all over the world.

Books for Cooks

Like the Travel Bookshop opposite, Books for Cooks has become something of a mecca for pilgrims – in this case serious foodies. Heidi Lascelles, founded the shop in 1983, largely in response to the meagre stock of cookery books available in even the biggest London bookshops. Despite housing around 8000 cookery books – including many foreign-language editions – the real secret of its success lies in the idea of testing recipes from the books on the shelves and serving the resulting dishes at lunch time. The test kitchen began in 1988 with Annie Bell as its first cook. In addition to the tiny restaurant (see Listings, p 53) Books for Cooks produces its own books, devised by French chef Eric Treuillé, who also runs seasonal workshops with the stress on perfecting basic recipes, from pasta sauces to bistro-style cooking, winter puddings and international dishes such as sushi, paella, polenta and Thai vegetarian cuisine. There are even sessions for children.

The next junction with Portobello is Westbourne Park Road, a busy bus route dominated on one side by Nuline, the ever-expanding builders' merchants, while opposite lies No.280, the location of the original blue door of *Notting Hill* fame. This was removed after the film, when the property changed hands and the new owners installed a substitute, firmly painted black. A few doors down at No.300, Intef Books (see Listings, p 53) is a welcome reminder of the area's cultural diversity, so notably absent from the film.

Richard Curtis on the dream that became *Notting Hill*

I suppose I started writing this film about 34 years ago. I was seven years old, and every night, to lull myself to sleep with a smile, I would have the same fantasy. It was my sister's birthday. Presents were unwrapped – and there didn't seem to be one from me. She would be unhappy, and then I'd say, 'Oh yes, well, actually, I did get you one little thing', then walk to a big cupboard and swing the doors open and there inside would be the four Beatles. They'd come out, chat, sing And I Love Her *and leave. And then I'd be asleep.*

Twenty-five years later, I was still having the same dream. The personnel had changed, but the basic plot was still the same. Now, when I couldn't get to sleep, I would imagine going to dinner with my friends Piers and Paula in Battersea, as I did most weeks. I'd casually say I was bringing a girl and then turn up unexpectedly with Madonna – usually Madonna, sometimes Isabella Rossellini – but usually Madonna. Piers would open the door and be very cool about it, though secretly thrilled. His wife Paula would have no idea who Madonna was and behave accordingly, and my friend Helen would arrive late and explode with excitement. By which time, I'd have dozed off again.

Five years later, we were doing the first week's filming of Four Weddings *and I was sitting in a cold room in Luton Hoo, beside James Fleet, asleep, trying to work out what I should write next. I remembered these dreams and thought it's not a bad idea for films to be about dreamy situations, and so I decided I'd have a bash at writing a film about someone very ordinary going out with someone very famous. This script is the result of that.*

After the crossing with Westbourne Park Road comes Lancaster Road, on which corner the first-floor terrace of Café Grove offers a perfect view of the Portobello action. Even during the week, it's usually busy outside Tesco's supermarket where one of the last traditional vegetable stalls is run by the Price family who also owns the last surviving greengrocer in Golborne Road. You'll find a lot more foodstalls here on Fridays and Saturdays, including fish, fruit & veg and olive oil. Two shops are also worth noting – the Grain Shop, justly renowned for delicious, vegetarian takeaways, and the Spanish supermarket, Garcia & Sons. The road then gives way to feather boas, cheap trinkets, cut-price make-up, CDs and new clothes, soon to blend into the glorious mix of junk, unexpected treasure and cutting-edge design under the Westway.

The Westway

The devastation caused by redevelopment plans to build the Western Avenue Extension (as it was then called) provoked one of the longest and most successful series of community-action campaigns in Notting Hill's history.

Until the building of the Extension, the fast exit from London, linking to the M40 out to the West of England, stopped at White City.

By the 1950s this had led to tremendous bottlenecks and accidents as frustrated motorists tried to find back routes for the final three miles into London via Notting Hill. The answer was to construct a new urban motorway, linking the existing road to the Marylebone Road in Central London. The project was designed in the late 1950s, site clearance began in 1964 and the road was officially opened by Conservative Minister Michael Heseltine in July 1970. Erected on concrete pylons just above roof height, it was an engineering triumph but a disaster in terms of social planning. Huge swathes of North Kensington became a building site; streets were chopped in two and around 700 houses were demolished to make way for the project.

Protesters caused total confusion on the day the road was opened and it took another two years of community action before all those immediately affected were rehoused. Local activists moved in yet again when it came to deciding what to do with the 23 acres that lay immediately beneath the Westway. Indecision and disagreements among local politicians had left this area derelict and abandoned. While an alliance of residents (see Frestonia, pp 132–3 & 211–14) had successfully campaigned for the building of co-operative, low-rent housing in Notting Dale, the travellers and totters who had been displaced to make way for the road were given nothing. Eventually, the independent North Kensington Amenity Trust was set up to organise the use of this land and to compensate the community for the destruction caused. In time, the Trust proved successful, filling much of the site with a mixture of amenities and private enterprises. Today it's a self-sufficient charity with an annual turnover of one million pounds.

The area under the Westway stands out as one of the most potent symbols of community action in Notting Hill. More than any other local landmark this concrete elevation and the life beneath it have captured the imagination of writers – Will Self, Michael Moorcock, Martin Amis and Anabel Donald, just to name a few. It's even been used as the title of a radio soap opera, *Westway*, the 'one and only global drama', broadcast twice-weekly by the BBC World Service (648 MW, omnibus Saturday 7.30pm, Monday 3.30am). Set in an inner-city health practice, the soap has its gritty moments, but it takes Amis, who lived for many years off Ladbroke Grove, to convey the truly sinister side of the Westway, as in this passage from *The Information:*

> *If anything was going to happen, it would surely happen under Westway. That black cavity, where the very walls and pillars were drenched in eel juice and snake's hiss, and tattooed with*

> *graffiti. If something was going to happen, it would surely happen under Westway.*

JG Ballard used the overhead motorway as the crash setting for his novel *Concrete Island*, and a totally different aspect is evoked in Michael Moorcock's *King of the City*. The description of a free rock concert under the Westway (see pp 205–7), on the ground now occupied by Portobello Green, is based on one of many such events that used to happen here during the 1970s. Nowadays this space is rarely used for music outside Carnival, though it did rock again one evening in July 2000, when the local Moroccan and Arabic-speaking Women's Centre, Al Hasaniya, hosted a memorable evening of Moroccan and Somali music, especially devised by these burgeoning communities.

To be fair to the Westway, or rather to the Amenity Trust and all the planners, community architects and local campaigners who fought so hard for the Portobello Green development, the mix of commercial and community enterprises that fill up the motorway bays on either side of Portobello Road is an impressive achievement. There can't be many places where refugee groups, youth projects, a Citizens' Advice Bureau, Social Services and an adventure playground share space with market traders, a flourishing clubbing venue and some of London's hottest fashion designers (see Listings for Subterania, p 89 and Portobello Green Arcade, pp 58–9).

Beyond the Westway

Past the Westway, up to the junction with Oxford Gardens, the north end of Portobello Road has several popular restaurants, as well as an eclectic mix of shops, from Honest Jon's for lovers of seriously cool jazz, to Sandie Stagg's Antique Clothing Shop and comparative newcomer Emma Bernhardt's treasure trove of Mexican kitsch. The road then follows the brick wall that used to enclose a Franciscan convent, later turned into the *Colegio Español* (Spanish school) that thrives here now. On the other side of the road, council housing occupies the site of the farmhouse which, until 1864, belonged to Portobello Farm. This section of Portobello represents the grotty end of the Friday and Saturday market, dominated by junk but not devoid of bargains for those dedicated enough to rummage through boxes of cracked china, or dig deep into the mounds of old shirts, jumpers, skirts and other second-hand clothes that gradually take over the battered trestle tables up to the crossing with Golborne Road. Although stalls peter out at the northernmost end of Portobello, the market carries on to the right, past the Victorian bulk of the former Caernarvon Castle (recently turned into yet another gastropub) and along Golborne Road.

The *Colegio Español*

In 1857 Father Henry Manning (later Cardinal) asked a nun, Mother Elizabeth Lockhart, to move from Greenwich into three adjoining houses at 34 Elgin Crescent, Notting Hill. From this base she and her small community of sisters taught in the school for poor girls attached to St Mary of the Angels (see pp 106–07) and within a year they were instructing about a hundred pupils as well as looking after several orphans. Father Manning encouraged them to become Franciscans and by the time the community moved to the convent at 317 Portobello Road in 1862, they were the first group of Franciscan Third Order women to live in England since the Reformation. The convent, designed by Henry Clutton (1819–1893), was a large building with grounds extensive enough to provide a triangular grass cemetery for the burial of nuns who died there. In 1897 the Franciscans left and were replaced by a Dominican Order, who set up an orphanage and home for young girls convicted of minor offences. This lasted until the 1970s when the convent was bought by the Spanish government and transformed into the *Colegio Español*, England's first and only Spanish school. Only open to Spanish nationals, for whom it is free, the school is attended by around 350 pupils aged five to 18 from all over London. Clutton's vaulted chapel, with its two banners designed in 1866 by John Francis Bentley, today serves as the school's assembly hall. Further information is available by telephoning 020 8969 2664.

You're now on the final stretch of Portobello Road and the last section to have received the kind of makeover treatment that still sits rather uncomfortably in Golborne Road. While George's Portobello Fish Bar looks positively jazzy these days, Cockney's Pie & Mash over the road has a determinedly timeless air, as does Valerie's Flowers and the aptly named Temptation Alley – a wonderfully old-fashioned haberdashery stuffed with buttons, ribbons and trimmings of every description. Just one restaurant has made it up here: the Brasserie du Marché aux Puces has established a successful niche as *the* neighbourhood brasserie for this end of Notting Hill, but it hasn't been easy. The juxtaposition of extreme wealth and some of the poorest housing in London makes for an explosive cocktail, and burglary is a common occurrence, unlikely to decrease as long as the more upmarket restaurants and retailers keep moving in.

ACCOMMODATION

HOTELS

The Gate Hotel

6 Portobello Road W11
020 7221 0707/ Fax 020 7221 9128
gatehotel@thegate.globalnet.co.uk
www.gatehotel.com
More bed & breakfast than hotel, The Gate has only six rooms, all simple, clean and equipped with refrigerator and tea- and coffee-making facilities. Probably the cheapest option, with prices ranging from £55–£70 single to £100 for a triple en suite, including continental breakfast.

Portobello Gold Hotel

95–7 Portobello Road W11
020 7460 4910
Mike@portobellogold.com
www.portobellogold.com
This five-room hotel is renowned for several reasons, from its origins as a notorious bikers' pub, the Princess Alexandra (affectionately known as the Alex), to its present status as having, in the Buzz Bar, one of the few existing licensed cybercafés – not to mention a recent surprise visit by President Clinton (see pp 45–6). It was also, in 1995, the first UK hotel to offer internet access in every room, recently made free to guests. Accommodation is otherwise basic, reflected in the rates: £47 to £75 for rooms with en-suite shower but not all with WC. Continental breakfast is included, and there's a lively downstairs bar, plus conservatory restaurant offering a range of global-style dishes at reasonable prices.

EATING AND DRINKING

CAFÉS, SNACKS AND TAKEAWAYS

Argile Gallery Café

7 Blenheim Crescent W11
020 7792 0888
Mon–Fri 10am–6pm; Sat 9am–7pm; Sun 11am–6pm
Argile started in 1988 as a gallery, adding the café – now its main business – soon after. Salads, sandwiches and home-made soups, all with a Mediterranean flavour, are served in a pleasantly unhurried atmosphere. Argile is licensed for wine and beer but also sells mouth-watering flavoured cappuccino and peach, lemon and orange teas. The walls are adorned with a mix of pictures for sale, chosen by the owners.

Café Grove

253a Portobello Road W11
020 7243 1094
cafegrove@cwcom.net
Mon–Sat 9.30am–8pm; Sun 10.30am–5pm
Café Grove is a relaxed place, popular with locals who like to sit for hours scribbling in notebooks over one cup of coffee. The food is reliable with some good salads, sandwiches and excellent chunky chips – all at very reasonable prices. The pace hots up on Saturdays, especially in summer owing to the roof terrace which provides a great view of Portobello.

The Coffee Stop

303a Westbourne Park Road W11
020 7243 1535
Mon–Sun 9am–6pm
This tiny 'holistic espresso and *panini* bar', as it describes itself, is a welcome antidote to the corporate invasion around the corner. Owner Dorothea Maria

Geusen's interest in New Age philosophies is evident in the books on display. Also proclaimed is her café's claim to fame as the spot where Hugh Grant buys the orange juice he's about to tip over Julia Roberts. There's even a sandwich called 'a blue door' (tuna, double cheddar, peppers, chives and onion), but the place is quirky enough to be forgiven. While sandwich prices start at £3.20, a half-hour's tarot reading will set you back £25 (or £15 for a mini-session).

Eve's Market Café

222 Portobello Road W11

Mon & Tues 7.30am–5.30pm; Wed 7.20am–5.30pm; Thurs 7.30am–3pm; Fri & Sat 7.30am–5.25pm

Formerly the Anglo-Yugoslav, Eve's is one of the few workers' cafés to survive. It's a typical English greasy spoon, popular with market traders, which may have something to do with the odd precision of the opening times.

Il Girasole

78 Tavistock Road W11

020 7243 8518

Mon–Sat 9.30am–7pm

Friendly Italian café offering genuine pizza *rossa* or *bianca* by the slice. Also a good place for sandwiches and coffee, with plenty of room to sit and watch the world go by, from inside or out on the plaza which fills with stalls every Saturday.

M Café

12 Blenheim Crescent W11

020 7229 3757

Mon–Sat 7.30am–10.30pm

After well over 20 years as a basic English 'caff', this bright, spacious outfit went through some rigorous changes in the late 1990s and now has the atmosphere of a de-greased greasy spoon. English breakfasts start at £1.70, a range of main courses (including meat & two veg) and dishes of the day at around £4, plus salads and sandwiches, with a BLT at £1.70. Another gem – low on pretension and very high on value with friendly, brisk service and a refreshingly mixed clientèle. Licensed too.

Makan

270 Portobello Road W10

020 8960 5169

Daily 11.30am–7pm

This friendly café/restaurant and takeaway specialises in Malaysian food from the more usual spring rolls and samosas to fish, chicken or squid *sambal* and green chicken curry (£4.50). The many vegetarian dishes include several with tofu, spicy pineapple curry and delicious chickpeas, spinach and dates (£4.25). Deservedly popular, especially at lunch time (12 noon–4pm) when there's a minimum charge of £2.50.

The Mannacafé

59a Portobello Road W11

020 7221 8416

Tues–Sat 9.30am–5pm; lunch 12.30–3pm

Caroline Bretherton uses only the freshest, usually organic, ingredients in the sandwiches and cakes served in this beautiful galleried space, attached to St Peter's Church and reached through a leafy courtyard. The friendly atmosphere is suitably serene and the food delicious and remarkably good value, including lunch dishes such as beetroot and goat's cheese risotto (£5.50), glazed chicken with rosemary potatoes and spinach (£6.50), and Greek salad (£2). A highly recommended alternative to some of the hyped-up eating places down the road.

Portobello Sports Café

3–5 Thorpe Close W10
020 8964 5484
Mon–Fri 12 noon–11pm; Sat & Sun till 6.30pm
If the space is anything to go by, this new venture above the Portobello Green Fitness Club is set to succeed, especially since it's under the same team as the excellent Sausage & Mash Café. Bleached wood floors, external balcony, a streamline bar, plus state-of-the-art pool tables, create a simple, modern feel with tempting food to match. The café is open to non-members till 6pm when it switches to members only; free for those already affiliated to PGFC, otherwise £5 a year for social membership. A welcome antidote to the lingering grimness of the Westway.

Ruby in the Dust

299 Portobello Road W10
020 8969 4626
Mon–Thurs 10am–11pm; Fri & Sat till 11.30pm (Sun 10pm)
Portobello seems the perfect location for this 'hippy chic' café cum bar/restaurant. Friendly staff, battered furniture (including a comfy sofa) and brightly painted walls scattered with Asian symbols make for a deliberately laid-back atmosphere. The food, with plenty of choice for vegetarians, is fittingly eclectic, ranging from traditional English breakfasts and bangers & mash to a chicken satay sandwich, warm tortilla wrap (both £4.50) or baked potato with Marrakech veg (£3.35).

Café Shiraz

72 Lancaster Road W11
020 7565 8258
Mon–Sat 9am–6pm
Run by an Iranian woman and her two sons, this clean and welcoming café/restaurant serves Persian specialities and continental patisseries. A haven of peace situated just off the often frantic Portobello Road.

RESTAURANTS

French

Brasserie du Marché aux Puces

349 Portobello Road W10
020 8968 5828
Mon–Sun 12 noon–4pm; Tues–Sun 7pm–11pm; breakfast Mon–Sun 10am–12 noon
Expect to hear fascinating smatterings of movie or fashion talk from your fellow diners in this wonderful restaurant. The bright turquoise exterior, bentwood chairs, and stylishly lived-in décor create the atmosphere of a local brasserie in the Quartier Latin, as the French owner intended. The menu offers good solid Gallic cuisine, and prices are not unreasonable (starters around £5–£6 and main courses £8–£10.) An all-day breakfast menu includes a truly perfect omelette and frites for £6.95. When things aren't too frantic (as they are over the weekend) you can get an excellent cup of coffee and read a book in peace.

Italian

Mediterraneo

37 Kensington Park Road W11
020 7792 0482
Lunch: Mon–Fri 12.30–3pm; Sat 12.30–4pm; Sun 12 noon–3.45pm
Dinner: Mon–Sat 6.30–11.30pm; Sun 6.30–11pm
This upmarket partner of the highly popular Basilico (below) serves generally good Italian food, from a range of pastas (no pizza) to dishes such as warm seafood salad, grilled seabass and pan-fried lamb on a bed of lentils and red onions –

deliciously tender. Good for lunch; slightly over-attentive waiters hover over the well-heeled clientèle who tend to favour this spot in the evenings. Prices range to around £6 for starters; £12–£16 for main courses. Wine is expensive.

Osteria Basilico

29 Kensington Park Road W11
020 7727 9957
Lunch: Mon–Fri 12.30–3pm; Sat 12.30–4pm; Sun 12.30–3.15pm
Dinner: Mon–Sat 6.30–11pm; Sun 6.30–10.30pm

Other restaurants may have failed on this prime site, but Osteria Basilico took off from the moment it opened in 1992. It's not the place for a relaxing evening – booking is essential and waiters can get frantic to the point of being rude – but the food is reliable and any long delays are alleviated by the usually swift arrival of delicious warm bread for dipping into olive oil. Recommended are the self-service *antipasti* (£6), Italian sausage served with spinach (£6), large crispy pizzas (£6.50–8) and it's always worth choosing from the daily specials. Tables upstairs are much more fun for people watching, augmented by pavement seating when weather permits.

Modern European

First Floor

186 Portobello Road W11
020 7243 0072
Dinner: Mon–Sat 7pm–11pm
Lunch: Mon–Sun 12 noon–3pm

The food is reasonably good and the service both friendly and discreet, but it's the spacious dining room with its atmosphere of faded grandeur that makes this restaurant so special. White linen table cloths add to the elegance while, at dinner, clusters of candles soften the dim light given off by a huge crystal chandelier. Starters on the eclectic menu include roast field mushrooms with olive toast (£5.25) and *zucchini* flowers stuffed with taleggio (£6.75), while a typical main course is grilled balsamic and lime chicken with roast vegetables (£12.50). The set lunch (Mon–Fri only) offers two courses for £10.50 – definite value.

192

192 Kensington Park Road W11
020 7229 0482
Lunch: Mon–Fri 12.30–3pm; Sat & Sun 12.30–3.30pm
Dinner: Mon–Sat 7–11.30pm; Sun 7–11.30pm

Notting Hill's first trendy wine bar (opened in the early 1980s) has a longstanding reputation as a lively, hip place to spend the evening shoulder-to-buttock in a party atmosphere around a bar area stuffed to the brim with fashion-conscious locals. The eating areas are generously placed and the menu, service and prices well tailored to the core clientèle. Although the enticing menu sometimes promises more than it delivers, the food is refined and the service charmingly laid-back. Recommended if you are neither very hungry nor hurried, and don't mind spending the odd buck over the odds for the sake of atmosphere. Starters from around £6; main courses £13.

English

Sausage & Mash Café

268 Portobello Road W10
020 8968 8898
Tues–Sun 11am–10pm

The S&M Café has taken a simple theme – traditional English bangers and mash – and made it a huge success by offering good food and terrific value with just the right touch of unpretentious style. Cream walls, rustic tables and green plastic seating provide the setting, while the menu lists a choice of five meat and three vegetarian sausages, three kinds of mash, salads and veg. Prices start at £5.75 for any two sausages, mash and gravy. Worth every penny. Licensed.

Spanish

Galicia

323 Portobello Road W10
020 8969 3539
Tues–Sun lunch 12 noon–3pm & 7–11.30pm
Authentic Spanish food, beer and wine are accompanied by a healthy disregard for the vagaries of fashion is this homely restaurant-cum-tapas bar. The cooking is plain and filling, with some good fish dishes such as *merluza a la gallega* (£10) and, especially recommended, *gambas al ajillo* – six fat prawns sizzling in garlic butter for around £6. There's rarely a time when you won't find a group of local Spaniards (usually men) propping up the bar at the front. Shut your eyes and you could be in Northern Spain.

Thai

Market Thai

240 Portobello Road W11
020 7460 8320
Daily 6–10.30pm
Local opinion is divided on this one: some say they love it, others say it's dreadful. It's either the food or the fantastic décor – all carved wooden screens and rich colours – but there's no denying that this is one of the most difficult eateries in the 'Bella to get a table without booking in advance. Main dishes cost from £4.95, and they do an excellent set menu at £13.95 per head (excluding drink). Note that the entrance is to one side on Lancaster Road rather than on Portobello Road.

BARS

The Beat Bar

265 Portobello Road W11
020 7792 2043
Daily 11.30am–11pm; Sat 11am–11pm
No credit cards
Blue and orange walls, and the requisite display of art-for-sale makes for an archetypal Portobello bar. The drinks list includes the usual designer beers from £2.50 a bottle and cocktails (£4 each, £12 for a jug). A major plus is the laid-back atmosphere, excellent Illy coffee, cosy seating, and a far-sighted policy of allowing you to bring in takeaways from the excellent Grain Shop a few doors down the road, provided you buy a drink.

The Market Bar

240 Portobello Road W11
020 7229 6472
Mon–Fri 12 noon–11pm; Sat 11am–11pm (Sun till 10.30pm)
The Market Bar has a surprisingly sumptuous urban rococo interior complete with Miss Haversham's front parlour curtains and dripping candles. There's no better place to be on a busy Saturday afternoon when the funk, reggae or soul is blasting out. Usual pub drinks, average £2.50 a pint.

Portobello Gold & the Buzz Bar

95–7 Portobello Road W11
020 7460 4906
Bar 10am–11pm; restaurant Mon–Fri 7.30pm to midnight; Sat 12.30–5.50pm, 7–11.30pm; Sun 1–8pm
Friendly staff, comfy benches, news-papers on a stick and a 'real' gas fire serve to make this one of the most congenial bars in the area. It even has the seal of approval from President Clinton who astounded local drinkers by dropping

in with his entourage for a lunch-time half-pint of organic lager last December. As well as bar food (starters from £2, main courses mostly around the £6.50 mark), the restaurant at the back (with a conservatory roof which opens in summer) offers an impressive menu with Pacific rim feel, specialising in vegetarian and seafood dishes including Irish oysters. It changes with the sign of the zodiac, a slightly cutesy notion but one that ensures seasonal ingredients are being used. The menu is also full of useful advice on which wines to choose from the comprehensive list. A two-course meal for two with wine will set you back about £50.

The **Buzz Bar** upstairs (020 7460 4906) was the second cybercafé to open in the UK. Unusually, it is run on an honesty system (signs exhort you to remember to pay at the bar on your way out) and the room is done up like someone's living room, with wicker armchairs and cushions everywhere. Fees: £3 per hour, minimum £1.50. Printing and scanning are also available.

Ground Floor

186 Portobello Road W11
020 7243 8701
Mon–Sat 11am–11pm; 12 noon–10.30pm; Sun 11am–10.30pm

Full of thirty-somethings dressed in black who look like they are 'working on a project right now', the atmosphere and décor is standard Y2K, with natural wood and leather sofas. Although bland, it's in a convenient position halfway along the Portobello Road, you can hear yourself think, prices are reasonable for this area and the staff are pleasant.

PUBS

Duke of Wellington

179 Portobello Road, W11
020 7727 6727
Mon–Sat 11am–11pm; Sun 12 noon –10.30pm

Now a free house, this was once owned by the brewers Finch's, hence its local nickname (spot the moniker on the clock above the wonderful round bar). A large, sprawling, noisy, smoky place, serving unexceptional pub drinks and spilling its customers out onto the pavements most Friday and Saturday nights, nonetheless it has the feel of a village local, which is essentially what it is.

Portobello Star

171 Portobello Road W11
020 7221 2442
Mon–Sat 11am–11pm; Sun 12 noon –10.30pm

Until the recent refit, this was the least spoilt of the pubs in the area, the main draw being Ray the barman who seemed to know every local character. Although it has lost some of its downmarket charm, it still hosts a healthy mix of dishevelled locals and market traders hanging out on a regular basis. In summer the front opens out for pavement tables, and there is bar food on offer.

The Sun in Splendour

7 Portobello Road W11
020 7313 9331
Mon–Sat 12noon–11pm; Sun 12.30pm –10.30pm

Once a perfectly decent old-fashioned London pub, this has endured so many attempts to inject it with 'character' that it has ended up with none at all; chalk boards announcing the promise of special deals, and too many tourists passing through deter most locals from drinking here. Still, the food is passable, there is a garden out back and the atmosphere is lively enough if you like that ersatz kind of thing.

ENTERTAINMENT

FILM

The Electric (see p 34)

MUSIC AND CLUBBING

Subterania (see p 89)

CHILDREN

Art 4 Fun/Creative Café
196 Kensington Park Road W11
020 7792 4567
Mon–Sun 10am–8pm
A concept brought over from the States where it seems stressed executives like nothing more than to unwind by making bowls out of balloons and plaster. As well as regular workshops, the café holds creative parties for children and adults (including hen nights) with pastimes from mosaic-making to T-shirt printing, and the 'famous ceramics painting party'. The basic studio fee is £3 plus the cost of the particular activity and materials you have chosen. Normal café fare is on offer, but you can bring in your own food and wine.

Playstation (see p 90)

SHOPPING

PORTOBELLO ANTIQUES MARKET

Portobello Antiques Market is a world in itself, a place where dealers trade with each other and visitors wander, some in search of a chance bargain, others hunting for specific curiosities. You'll find almost anything here, from twentieth-century costume jewellery to antique prints and maps, enamel boxes, Georgian silver, oriental art and old teddy bears. The list is endless.

Below is only a tiny selection, mostly in order of specialisation and attempting to pick out some of the quirkier or more specifically British antiques that make the market unique. However, a lot of the dealers, especially those with market stalls, tend to offer a wide range of goods which defy categorisation. Unless otherwise stated, all are Saturday traders only. As part of Portobello Market, the list incorporates Westbourne Grove (see pp 103–08).

The dealers themselves say that the strength of the pound, the difficulty of finding stock, and rising rents are making life tough for those who trade in Portobello, and rumours abound that this arcade or that is about to be sold to some high street retail chain. Despite the prevailing pessimism, there's a certain family atmosphere and, as in all extended families, everyone knows everyone else; if you're looking for a particular treasure, ask around and you'll be directed to the right person.

A guide to the market can be found on a lot of the stalls and is also available from the Portobello Road Antique Dealers Association (PADA) at 12 Vernon Yard, London W112DX. Tel: 020 7229 8354. Fax: 020 7243 3419.
Email: info@portobelloroad.co.uk

Internet: www.portobelloroad.co.uk.
Office open: Tues & Fri 9.30am–2.30pm
There is also a Saturday information booth at the junction of Portobello Road and Westbourne Grove. The PADA members subscribe to a code of practice printed on the back of the guide.

Trading begins at around 5.30am; most stallholders are in place by 8am. The old timers tend to slope off home by about 2pm, some do antiques fairs at certain times of the year, and not all come in every week, so if you're intending to see a specific person it's always worth checking first that they'll be there.

Beatlemania

The Beatles Stall

The Good Fairy Arcade
100 Portobello Road W11
A range of Beatles' memorabilia including original singles, picture discs, albums, magazines, photographs and some of the kitsch merchandise produced for their fans. Great fun. Prices start at around £4.

Clocks

John Carnie Antiques

Arbras Gallery
292 Westbourne Grove W11
020 7221 6710 (Sat)
07973 197974 (Mobile)
After spending 20 years at Bermondsey market, John Carnie moved to Portobello seven years ago. Although he only advertises as a specialist in clocks, watches, and barometers, he also has a number of delightful music boxes, live steam trains (the biggest of which could pull 14 children), and various mechanical eccentricities. As he put it himself, these are 'toys for old boys'.

Costumes and vintage clothing

Sheila Cook Textiles

283 Westbourne Grove W11
020 7792 8001
www.sheilacook.co.uk
sheilacook@sheilacook.co.uk
Wed–Sat 10am–6pm; all other times by appointment
Sheila Cook has had shops in the area for the past 30 years. Her unique collection of textiles, costume, and accessories dates from the late eighteenth century to the 1970s and cuts across the fashion and antique world, appealing as much to the public as to the film and television designers who hire from her. Rummage around for wonderful woven paisley shawls, or that little Forties' garden party dress, or ask for help from the bevy of young and friendly assistants.

General

Alice's

86 Portobello Road
020 7792 2456
Tues–Sat 9am–5pm
Unmissable with its bright red façade, Alice's has been here forever. In the Sixties this was the place for Edwardian policeman's cloaks and military costumes of the type worn by the Beatles on the cover of *Sgt Pepper's Lonely Heart's Club Band*. Nowadays the shop sells a cheerful selection of painted furniture, decorative pieces, painted advertising boards, pine, toys and other objects – both reproduction and genuine antiques.

Delehar

146 Portobello Road W11
020 7727 9860 (Sat)
01923 829079 (Other times)
This family-run business was established in 1911. The third generation now offers an eclectic selection of some of the best-quality antiques you will find anywhere.

Flora Offard specialises in costume jewellery from the 1880s to 1960s. Unlike the exquisite eighteenth- and early nineteenth-century English paste her sister Marion Gettleson has in the neighbouring cabinet, this is immediately wearable and chosen for style, not just designer signatures. Marion's main area of expertise is, well, indefinable; let's say esoteric decorative objects, games and curiosities. Peter Delehar is an expert in scientific and medical instruments. The back of the shop is the third sister Valerie Jackson-Harris's domain. One of Britain's top dealers in ephemera, a term covering a wide range of marginalia from valentines to royal commemoratives, she has particularly fine material relating to London. The entire family is passionate about what they do and generous with their time and knowledge.

Glass and crystal

Alan Milford

Stand 5/6 Dolphin Arcade,
155–57 Portobello Road, W11
01273 503582

As one of the other dealers put it, 'Alan Milford will sell you a humble tumbler for a few quid, but if you ask him nicely to find you a rare piece for £10,000 he'll do that too'. An extremely knowledgeable specialist in seventeenth- to eighteenth-century drinking glasses, he also has French paperweights and European and Chinese pottery and porcelain.

Jewellery

The market is awash with costume jewellery dealers, and sifting through great trays of brooches, rings, and earrings is one of the joys of being here. Dealers specialising in period jewellery include:

Kleanthous Antiques Ltd

144 Portobello Road W11
020 7727 3649
antiques@kleanthous.com

Costas Kleanthous is the chairman of the Portobello Road Antiques Dealers Association, which has been trading since 1969. Kleanthous has a wide range of stock, but particularly period jewellery ranging from the Georgian era through to art deco. Also a wide selection of vintage wrist and pocket watches.

John and Linda Semple

Unit 44, Admiral Vernon Antiques Market
141–49 Portobello Road W11
01526 323312

Mainly designer pieces including Arts and Crafts and art deco, both of which are enjoying a return to vogue. Of particular interest if you're looking for something British is the jet jewellery fashionable during the Victorian era.

Needlework

Erna Hiscock

Chelsea Galleries
69 Portobello Road W11
01233 661407

Samplers are needlework panels produced between the seventeenth- and nineteenth-centuries by young girls in order to show their skills with a needle, rather as we put together a CV. Others would embroider maps of the British Isles to learn the counties. Erna Hiscock has the largest collection of these hugely decorative pieces of English social history, with prices ranging from £60 to £10,000. You will also find children's ceramics on this stand, as this is the field of Erna's partner John Shepherd (see pottery and porcelain, p 49).

Pens

Battersea Pen Home

Portobello Studios Antiques Arcade
101–03 Portobello Road
0870 900 1888
www.penhome.com
Vintage fountain pens (Parker, Watermans, Swan and others) bought and sold with all repairs and servicing by the Pen Home.

Perfume bottles and boxes

Lawrence Gould

Harris's Arcade
161–63 Portobello Road
020 8459 7957/0860 875150 (Mobile)
The only word for polyglot Lawrence Gould and his daughter Nicky is boisterous. Lawrence started as a keen collector who had to sell to make space, Nicky joined him 17 years ago. Trading insults and jokes at the top of their voices, it's quite a double act, but they really know their stuff. Eighteenth- and nineteenth-century English and continental perfume bottles, and Bilston enamel patch boxes (a British speciality), make up the bulk of their stock and they have the kind of pieces you'd expect to see in the V&A (and some of them have indeed ended up there). With their international client base, you can catch them at Olympia and Miami Beach Antiques Fairs as well as at Portobello.

Pewter

Hilary Kashden

Outside Admiral Vernon Arcade
141–49 Portobello Road W11
020 8958 1018
Hilary has been doing Portobello on and off for 35 years, dealing in pewter, a material consisting of 90 per cent tin, which fulfilled the role of plastic in the fourteenth to nineteenth centuries. Although produced all over Europe, British pewter is often reckoned to be of the best quality. It was used to make all manner of affordable domestic and tavern ware, enjoying its finest moment in the seventeenth century, until porcelain came along as a cheaper alternative. Designs have been copied from those used for silverware and Hilary has some splendidly decorative pieces, especially flagons, plates, candlesticks and spoons. She also has a small display cabinet of curios including pilgrim badges.

Picture frames

Justin Skrebowski

The World Famous Portobello Market
77 Portobello Road W11
020 7792 9742/07774 612474 (Mobile)
justin@skreb.co.uk
Sat 8am–4pm or by appointment
Specialises in old frames – from 1700 to 1940 – in particular for watercolours and prints. Also folio stands/browsers and easels.

Portrait miniatures

Stewart Antiques

Stall 18 (Ground Floor), Lip
020 7727 2027 (Sat)
020 8446 2537 (Home)
One of the most respected dealers in portrait miniatures, Mr Stewart sports a bow tie and a charming Middle-European accent. An enormous selection of fine portraits, mainly painted on ivory and enamel, includes boxes, rings, and brooches, both English and continental.

Pottery and porcelain (British)

John Shepherd

Chelsea Galleries
69 Portobello Road W11
01233 661407
John Shepherd started his career as an archaeologist specialising in medieval

pottery, before dealing in English ceramics dating from the Middle Ages up to the 1840s. His stock is mainly blue and white, and creamware, with a growing amount of children's ware to complement the needlework displayed by his partner Erna Hiscock (see p 49).

Ray Walker Antiques

Burton Arcade
296 Westbourne Grove W11
020 8727 7920 (Sat)
020 8464 7981 (Home)
0780 1225866 (Mobile)

Everyone I asked about pottery and porcelain directed me to Ray Walker. During the nineteenth century hundreds of small factories all over Staffordshire produced the animal and portrait figures that almost epitomise British ceramics, and this dealer has a tremendous selection, as well as other typically British pieces including highly decorative lustreware. Prices reflect the popularity of such pieces, and you won't be picking up a bargain but making a solid investment. In the same arcade Aurea Carter is a highly respected porcelain dealer, and Judy Bland specialises in bargeware.

Prints and maps

The Portobello Print Rooms

109 Portobello Road W11
020 7243 2203 (Sat)
020 8858 2560 (Weekdays)

The biggest selection of original maps, prints and engravings in Portobello, helpfully classified by subject. Every possible category is covered, from furniture design to birds, but if you're looking for something particularly British there are maps starting from the seventeenth century, views of London and the rest of England, charming song sheets (the forerunners of hit singles), sporting and coaching prints, and the crude satire of eighteenth- to nineteenth-century political cartoons. Marguerite Burr has been here for 30 years, and her son has recently opened his own shop around the corner at 297 Westbourne Grove. All the pictures have new mounts and prices are reasonable, starting at around £15.

Silver

Wynyard RT Wilkinson

Red Lion Arcade
165–69 Portobello Road
01787 237372

The unanimous word on the street is that if you're looking for good-quality silver at sensible prices, then this is your man. Extremely knowledgeable and highly respected in the trade, he has produced two books on Indian silver, as well as a history of hallmarks. Areas of specialisation include flatware (or spoons and forks to you and me); cutlery, which apparently should only mean knives; full sets of twelve times everything, known as 'canteens'; and an array of collectibles from port labels to a novelty shot measure shaped like a top hat. Pieces date from 1650 to 1980 and come from England, Ireland, Scotland, North America, the Commonwealth and India (both local and colonial work).

Stained glass

Neil Phillips

99 Portobello Road W11
020 7229 2113
Mon–Sat 9am–5pm

Phillips specialises in stained glass windows and ecclesiastical antiques, with a client base ranging from major rock and movie stars to specialists in medieval glass and Japanese air pilots. Eddie Phillips opened the shop in 1963 and many customers drawn here then by his flamboyant charm are still coming back today. It's now managed by his son Neil, who specialises in rare windows but also sells handbag-sized 'hangers' for those who want to purchase a smaller piece of this rare and beautiful art. There are also tiles by Pugin at surprisingly realistic prices and occasional pieces of Arts and Craft metalwork and furniture.

Tartanware

Eureka Antiques

Geoffrey Van Arcade
105 Portobello Road W11
020 7229 5577 (Sat)
0161 941 5453 (Weekdays)
0498 573 332 (Mobile)

You can be forgiven for not knowing what this is. A prolific cottage industry between 1830 and 1870 in and around the village of Mauchline, Ayrshire, produced a host of objects such as boxes and cotton reels for the souvenir market. Made from sycamore they were covered in hand-printed or, more rarely, painted paper in every clan tartan going. Noel Gibson has been dealing for 40 years, 15 in Portobello, and his clients range from the Scottish aristocracy to North Americans looking for their family tartan. Some pieces have hand-painted miniatures, mainly local views, on them, and others are decorated with ferns (unsurprisingly known as 'fernware').

Teddybears

Heather's Teddies

The World Famous Portobello Market
77 Portobello Road W11

Heather has been dealing for 17 years and collecting teddies for a lot longer. She even has her own limited edition of new bears, which cost £500 for the whole family of four. The antique beasts are mainly English (Merrythought, Chad Valley, Chiltern and Dean's being the manufacturers to look out for) and German, with some representatives of the rest of Europe. Steiff's is the one name everyone has heard of, and, of course, Heather has a good range of these. Prices go from £55 into the thousands.

Toys and games

Pierre Patau

Stand 5, Admiral Vernon Arcade
141–49 Portobello Road W11
020 7834 1423
www.antiquetoysngames.com
Pierre@patau.freeserve.net

A member of the Ephemera and Magic Lantern Societies, Pierre has stock dating from the eighteenth century to World War I. He specialises in games, juvenilia, magic, movable books, and pre-cinema, which basically means all sorts of entrancing optical toys that kept both children and adults amused on rainy Sundays before the advent of the moving picture. If you think kaleidoscopes are cool, have a look at such marvels as a Chinese Shadow Theatre. Prices range from £10 to 'the sky's the limit'.

Wristwatches

See **Kleanthous Antiques** under Jewellery

ART SUPPLIES

Lyndons Art & Graphics

197 & 164 Portobello Road W11
0207 727 4357/020 7727 5192
Mon–Sat 9.30–6pm; Sun 11am–4pm

Much used by local artists, the art shop on the corner of Portobello Road and Blenheim Crescent stocks such a wide-ranging collection of artist's materials that each visit feels like a voyage of discovery. Downstairs is crammed with papers, cards, notebooks and other materials; upstairs concentrates on brushes, pencils and paints, plus photocopying and laminating services. Only a block away, the stationery shop has racks of cards on the pavement and sells a comprehensive range of office supplies, including printer cartridges.

BOOKS

Books for Cooks

4 Blenheim Crescent W11
020 7221 1992
www.booksforcooks.com
Bookshop Mon–Sat 10am–6pm; lunch Mon–Sat 12 noon–3pm
A staggering range of cookery books, delicious coffee and the best-value three-course lunch you're likely to find in London make this a consistently popular haunt for visitors and residents alike. Even on Mondays this tiny shop can be packed with customers leafing through volumes as diverse as *Chocolate Passion, Goose Fat and Garlic* and *Cooking with Ganja*. (also see p 36).

Garden Books

11 Blenheim Crescent W11
020 7727 1992
sales@garden-books.co.uk
Mon–Sat 9am–6pm
Garden Books is the latest addition to the bookshops of Blenheim Crescent. Started in 1996 by Valerie Scriven and Rob Cassy, this beautiful-looking shop stocks a wide range of books about every aspect of gardening, from the practical to the inspirational. It includes a large selection of environmental and interior design books. The owners have also written their own tome, *Everything You Need to Know About Gardening* (£12.99).

Intef Books

300 Westbourne Park Road W11
020 7243 3620
Mon–Sat 10am–6pm
It's easy to miss this unexpected bookshop, despite its temple-like wall, obelisk and the prayer in blue hieroglyphics that adorns the top of the building's white façade. Owner Amon Saba Saakana specialises in books on and artefacts from ancient Egypt and related civilisations, in the belief that the European emphasis on Greece as the gestator of culture and civilisation is misleading. A prolific author himself, he has an almost missionary zeal about correcting the lack of attention paid to the role of ancient Egypt in influencing both Greece and Rome. Many books are imported from North America, and Saba also publishes scholarly African texts under the imprint Karnak House.

Portobello Bookshop

328 Portobello Road W10
020 8964 3166
sales@portobello-books.com
Mon–Fri 11am–5pm; Sat 9am–5pm
Proprietor Lawrence Thompson sells first editions, out-of-print and second-hand books, with an emphasis on non-fiction, especially in the areas of photography, film, art and architecture.

The Travel Bookshop

13 Blenheim Crescent W11
020 7229 5260
www.thetravelbookshop.co.uk
post@thetravelbookshop.co.uk
Mon–Sat 10am–6pm; Sun 11am–4pm
Blenheim Crescent's first bookshop has a distinguished reputation with travellers and would-be travellers all over the world. Since 1999, it's also become a curious source of pilgrimage for the countless fans of Richard Curtis's film (details, p 36–7).

FASHION

Bella Parkinson

Stall under the Westway
No phone
Fri & Sat 9am–5pm
Currently one of the most innovative young designers in the market, Bella works from a central theme and then expands on her collection of feminine tops, skirts and jackets in various textures, from silks to wool depending on the season. Clothes are complemented by original accessories and jewellery.

Crazy Tights

Stall E 136, just before the bridge, heading north Portobello Road W10
Friday & Saturday 8am–6pm
Stallholder Ozra sells a riotous mix, from black lace to tights in every conceivable pattern and colour, including a few Mary Quant items from the 1980s. Adult and children's sizes start from around £3.

Euforia

61b Lancaster Road W11
020 7243 1808
www.euphoria.uk.com
Mon–Sat 11am–7pm
Avant-garde creations and an eclectic mix of footwear and accessories share space with carefully selected pop-culture books, collectors' fashion and lifestyle magazines. Owner Annette Olivieri is a leather expert; among the clothes she designs and makes herself are some gorgeous ruched jackets and coats with delicate string-tie fastenings and necklines. Popular with the fashion in-crowd.

Graham & Green

10 Elgin Crescent W11
020 7727 4594
info@grahamandgreen.co.uk
www.grahamandgreen.co.uk
Mon–Sat 10am–6pm; Sun 11am–5pm
Antonia Graham's fashion shop stocks an original range of contemporary designer clothes skilfully selected by buyer Cushion Katz. Several labels such as Claudie Pierlot, Yoshiki Hishinuma and Capucine Puerari are more or less exclusive to this store, which also sells jewellery, bags – including wonderful creations by Orla Keily – and the odd mirror, table or lamp, also by modern designers.

Griffin

297 Portobello Road W10
020 8960 9607
www.griffin-studio.com
Mon–Sat 10am–6pm
The multi-talented Griffin studio designs menswear for Kenzo, Iceberg and other big names, but this is their first retail outlet for the Griffin label. The shop/installation space provides a refreshingly different experience: there are no rails or shelves, just garments hung on bare slate walls on which shoppers are invited to draw. That was autumn 2000. With every season's collection, the décor will change. The clothes – stylish hooded coats, trousers and shirts in off-beat streetwear style – are also worth coming for. Everything is user friendly, from jackets that will keep you warm in the coldest winters, to trousers with pockets for everything

---

Justin Kara

253 Portobello Road W11
020 7792 6920
Mon–Sat 10.30am-6pm
Former market-stall owners artist/architect Kara and Justin, an interior designer, decided to open a women's fashion and lifestyle shop that represented young designers not found elsewhere in London.

The result is jewel-crusted handbags from Vesna, a Croatian designer, customised dresses by Mai Hui Luin and a great mix of skirts and tops by the Swedish studio Miracle Agency and English designer Susy Harper. Also on sale are mosaic panels and a beautiful mirrored bust by Celia Gregory (£800).

The London Beachstore

178 Portobello Road W11
020 7243 2772
Mon–Wed 10am–6pm; Thurs–Sat 10am–6.30pm; Sun 12.30–5pm
Buy your surfboard from Low Pressure (below) and you have all you need for the beach without even having to leave Portobello, apart from the sea, that is. The stock's seaside theme is echoed by the shop's wave-like interior where the clothes and accessories on display are original, stylish and functional. When the beach is out of season, owners Dickon, Ben and Dave will show you the latest in snowboarding and après ski wear. Also available is the gear needed for the fastest growing water sport in the world – kite surfing.

Low Pressure

23 Kensington Park Road W11
020 7792 3134
shop@lowpressure.demon.uk
Mon–Sat 10am–6pm
International, surf-crazy staff dispense good advice as well as all the toys, clothes and accessories you might need for an active beach holiday. This includes a fair selection of swimwear for men and women, plus a good range of surfboards – some second-hand. Low Pressure publishes its own Stormrider guides, so far covering Europe and 'the world', with North America coming out in 2001. Snowboard guides to Europe and the USA are also on sale.

Nothing

230 Portobello Road W11
020 7221 2910
www.nothingshop.co.uk
Mon–Sat 10.30am–7.30pm; Sun 12 noon–5pm
Nothing is an own-label store selling street clothes for women. The collection, designed for easy wear with a twist, includes funky T-shirts, bags, belts and other accessories. Fabrics used are denim, tartan, wool, 100 per-cent cotton and showerproof synthetics – essential for London.

The Portobello Road Cashmere Shop

166 Portobello Road W11
020 7792 2571
eldon.cashmere@ukgateway.net
www.portobellocashmere.com
Fri 10am–5pm; Sat 9am–6pm; weekdays only over the Christmas period (Nov–Jan)
Devoted to the best-feeling wool in the world, this shop sells great-value cashmere in a range of good colours. Using only Scottish wool, owner Annemarie Beatty designs many of the gloves, scarves, sweaters and cardigans herself – usually are made in Hawick. European *Vogue* has described it as 'the kind of shop you have to keep popping into'. Many locals would agree.

Also look out for second-hand cashmere on **market stalls** under the Westway (Fri–Sat) and on Fridays between the junctions of Cambridge Gardens and Oxford Gardens.

Sub Couture

204 Kensington Park Road W11
020 7229 5434
subcouture@x-stream.co.uk
Mon–Sat 10.30am–6.30pm; Sun 12 noon –5pm. Staff are happy to stay late on request
Nestling quietly among the restaurants

and wine bars, Sub Couture offers a selection of contemporary designer wear from bohemian to classic, including accessories and shoes across 32 labels, from Christian Lacroix, Amaya Azaruga, Bruns Bazaar, Kenzo and Missioni to Cutler & Gross. The shop's look changes weekly to coincide with the arrival of new collections. The clientèle's ages range from 25 to 45 and everyone is treated with the personal touch and honest advice. Tailoring service available.

Supra For Girls

212 Kensington Park Road W11
020 7221 6857
Mon–Sat 10.30am–6.30pm
This shop is a favourite of Natalie Imbruglia and rock chicks who still like to wear their Levi's, twisted of course, but teamed up with some seriously fashionable T-shirts and accessories. Labels include Mr Friendly, Zakee Shariff and PPQ. A small selection of trainers and shoes is also available.

Titri

82a Portobello Road W11
020 7229 2023
www.titri-online.com
sales@titri-online.com
Tues–Sat 10am–5pm
This tiny shop is packed with delectable clothes and soft furnishings from India. Owner Mark Akroyd travels there regularly to replenish his stock and to supervise the hand-embroidery on shawls and linen commissioned from Kashmir and Lucknow. He's also the distributor for Brigitte Singh who takes her ideas for block prints from the decorative arts of seventeenth-century India. Includes a small selection of good-value jewellery.

Utuinana

Stall under the Westway
Fridays only 8am–4pm
A rich mix of urban and evening wear in antique silk, organza, chiffon and hand-embroidered denim are sold on this stall, which originates from the shop of the same name in West Hampstead. Birds of paradise feathers, chokers, arm pieces and sterling silver jewellery help complete the picture.

For more Fashion, see **Portobello Green Arcade**, (p 58)

Vintage and second-hand

The Antique Clothing Shop

282 Portobello Road W10
020 8964 4830
Fri & Sat 9am–6pm
Several vintage clothes shops have been squeezed out by trendy streetwear boutiques, but this rich resource, much favoured by models and stylists, at least seems to be surviving. Clothes and accessories span many eras from Victorian bustle dresses, pantaloons and bonnets to Sixties' flares and bright satin shirts – all at surprisingly reasonable prices.

Still

61D Lancaster Road W11
020 7243 2932
Mon–Sat 11am–6pm; Sun 12 noon–5pm
In this lovely calm space, just around the corner from the bustle of Portobello Road, owners Sophie and Steve sell a tasteful selection of vintage clothes, enhanced by new designs made from vintage fabrics. Prices range from £15 for a hand-rolled silk scarf to hundreds of pounds for rarer collectors' items.

Children's clothes

Chi Chi

Stall 125E Fridays
Stall 5 Saturdays

Chi Chi specialises in young children's clothes from newborn to three years, and wonderful toys, which you may be sorely tempted to buy for yourself – no Mickey Mouse or Power Rangers, but innocent motifs and images of teddy bears in pastel shades. Isla also paints children's murals by commission.

See also **Cheeky Monkeys** (p 63) and **Sasti** (p 59)

Jewellery

Andea Jewellery

203 Portobello Road W11
020 7221 5690
Mon–Sat 10am–6pm; Sun 11am–5pm

Long established wholesalers in the area, Andea specialises in silverwork designed and made in Mexico – not just rings, bracelets and necklaces, but gift items such as babies' rattles, paper knives and key rings. Prices can vary from £2.25 for plain hoop earrings to £400 for a heavy silver necklace. It's also a good place for Chinese pottery, silk cushions and ancient stoneware for the house or garden.

Maynard Glass

Outside HSBC bank
0958 733928 (Mobile)
Thurs 9am–2pm; Fri 9.30am–5.30pm

At the other end of the market, on the corner of Colville Terrace, newcomers Marysia and Peter specialise in Venetian glass jewellery, chandeliers and masks. Prices are well below what you would pay in a shop, and they also make items to order so you can choose your own colour scheme and design.

Necklace Maker Workshop

259 Portobello Road W11
020 7792 3436
stephanietomalinbeads@compuserve.com
Mon–Fri 11am–5.30pm; Sat 10am–6pm

Stephanie Tomalin has been selling beads here since 1982 and every year her collection seems to grow. The shop is positively bursting with loose beads of every kind, from cheap tubes of embroidery beads to rare, antique, precious and exotic items from Afghanistan, Egypt, India and Africa. The cheaper ones are sold by weight while rarities such as excavated beads from West Africa cost £85 a string. Pendants, threads and fasteners are also on sale and, for those who need it, threading tuition can be booked by appointment.

Ruby Red

341 Portobello Road W10
020 8969 5051
www.rubyred.co.uk
Tues–Sat 11am–6pm

Designers Lucy Goldman and Sam Salmons design and make their jewellery in a workshop at the back of this enticing shop, right up the northern end of Portobello. Both work in silver, gold and stones, and like doing commissions with the customer involved at every stage. They show the work of 13 other jewellers and plan to launch a jointly designed Ruby Red collection in 2001, anticipated to be 'cutting-edge and cheeky'. Prices range from £50 to £1,000.

See also **Portobello Green Arcade,** (p 58)

Haberdashery

Temptation Alley

361 Portobello Road W10
020 8964 2004
Mon–Sat 10am–5.30pm

This treasure trove of trimmings is indeed a dressmakers' heaven, packed with a chaotic collection of ribbons, lace and braid – in boxes, on the counter, hanging from the ceiling – and all manner of catches and cottons and buttons.

PORTOBELLO GREEN ARCADE

Debonair

Unit 23
020 8960 7679
Tues–Sat 10.30am–6pm
Deborah Nicholls is another example of a market trader made good. Her speciality is jewel-coloured leather, torn and ripped in just the right places to show maximum cleavage or leg. No two pieces are the same and some are multi-purpose, depending on how you tie them. The shop, complete with a Sixties' fridge display-unit, doubles as an ever-changing installation space. Deborah also does beaded jeans and a selection of leather/feather necklaces and wristbands.

Isis

Unit 3
020 8968 5055
Mon–Sat 9.30am–5.30pm
Isis has been selling modern silver jewellery in Portobello Green since its inception. As for most designers in the Arcade, the combination of work space and shop means that Linda Atkinson can design and make her jewellery as well as sell it on the spot. She also displays the work of other contemporary jewellers who complement her own pieces. Prices range from £2.50 to £250.

Olivia Morris

Unit 19
020 8962 0353
livmorris@aol.com
Tues–Sat 10am–6pm
In 1998, Browns and Pineal Eye snapped up Morris's handbags called Slag Bags. Since then, she has moved on to design cutting-edge, sexy footwear collections for British designers Anthony Symonds, Boyd and further afield for DKNY. She also stocks her own label of unconventional hand-finished mules, courts and boots in leather and suede.

Preen

Unit 5
020 8968 1542
Tues–Sat 11am–6pm
Popular for its hybrid style of clothes, fusing antique with modern, masculine with feminine, Preen is immediately recognisable for signature touches of small but significant detailing, such as puffs and tucks, as well as the imaginative use of recycled pieces. A favourite with celebrities such as Kate Moss, Liv Tyler and Kylie Minogue, the company has had phenomenal success in Britain, New York and Tokyo, and is much sought after by buyers and press during London Fashion Week.

Puppy and Bedstock

Unit 26
020 8964 1547
bedstock@msn.com
www.Puppy-Bedstock.co.uk
Mon–Sat 10am–6pm
The great allure of this bedding boutique is that it sells only 100 per-cent cotton percale bedlinen and towels, with more than 450 colour dyes to choose from. The Union Jack pillow cases and red scattered-rose designs are very popular, and you can have your bedlinen made to measure in any size.

Sarah Bunting

Unit 22
020 8968 2253
sarahbunting@enterprise.net
Mon–Sat 10am–6pm (or later by appointment)

Sarah Bunting does many jewellery commissions for engagements and weddings, which she designs and makes in her studio-cum-shop. She loves working alone and produces pieces in silver, gold and platinum using both precious and semi-precious stones. Bunting is one of 35 English and European designers who show annually in the Dazzle exhibition at the National Theatre.

Sasti

Unit 8
020 8960 1125
Mon–Sat 10.30am–6pm
Exciting children's wear and accessories (age range is 0–6 years) for those who want something trendy and different to the high street. Labels include Squirt knitwear, Our Life, and 10 Fingers 10 Toes. Includes a lovely play area with toys to keep non-shoppers happy. The shop also sells various market stallholders' goods, providing a good price range to choose from.

Supra for Boys

Units 1 & 2
020 7243 2354
www.supra-london.com
Mon–Sat 10.30am–6.30pm
Supra caters for up-and-coming media/internet savvy men and tourists searching for the laid-back trendy look. Labels include Stussy, Maharashi, the cult label Silas and Rolling Rock. In the words of owner Chris Malcolm, 'high-end streetwear and limited edition trainers for music/media/fashion/drug dealers and others'.

Zarvis

Unit 4
020 8968 5435
www.zarvis.com
Wed, Fri & Sat 11am–6pm
Vivian Zarvis already mixes medicinal and cosmetic herbs in her tiny but enticing shop, but dreams of being able to have a large space in which she could use a giant pestle and mortar to blend her concoctions. Way ahead of her time, Vivian has been using simple glass bottles and aluminium tins with hand-written labels for her brews for years. She studied Ayurvedic medicine in India, but rather than treating people who are ill encourages people to be good to themselves. She sources her ultra-pure ingredients from all over the world and sells tempting tins with names such as 'Dreamtime' and 'Redemption'. You could spend a fortune in this shop but could also get away with buying sandalwood soap for £1.

FLOWERS AND PLANTS

Tom's

Corner of Elgin Crescent and Kensington Park Road
020 7792 8510
Mon, Thurs, Fri & Sat 9am–6.30pm; Tues & Wed 9am–6pm; Sun 10am–5pm
High rent increases forced Tom out of his Elgin Crescent shop but he kept a stall on this corner site and now also works out of a tiny studio in Clarendon Road (see p 156).

Valerie's Flowers

337 Portobello Road W10
020 8969 2927
Mon–Sat 8.30am–6pm
Being at the 'wrong' end of Portobello Road, Valerie Pile is able to offer very competitive prices. With its tiled floor, the shop has an old-fashioned feeling but Valerie, who did her apprenticeship with Moyses Stevens, does contemporary arrangements for all occasions and will also deliver locally.

FOOD AND WINE

The Breadstall

172 Portobello Road W11
020 7221 3122
Daily 8am–6pm. No credit cards
The Vince family started with a stall in the market, then opened this shop in 1998. One of the most welcome additions to the area, it has an enormous range of breads, including baguettes made with proper French flour and delicious olive focaccia. Bagels and rye bread are delivered daily by taxi from the Brick Lane bakery and the Cornish pasties come from Bodmin. They also offer a choice of sandwiches and patisserie. Try the wonderful lemon tarte or the chocolate brioche (which makes a great version of bread and butter pudding).

Mr Christian's

11 Elgin Crescent W11
020 7229 0501
Mon–Thurs 7am-7pm; Fri & Sat 5.30am–6.30pm; Sun 7am–5pm
Friendly, knowledgeable staff, delicious home-made dishes and quality goods from small suppliers have ensured this deli's popularity for more than 25 years. A team of six work full-time in the downstairs kitchen to produce a mouth-watering array of food, from pastries, tarts and flapjacks to soups, stews, salad dishes and sandwiches. The chocolate brownies are a dream. A huge choice of cheeses, pâtés, olives and sauces grace the delicatessen counter, while oils, vinegars and packaged goods spill over into the small room at the back.

Corney & Barrow

194 Kensington Park Road W11
020 7221 5122
wlws@corbar.co.uk
Mon–Sat 10.30am–9pm
An Aladdin's cave of wine with the emphasis on traditional, fine and rare older vintages, which often come in tempting bin-ends. House wines start at £3.95 and, although prices can be as high as £895 a bottle, the qualified, knowledgeable and friendly staff will help find something for everyone. It also stocks a good range of olive oils and the best local selection of Cuban cigars, as well as specialist whiskies and wine accessories. Tastings and discounts can be organised through the company's wine society and although much of its trade is local (they deliver), wine is despatched all over the world.

Felicitous

19 Kensington Park Road W11
020 7243 4050
Mon–Fri 9am–9pm; Sat 9am–7pm; Sun 9am–5pm
A food shop that prides itself on its specialised groceries stocking only the 'best of the best'. The products are individually sourced and the take-away food is of restaurant quality. The chef, Tom Kime, is extremely versatile, having worked at the River Café and for Rick Stein, as well as doing a course in 'Royal Thai' cookery. Much of the business is devoted to outside catering and Felicity Osborne, the owner, does all the behind-the-scenes organisation for weddings, christenings and parties.

The French Cheese Stall

Opposite the Tea & Coffee Plant
Portobello Road W11
Saturdays only
Yann Leblais used to have a cheese shop in Normandy and now brings a fantastic assortment of really good-quality French cheeses, pâté, rillettes, honey, and saucissons over on the ferry every week. The choice of goat's milk cheese is

especially impressive. Prices are reasonable, and there are always good deals of the day starting from £1.50.

P De La Fuente

288 Portobello Road W10
020 8960 5657
Mon–Sat 9am–6pm
Smaller and less well known than Garcia & Sons below, this friendly Spanish grocers offers a similar range of food and wine, from chorizo and whole hams to cakes, biscuits, sugared almonds and reasonably-priced traditional wines. One of the best buys is Parma ham which is astonishingly cheap.

R Garcia & Sons

248–50 Portobello Road W10
020 7221 6119
Tues–Sat 8.30am–6pm
This traditional Spanish supermarket sells an impressive selection of wines, oils, olives and cheeses as well as a wide choice of tinned foodstuffs, cakes and preserves. Earthenware pots are another good buy and Christmas always brings a wide selection of Italian panettone.

The Grain Shop

269a Portobello Road W11
020 7229 5571
Mon–Sat 9.30am–6pm
Lunch-time queues testify to the enduring success of this wholefood shop, which started life here as Ceres in the early Seventies. Take-away vegan and vegetarian food constitutes the main draw, with a choice of about ten hot dishes, and salads in small, medium or large portions, in whatever combination you fancy. Everything is cooked on the premises, including the pastries, cakes and bread – at once wholesome and delicious.

Kingsland, the Edwardian Butchers

140 Portobello Road W11
020 7727 6067
Mon–Sat 7.30am–6pm
Wood panelling, striped aprons and top hats provide the Edwardian element of this traditional English butchers, which offers free-range eggs, chutneys and cheeses, in addition to organic and non-organic meat. Expect to queue on Saturdays and especially at Christmas when Kingsland provides an excellent and far cheaper alternative to the famous Lidgate on Holland Park Avenue (see p 156).

The Organic Market

Under the canopy beneath the Westway
Thurs 9.30am–6pm
Sadly, this market has never really taken off, even though some of the food is well worth seeking out. Home-grown fruit and vegetables are joined by overseas produce such as cheeses, biscuits and nougat from Sardinia, and unusual honeys and preserves from Provence. Local resident Catherine Bessin sells the honey, which comes in flavours such as thyme, rosemary, pine and chestnut, all available for tasting. Chestnut jam is especially recommended. There's also a good second-hand bookstall.

Portobello Wholefoods

266 Portobello Road W10
020 8968 9133
Mon–Sat 9.30am–6pm; Sun 11am–5pm
This slightly shambolic business may lack the panache of the nearby Grain Shop but it does sell a far wider selection of goods. Grains, cereals, dried fruit, nuts, pulses, honey, jam, eco-friendly cleaning materials, soaps and potions are the mainstay, with a limited selection of organic bread, fresh fruit and vegetables.

The Spice Shop

1 Blenheim Crescent W11
020 7221 4448
www.thespiceshop.co.uk
Mon–Sat 9.30–6pm; Sun 11am–5pm

Starting from a market stall, Birgit Erath has built up an impressive business around her passion for spices of all kinds. Opened in 1995, her tiny welcoming shop is crammed with more than 1,500 herbs, spices and blends, plus nuts, beans, grains and dried fruit, each of which she will happily discuss in great detail. Weather permitting, pots of fresh herbs, nuts and ropes of garlic adorn the bright yellow façade.

The Tea & Coffee Plant

170 Portobello Road W11
020 7221 8137
coffee@pro-net.co.uk
www.coffee.uk.com
Tues–Fri 10.30am–6.30pm; Sat 9am–6pm

It's almost impossible to pass this shop without being tempted in by the smell of freshly roasting coffee. Inside you're spoilt for choice. The most expensive beans are Jamaican Blue Mountain at £45 a kilo, but the majority are at the lower end of the market and very good value. Most coffees are directly sourced, with an assortment of organic, fair-trade and decaf varieties. You can also buy teas, chocolate and equipment and, on Saturdays, sit and enjoy freshly squeezed orange juice and delicious home-made brownies outside on the pavement.

GALLERIES

Apart

138 Portobello Road W11
020 7229 6146
apart@tinyworld.co.uk
Tues–Fri 10.30am–6pm; Sat 11am–6pm; Sun 11am–5pm

Apart occupies about 750 sq metres of a split-level light and airy space in what was a run-down antiques arcade. It shows contemporary art in a unique way – being more like a shop than a gallery – and hanging a constantly changing selection of work. If you buy something you take it with you immediately, the gallery takes 45 per cent commission and another painting is put up. Paintings are left up for a maximum of six weeks and no more than four works by any one artist are shown simultaneously.

East West

8 Blenheim Crescent W11
0207 229 7981
www.eastwestgallery.co.uk
david@eastwestgallery.co.uk
Wed–Sat 10am–6pm; and by appointment

David Solomon and Jill Morgan travelled around Eastern Europe in a camper van, meeting painters, before opening in 1990 with a show by an artist from Belgrade. Their appearance on the art-scene was a baptism by fire, for within a short time 24 galleries in the neighbourhood (briefly known as the second Cork Street) closed. David had trained as an accountant, Jill as a painter, but neither had any experience running a gallery, However, they survived and now organise 12 exhibitions a year featuring interesting work from around the world. Both are great believers in drawing and most of the paintings exhibited are figurative. They do not consider themselves leading-edge but rather show painters who have an intelligence behind what they do and who they believe will endure.

The Special Photographer's Company

21 Kensington Park Road W11
020 7221 3489
info@specialphoto.co.uk
www.specialphotographers.com
Mon–Fri 10am–6pm; Sat 11am–6pm

This three-tiered gallery specialises in contemporary photography and a selection of vintage prints by established photographers. Regular exhibitions feature the likes of Bill Peroneau (seascapes), Sheila Rock (horses), Lois Greenfield (dance) and several portraitists, often focusing on musicians and other celebrities. In addition, last autumn provided a rare opportunity to see and buy the work of Bill Brandt, one of England's greatest photographers, who lived in Notting Hill and died in 1983. Prices range from £80 to over £2,000.

GIFTS, TOYS AND PARTIES

Banana Moon

183 Portobello Road W11
020 7727 6426
Mon–Thurs 10am–5.30pm; Fri & Sat 10am–6pm; Sun 11am–5pm
Banana Moon sells funky kitchen and bathroom accessories, but it's the more unusual items such as dancing animals (£10–£15), customised American cufflinks (£20–£30) and plastic chandeliers from the Netherlands (£23) that make it worth checking out. It's also a good place for greetings cards, wrapping paper and contemporary art posters (around £16), recently boosted by a contract with the Tate Modern.

Barnett Novelty House

17 Kensington Park Road W11
020 7727 7164
Mon–Sat 9am–6pm
It didn't take long for Barnett's to bounce back from the fire which virtually destroyed the toyshop last summer. The refurbished space sells a reliable selection of all the most popular commercial toys from board games to Barbies, plus bikes, skateboards, and lots of smaller items like stickers, jokes and tiny bouncing balls.

Cheeky Monkeys

202 Kensington Park Road W11
020 7792 9022
Mon–Fri 9.30am-5.30pm; Sat 10am–5.30pm; also open Sun 11am–5pm during the run up to Christmas
The first of five in the Cheeky Monkeys chain, this is an old-fashioned toy shop, without a video game in sight. Adults enjoy themselves here as much as children, ooohing over the beautiful traditional toys, including dolls' houses, fancy-dress costumes and an enormous range of those little gizmos you always longed to buy with your pocket money. There are also books and games, many of them with an educational bent, and a small range of clothes. The shoe shop downstairs, Shoe-Time, is a separate business, but is run with a similar ethos. It also offers Start-rites.

Purple Planet

318 Portobello Road
020 8969 4119
Mon–Sat 9.30am–5.30pm
Right up the northern end of Portobello, Purple Planet stocks a tantalising range of party trimmings, not only for children but weddings and other occasions. Candles, cards, cake decorations and every shape, colour and size of balloon are joined by some fiendishly wicked masks, skeletons, giant rubber spiders and other ghoulish props at Halloween.

Sitara Gift Shop

239 Portobello Road
020 7792 1970
Mon–Sat 9.30am–7pm; Sun 1pm–5pm
Candles, paper lanterns, wind chimes, inflatable furniture, slipper socks, plastic flowers and much more are crammed into a chaotic space that's well worth sifting through, especially for candles. From

mosaic cubes and colourful tea lights to tall church candles, Sitara has a huge variety and is cheaper than almost anywhere.

Spices & Rices

13 Portobello Road W11
020 7792 0263
www.spicesandrices.com
Mon–Fri 10am–6pm; Sat 9.30am –6.30pm; Sun (before Christmas) 11am–4pm
The exotic scent is what hits you first on entering this eclectic shop that draws almost everything on sale from its owner's base in Indonesia. Popular items include rice-paper lanterns (£2.50), hand-crafted books made from pineapple paper (£3–£25), handsome oil torches for lighting your garden at night (£50 per pair) and bamboo ladders (£35.25). The shop also stocks high-quality essential oils in 'breathing bottles', St Eval scented candles and a whole range of original gifts, large and small.

Verandah

15b Blenheim Crescent W11
020 7792 9289
Mon 1–6pm; Tues–Sat 10am–6pm
Happily, when Simone Russell took over this long-established treasure house of ceramics, lanterns, colourful baskets, Mexican mirrors, painted trays from Thailand, flying teddies and other knick-knacks, she inherited many of her predecessor's stockists. She also cut down on the clutter, but this is still a great place for original presents, especially at Christmas when the shop shimmers with brilliantly coloured decorations from different parts of the world.

Zarvis (see Portobello Green Arcade, p 59)

HOME

Bellhouse & Co

33 Kensington Park Road W11
020 7221 0187
Mon–Fri 9.30am–1pm & 2pm–5.30pm; or by appointment
Bimbi Bellhouse started her interior design and supply shop in 1984. She has a massive choice of fabric and carpet samples and will undertake any job, whatever the size. Prices are reasonable. She makes curtains in-house and has her own painters, decorators and carpet layers.

Emma Bernhardt

301 Portobello Road W10
020 8960 2929
Tues 12 noon–5.30pm; Wed & Thurs 10.30am–5.30pm; Fri 9.30am–5.30pm; Sat 10.30am–6pm
Former magazine stylist Emma Bernhardt draws much of her inspiration from the wonderfully colourful and gaudy ephemera she discovered on a first trip to Mexico. Soon after returning with a huge sack of mainly plastic goodies, she set up this now flourishing business selling a riotous mix of plastic skulls, flower garlands, votive candles, kitchenware, hats, shopping bags, feathered angel wings and, increasingly, clothes. Not cheap but certainly cheerful.

Ceramica Blue

10 Blenheim Crescent W11
020 7727 0288
www.ceramicablue.co.uk
shop@ceramicablue.co.uk
Mon 11am–5pm; Tues–Sat 10am–6.30pm; first Sun of month 12 noon–4pm
New Zealander Lindy Whiffen opened her first small shop in Clarendon Road in 1987, moving to Blenheim Crescent, 'the best street in the area', two years later.

Ceramica Blue stocks the best of international tableware from Italy, Spain, France, Tunisia, Colombia, South Africa, New Zealand, England, Wales, Holland and Thailand. Lindy travels widely, always on the lookout for new stock. The most recent addition is table linen from France.

The Cloth Shop

290 Portobello Road W10
020 7968 6001
www.clothshop.co.uk
Mon–Sat 10am–6pm
An original combination of antique linen sheets, Welsh blankets, saris and dyed muslin pack the shelves of this likeable shop, which also stocks a large range of cotton furnishing-fabric in strong pinks, reds, greens and other good plain colours. Prices start at £65 for Welsh blankets, £60 for antique sheets and £16 for saris.

David Wainwright

63 & 251 Portobello Road W11
020 7727 0707/020 7792 1988
Mon–Sat 9am–6pm; Sun 10am–6pm (Sun No.251 only)
Both shops stock the same mix of old and new furniture – mainly teak from India and Indonesia – coloured glass, stoneware, rustic hooks and pulleys, leather buckets and silver jewellery, with an increasing number of items from China and Tibet. Prices are on the steep side but Wainwright, who has probably been in the trade longer than he'd care to remember, has a very good eye for global style.

Decordence

126 Talbot Road W11
020 7792 4122
Mon–Sat 10am–6pm
Yet another interior/lifestyle shop, Decordence sells a now familiar combination of cushions, lights, mirrors, bedspreads and exotic hangings. Its strengths lie in the few items you may not see elsewhere, such as printed suede cushions (from £100) and strings of wonderful flower lights made from hand-made paper (up to £75) – perfect for building your own fairy grotto.

Gong

182 Portobello Road W11
020 7565 4162
Mon–Sun 10am–6pm
Eastern style permeates this shop, which opened just two years ago. Belgian owner Jo Plismys began by selling mainly Chinese ceramics and furniture, but has since added an increasing number of well-chosen objects from Africa and the Mediterranean. Crackle-glazed vases and bowls in 15 subtle shades (£30–£50), plain bamboo lamp stands, finely made Chinese mats (£85 new, £285 old) and leather shopping bags from Mali (£45) are just some of the items on display. Gong is also the place to buy bamboo curtain poles, reasonably priced and tastefully stained in various shades of brown.

Graham & Green

4 & 7 Elgin Crescent W11
020 7727 4594
www.grahamandgreen.co.uk
Mon–Fri 10am–6pm; Sat 9.30am–6pm; Sun 11.30am–5pm
Each of these different-style shops is a great source of presents (especially if you're feeling generous), as well as an inspiration for ideas on how to embellish your home. No.4 is cluttered with sumptious embroidered cushions and throws, kelims, mirrors, wooden candlesticks, hats and hand-painted furniture, while No.7 has a more modern, cutting-edge feel. Here mock-leather bags, baskets, ceramics and chrome gadgets jostle for space with the latest in Italian

lighting. Rent increases make it hard for any independent business on this patch, but originality and a knack for keeping up with the times will surely enhance G & G's chances of survival.

The Java Cotton Co.

3 Blenheim Crescent W11
020 229 3212
Mon–Sat 10am–6pm
Judith Kennard's cosy shop specialises in hand-blocked Javanese cottons sold by the metre but also made up into various items, from lovely soft bed quilts to hand-drawn silk batik sarongs. Patterns come in muted shades of green, yellow, blue and pink. Prices are reasonable, from £195 for a single quilt (£245 double) with material at around £22 a metre. This is also a good place for small presents, such as mirrors, make-up bags, hotwater bottle covers (a favourite at £10.95) and brightly painted wooden egg cups (£3.45).

Paintworks

5 Elgin Crescent W11
020 792 8012
Mon–Sat 10am–6pm; Sun 11am–4pm
Nicky Foster's Paintworks combines selling an impressive range of historical and contemporary colours with advice and studio workshops on how to use them. Paints include 18 colourwashes for use over emulsion and 30 matt woodpaints for staining, stencilling or applying as a solid finish. Colours range from a wonderfully subtle Indian pink to Corsican blue, Corinthian mauve and metallic silver and gold. Prices start at around £20 for 2.5 litres of emulsion to £32 for the same amount of eggshell, and you can buy crackleglaze, acrylic varnish and other finishes too.

For great bedlinen see **Puppy and Bedstock** (Portobello Green Arcade, p 58)

Wigwam

25 Kensington Park Road W11
020 7727 8888
info@wigwamdesign.co.uk
Mon–Sat 10.30am–6pm
Most of Wigwam's fabrics, scarves and throws come from Bali, Vietnam and India. It stocks a few clothes – by East, Noa Noa and Amano – and some jewellery, but the emphasis is increasingly on furnishings, with brightly-coloured cushion covers starting at £16.

MUSIC

Intoxica

231 Portobello Road W11
020 7229 8010
Mon–Sat 12 noon–4pm
Founded in 1975, this collectors' paradise changed around six years ago from a specialist Sixties-only shop to one which sells across-the-board specialist records. Nowadays you'll find as many records by Yusef Lateef as the Yardbirds. Through the street-level shop, containing Sixties' vinyl, some with the rarity value of a Ming vase, steps lead down to a cellar where jazz buffs will be amazed and delighted to find a huge selection of jazz esoterica. This space also doubles as an art gallery, with some wonderful jazz and pop memorabilia for sale.

Minus Zero Records & Stand Out Collections

2 Blenheim Crescent W11
020 7229 5424/020 7727 8406
Fri & Sat 10.30am–6.30pm; mail order in operation for the rest of the week
As proprietor Phil explains, the arched wooden door of No.2 Blenheim Crescent leads into two separate, yet oddly similar, shops: to your left, Minus Zero takes its name from a well-known Dylan album and specialises in highly collectable pop,

rock and folk, mainly from the mid- to late-Sixties, while in Stand Out Collections on the right, the equally affable Bill sells much the same. A glance through the catalogue will render the most avid enthusiast speechless as undreamed of Jethro Tull albums and ancient recordings by the Incredible String Band nestle alongside bands even more obscure than the Eleventh Floor Elevators.

Sounds

236 Portobello Road W11
020 7467 0708
Mon–Wed 10am–9pm; Thurs–Sat 10am–7pm; Sun 12 noon–6pm
This intimate premises caters to a younger clientèle and has an excellent range of soul, R & B and dance music. Judging by the Friday and Saturday crowd, the music on offer, plus a nicely-chilled vibe, make it a popular choice with cutting-edge youth. Sifting through the wide-ranging music revealed some intriguing Seventies' remixes and, somewhat incongruously, the latest Corrs album.

Rough Trade

130 Talbot Road W11
020 7229 8541
Mon–Sat 10am–6pm; Sun 1–5pm
A spearhead organisation at the start of the punk era, Rough Trade continues to thrive into the twenty-first century thanks to its ongoing policy of promoting some of the most obscure and vibrant music of the day. Prospective purchasers can check out the panoramic range of vinyl on the decks provided or trawl through the racks of fliers advertising forthcoming events throughout London. The shop also stocks a wide variety of fanzines and mags.

Honest Jon's

276 & 278 Portobello Road W10
020 8969 9822
www.honestjons.co.uk
Mon–Sat 10am–6pm; Sun 11am–5pm
One of the best-known music haunts in London, Honest Jons began trading in the early 1970s, moving to its present position in 1979. There are two shops, side by side – one specialising in jazz, the other dealing with every other aspect of groove dance and remix imaginable. Roots music with passion is the order of the day and careful sifting is guaranteed to unearth some gems.

NEWSAGENTS

Rococo

12 Elgin Crescent W11
020 7727 5209
Mon–Sat 5am–7pm; Wed & Sat till 7.30pm; Sun 5am–5pm
With nearly 2000 magazine titles jammed into its shelves, this has to be one of the best-stocked newsagents in town. It has a good selection of foreign journals and newspapers, and will order anything that is not in stock. Stationery, cards, sweets and lottery tickets also sold.

MIND AND BODY

BEAUTY THERAPY

Portobello Green Room

The Body Shop
194 Portobello Road W11
020 7243 8211
Mon–Sat 10am–6pm (5.30pm Thurs)
The first ever London Body Shop started around the corner at 23 Blenheim Crescent. So too began the Green Room, a separate but complementary enterprise offering natural face and body treatments using only Body Shop products. Soothing New Age music is played as you wait for

your luxury hydrating facial to take effect, interrupted only by the cries of the market traders below. A relaxed and friendly atmosphere and fair prices, especially if you can pay for a course, are guaranteed to keep the regulars coming.

Saint's Tattoo Studio

201 Portobello Road W11
020 7727 8211
Wed–Sun 1–6pm; no appointment necessary
Marc Saint started here in 1983, and ever since the demand for tattoos and body piercing has escalated beyond his wildest dreams. Today he sees around 20 customers on a quiet day, 30 on Saturdays – most of them women. The slightly dodgy air of the place, with its two-way mirror and cubby hole doorway into the back studio, belies its official certification. Saint has his own rules too: no one under 18 or over 80 and nothing on the face.

HAIRDRESSERS

Base Cuts

252 Portobello Road W11
020 7727 7068
basecuts@lineone.net
Mon–Sat 10am–6pm; Thurs 10am–6.30pm
Wrought-iron mirrors give a Gothic touch to this friendly salon right in the heart of Portobello. Prices are fair – cut & blow dry £25–£30 for women; £20–£25 men – while its position, on a corner site beside the plaza, means plenty of outside action to keep you entertained.

Children of Vision

195 Portobello Road W11
020 7792 2494
Mon–Sat 10am–7pm
This wacky hairdressers with its slightly sinister title specialises in dreadlocks, extensions, plaits and colour – the wilder the better. Not for the middle-aged or fainthearted.

HEALTH AND FITNESS

Portobello Green Fitness Club

3–5 Thorpe Close W10
020 8960 2221
Mon–Fri 6.30am–7pm; Sat & Sun 9am–7pm
PGFC is a non-profit making organisation dedicated to encouraging fitness in the community through a wide range of exercise, from gym workouts to pilates, aerobics and boxing, as well as physiotherapy and seminars on nutrition. Many of the clients are schools and old-age pensioner groups but thanks to the addition of the Sports Café upstairs, individual membership is set to grow. Monthly membership fee £39–£45; minimum age 18. Welcome evenings to find out more about the Club are held in the café on the first Monday of every month.

HOLISTIC HEALTH

Bliss

333 Portobello Road W10
020 8969 3331
Clinic Mon–Fri 9am–9pm; Sat 9am–6pm; Sun 11am–7pm. Shop Mon–Fri 9am–9pm; Sat 9am–6pm; Sun 11am–7pm. Café Mon–Sat 10.30am–6pm; Sun 11am–5pm
A combination of 'creative' health centre, café, clinic and shop, Bliss offers a range of complementary health treatments including aromatherapy, reflexology, acupuncture, Reiki, Alexander technique and massage. The company was founded by acupuncturist Aliza Baron-Cohen and nutritionist Helen Thorp with the aim of

making these kind of treatments available to a wider public. Prices vary from £15 (for concessions), with an average of £35, while £150 will buy you a day of 'Ultimate Bliss' incorporating four treatments and consultations. Books, tapes, herbs, homeopathic remedies and essential oils are sold in the shop. The café, serving a reasonably priced variety of vegan, veggie, chicken and fish dishes, has been slower to take off.

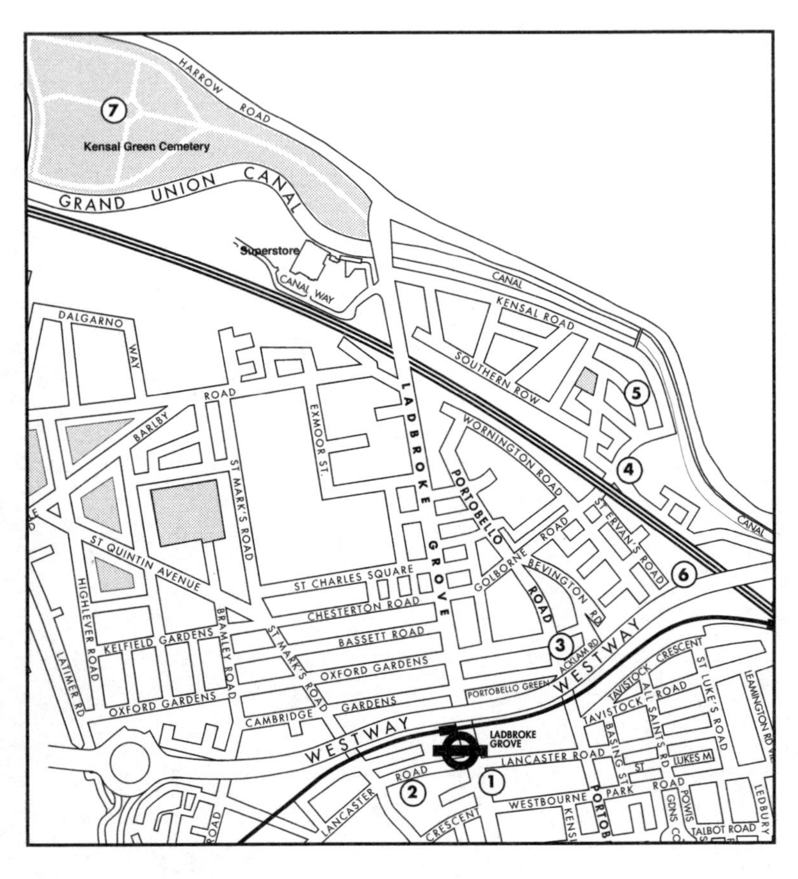

1 The Serbian Orthodox Church
2 The London Lighthouse
3 The Westway and Subterania
4 Trellick Tower
5 Meanwhile Gardens
6 The Muslim Cultural Heritage Centre
7 Kensal Green Cemetery

3. Ladbroke Grove, Golborne Road and Kensal Green Cemetery

This chapter concentrates on the northern section of Ladbroke Grove, from just before the Westway, past the right turning into Chesterton Road leading to Golborne Road, and over the Grand Union Canal to Harrow Road and Kensal Green Cemetery. Though officially North Kensington, Ladbroke Grove and Golborne Road are still wrapped up in both the history and the current life and character of Notting Hill. The cemetery, too, has strong links with the region as a whole.

Even with creeping gentrification, the Grove, as this end of Ladbroke Grove became known in the Fifties, stands a world apart from the lofty houses and communal gardens that border the southern stretch leading up to the Gate. Its main focus of interest is the Westway. Otherwise this shabby road is not much more than another busy thoroughfare, principally used as a source of public transport into and out of the area west, towards Notting Dale, and east in the direction of Paddington via Portobello market and Westbourne Park. It's also the place from which to take the No.52 bus up to Harrow Road and the unexpected delights of Kensal Green Cemetery.

Golborne Road is packed with contradictions. By turn blighted and revered for its position in the looming shadow of Trellick Tower (once the tallest high-rise in Britain), it has recently become a magnet for shops, restaurants and galleries cashing in on the wave of well-to-do residents who have moved here in the last decade. These, together with the Friday and Saturday flea market and the street's proximity to the more down-at-heel end of Portobello, are the main attractions. But more than any other part of Notting Hill, it's the different communities that have settled here over the years, from Ireland, Wales, the Caribbean, Serbia, Poland, Spain, Portugal and Morocco, which have shaped the neighbourhood's character.

In and around the Grove

The northern strip of Ladbroke Grove has virtually none of the early Victorian grandeur bestowed on the southern slopes of Notting Hill. This is largely due to its location, downhill and away from the royal cachet of Kensington, and the relatively late development of housing, which only commenced after 1864 and the inauguration of the Hammersmith and City railway at Ladbroke Grove Station (formerly Notting Hill). Today, looking south, the blue metal railway bridge is almost totally eclipsed by the concrete swathe of the Westway. Martin

Fitzpatrick, writing for the local website, mynottinghill.co.uk, sums up its impact (with embellishment from Will Self):

> *Today the Westway is part of the furniture and quite a few have come to appreciate and even admire it. Writing in the Evening Standard a few years back, the novelist Will Self described the Westway as a 'monument to the best that architectural modernism has to offer. A road sweeping across the city's cubist scape depositing you, dazed by the hubbub after the cool heights, in the bebop beat of central London'. Groovy! And there's no doubt the Westway has indeed become a potent symbol of modernity. It has featured in songs by seminal punk band, The Clash, and is also something of an off-the-shelf image for film-makers wishing to portray gritty urban realism. Even so, there may still be a few – perhaps among those who look out at it each day from their homes or drive along it between the rain-stained tower blocks – who feel that, while we may have come a long way in terms of high-speed transport and indoor plumbing, we haven't done quite so well for the human spirit.*

Coming up to the Westway, one of the few notable buildings is North Kensington Library on the corner of Lancaster Road. Opened in 1891, it was the first purpose-built library in the borough and the architect Henry Wilson won a prize for its design. Other close landmarks are the Church of St Sava, next door at No.89 Lancaster Road, which is owned by the Serbian Orthodox Church, and the London Lighthouse at Nos.111–17, Europe's leading hospice for people suffering from AIDS/HIV. The Lighthouse has a cheap café, best visited in summer when you can eat outside in the beautiful scented garden. But if it's top-class food you're after, visit Alastair Little's restaurant at No.136a.

The Church of St Sava

Walking into the unprepossessing-looking Church of St Sava is enough to take your breath away; nothing prepares you for the candles, chanting, icons, incense and the sight of the vast wooden dome that reaches over the carpeted floor of the great basilica. The building was originally constructed in 1901 as the Anglican church of St Columb, and was renowned for its High Church liturgy long before its sale to the Serbian Orthodox Church in 1951. Six years later, St Sava's was decorated with copies of frescoes from monasteries in Serbia; the iconostasis is new and was made in Macedonia.

The Serbs and the British were allies in the Second World War, and in the early Fifties many soldiers who had belonged to the Royal Army fled to England, forming the core of what is now a large local community. The church was consecrated by the theologian Bishop Nikolai Velimirovic, who, having survived Dachau concentration camp, settled in London. Now the church is run by Father Milun Kostic, who has been here for 23 years, and Father Radomir Acimovic. The adjoining community centre is open on Saturdays and Sundays. Services are held on Sundays and feast days at 10.30am; Vespers, Thursday 8.30pm and Saturday 6pm. Everyone is welcome at the services, but the church is not open at other times except by special request. For further information, telephone 020 7727 8367.

The London Lighthouse

The London Lighthouse opened its doors in 1986 as one of the first ever organisations dedicated to the provision of high-quality community care to people affected by HIV and AIDS. It has since gone through numerous changes, expanding its services to embrace the needs of children with HIV/AIDS, affected families and African communities, as well as offering further training and support. At the same time, financial pressures have forced it to shrink in size. Not only has government funding dried up, but the lack of publicity now given to HIV and AIDS (despite a trebling in numbers of people in London affected) coupled with the loss of such a high profile sponsor as Princess Diana, has taken its toll. In order for the Lighthouse to survive, in 1999 part of the original building was sold off to the Notting Hill Housing Trust for use as sheltered housing. Fortunately, it has managed to retain most of the big airy space downstairs, along with its tall palms, comfortable seating and tropical fish. As part of its policy to break down barriers and prejudice, the Lighthouse has always been open to the public and visitors are welcome. For more information, telephone 020 7229 1200, send an email to enquiries@london-lighthouse.org.uk or check out the Lighthouse website at www.london-lighthouse.org.uk.

Under the Westway, despite the presence of trendy bars such as Belgo and the Ion Bar with its fringe of pots of tall bamboo, Martin Amis's menacing image of a black cavity tattooed with graffiti (see p 38) still somehow sticks. Improvements are underway, spearheaded by the Westway Project, which has already introduced a new coat of paint and better lighting to brighten up the pedestrian stretch leading to Portobello Road and Acklam Road beyond. Saturdays see this walkway crammed with market stalls, mainly selling music, jewellery and clothes. Other days it's quiet, especially at night when any action tends to be concentrated underground in the aptly named Subterania. Formerly Bay 63, this club was built on the spot once occupied by Acklam Hall, itself a focus of musical innovation in the Seventies.

Punk meets reggae in the Grove

Talk to anyone about music in the Grove and they invariably come up with the name of Wilf Walker. The following is as much Wilf's story as it is a glimpse of the ways in which music evolved in and around Acklam Hall in the 1970s.

Ladbroke Grove has a rich musical history, from the early days of West Indian clubs and shebeens, to the germination of home-grown steel bands, through to the development of reggae and its unexpected alliance with punk in the mid-1970s. A key venue during the Seventies was Acklam Hall in Acklam Road, later to become the club Subterania. Like so many developments in Notting Hill, the use of Acklam Hall as a regular music venue was a direct result of community action, this time in the form of a project called Public Pictures which was dedicated to painting murals on the concrete walls under the Westway. Money was needed for paint, so John Tabieri, then manager of local pub band the 101ers (later to lose Joe Strummer to The Clash), organised a string of benefit concerts in Acklam Hall. He was supported in this by aspiring music promoter Wilf Walker, also a community activist, who went on to become a key figure in Notting Hill's music scene.

Wilf had arrived in Notting Hill from Trinidad via Shepherd's Bush in 1961. Unusually for a West Indian, he began his career by putting on white rock performers such as Hawkwind, the Pink Fairies, Quintessence and John Otway in 1974, some of whom had supported the mural project. But after the Carnival riots of 1976, knowing of his previous involvement in benefits, members of the black community approached Wilf to raise funds for Carnival defendants. Only then did he start to connect with the growing number of London reggae bands. A benefit took place, headed by Aswad from Westbourne Grove, but it was a decision by US band The Last Poets to play their first-ever UK gig at Acklam Hall that gave Wilf his big breakthrough. Born out of Harlem and inspired by the South African black consciousness movement, these fathers of rap and hip hop excelled in the poetry of outrage and rebellion, to the accompaniment of African rhythms. Jimi Hendrix was among their admirers and their arrival in Ladbroke Grove created a storm of media interest that launched Wilf's career as a full-time promoter. From then on, riding on the wave of the British Rock Against

Racism movement, he was able to set up an office under the Westway and transform Acklam Hall into a regular performance place. This was the era of punk, and every Friday night Wilf put on two punk bands and one reggae act. Unlike mainstream promoters, he recognised the links between these two very different types of music. In the words of Anthony Marks, writing in the anthology *Black Music in Britain:*

> *Like Rastafaris, punks viewed the musical and political establishment as an enemy; unlike the Rastafaris, punks were prepared to fight the system on a very basic level. The alliance of punk and reggae groups in the late 1970s for Rock Against Racism concerts prompted a surge in interest in reggae, as well as a heady optimism engendered by the sense of working for a common aim.*

So it was that bands like The Slits, The Raincoats and The Members shared a stage with Aswad, Merger, Sons of Jah, Barry Ford and King Sounds. In addition, two other elements favoured the rise of reggae here: the presence of Chris Blackwell's Island Recording Studio in Basing Street (now Sarm West, p 99) and the occasional visits of Bob Marley, who used to hang out with young bands when visiting his wife Rita's family in the Grove.

Wilf's Friday night concerts went on for 18 months, until petty theft and attacks by skinheads drove him to concentrate his energies elsewhere. Among other things, he went on to join the Notting Hill Carnival Committee and initiate the staging of live acts during Carnival, first under the flyover, then in Meanwhile Gardens and Powis Square. In true community spirit a mix of big names – Courtney Pine, Carol Grimes, the Passions, Sugar Minnott – were featured alongside local unknowns who were picked from a mountain of tapes sent in to a central office. But this too changed and with the new corporate face of the Carnival from 1992, Wilf abandoned his efforts in favour of schemes he could more easily believe in. Today he is still promoting black music, as well as helping to run the Nectar restaurant and to stage other events at the Tabernacle in Powis Square (see Listings, p 115).

Moving up Ladbroke Grove takes you past several well-kept residential streets on the left, all of which eventually cut through the St Quintin's Estate on the fringes of Notting Dale. One of these, Cambridge Gardens, is said to have had a ghost in the form of a phantom No.7 bus which, in the 1930s, haunted the junction with St Mark's Road. The story goes that a young motorist was killed here in June 1934 when, for no apparent reason, his car swerved off the road, hit a lamp-post and burst into flames. Witnesses reported having seen a London Transport bus tearing down the road towards them and 'how they desperately swung their vehicles off the road to avoid it'. When they looked back no bus was ever seen. The No.7 still takes this same route down Cambridge Gardens.

Most of the Victorian houses off Ladbroke Grove have been divided into flats, either by private landlords or by one of the many housing trusts which provide accommodation for people on low incomes. This may insure against the total gentrification of Notting Hill, but it has not prevented the mushrooming of cars that every night sit double-parked in lines along the likes of Oxford Gardens and Bassett Road. Amis, who once lived in Chesterton Road, hits the nail on the head again in this quote from *Money:*

> *The car and I crawled cursing up the streets to my flat. You just cannot park around here any more. Even on a Sunday afternoon you just cannot park around here any more. You can double-park on people: people can double-park on you. Cars are doubling while houses are halving. Houses divide, into two, into four, into sixteen. If a landlord or developer comes across a decent-sized room he turns it into a labyrinth, a Chinese puzzle. The bellbutton grills in the flaky porches look like the dashboards of ancient space ships. Rooms divide, rooms multiply. Houses split – houses are triple-parked. People are doubling also, dividing, splitting. In double trouble we split our losses. No wonder we're bouncing off the walls.*

Running west off Ladbroke Grove, Chesterton Road is one of the prettiest streets around here, especially in spring when clouds of cherry blossom briefly transform it into an Impressionist painting. These days some house is always being renovated, not just by private occupiers but by the housing trusts, which began buying up properties here in the 1970s and now own probably half of the street. Before then, the buildings were nearly all inhabited by poor Irish and West Indian tenants, some of whom, like Mary Gaine, have stayed on. Mary came over from Tipperary in the late 1950s and with her husband Tom moved into a two-room flat at No.48 in 1962. With no bathroom and only one toilet shared between four floors, they raised four children. Sixteen years later the landlord died and the building was bought by the Notting Hill Housing Trust. Mary still remembers the day in 1978 when the family was rehoused in a three-bedroom flat over the road, and the feeling of excitement at turning on the tap and seeing hot water gush out. A widow now, she still lives in the same flat with two of her sons and maintains that 'I'd die a slow death if I moved out of this road'. Not so Martin Amis, who no longer lives next door.

Golborne Road

On the other side of Ladbroke Grove, the eastern end of Chesterton Road becomes Golborne Road as houses give way to commercial premises, and the Moroccan foodstores, Portuguese pâtisseries, restaurants, and shops selling furniture, bric à brac and exotic fabrics, each stamp their own impression on the traditional Victorian façades. Moroccans, Portuguese and Spanish were among the many nationalities who settled here in the 1960s, drawn to North Kensington by its proximity to the West End of London, where they came to work in hotels, schools, the National Health Service (NHS) and other service industries. A number of escapees from Franco's Spain also came during the Spanish Civil War. People continue to arrive from overseas, most recently refugees from Somalia, Sudan and Ethiopia, but in the last few years it is the Moroccan community that has most made its mark on Golborne Road. The street has Moroccan cafés, restaurants, stalls and shops selling pottery, slippers, various foods, spices and herbs, carpets and music. Less visible are the community organisations providing services and facilities, both to Moroccans and the wider Arabic-speaking community (predominantly refugees and asylum seekers). Two of the main organisations are Al-Hasaniya Moroccan Women's Centre, tucked away on the ground floor of Trellick Tower, and the Moroccan Information and Advice Centre, situated next to the Lisboa café. Down Acklam Road, overlooking the railway, is the newly-built Muslim Cultural Heritage Centre, providing a mosque and activities for the local Muslim population.

The Moroccan community of North Kensington

North Kensington's Moroccan community dates back to the 1960s when migrant workers directly recruited in Morocco by British employment agencies arrived in West London. Single men and women were later joined by their families, who now have children themselves, and the community today numbers between 8,000 and 12,000, some 80 per cent of whom originate from Larache, a small town on Morocco's northern coast.

The social costs of displacement and immigration have been heavy. In the words of one Moroccan community worker: 'The generation gap is bigger than ever, and our community is on the brink of complete disorientation.' Her conclusion, that 'most of our immigrants came to alleviate their economic situation, but in the process they lost much more', may seem pessimistic, but there are a multitude of initiatives aimed at challenging their situation. On Saturdays and weekday evenings, locally run supplementary schools and homework clubs provide support for children let down by the education system; various youth clubs provide a focus and support to young people; there are specially run computer classes; and cultural events are organised, such as the hugely successful concert which livened up life under the Westway in July 2000 (see p 39).

While most Moroccans maintain regular contact with Morocco and travel down each summer, the community is quite insular and self-contained, and remains relatively disadvantaged as a result of high local unemployment and poor housing. As a whole, Golborne Ward is the sixth most disadvantaged ward in London, with minority ethnic communities experiencing the highest deprivation.

Despite the somewhat difficult social history of the community, many of the younger generation have successfully overcome the disadvantages of their parents such as language and integration, and work in a wide range of professions. Some have maintained the cultural and religious characteristics of their parents, with others adopting more noticeable religious and cultural practices, indicating their Muslim identity (even British-Muslim) as much as their national one. You'll see, for instance, younger women wearing both the *hijab* (scarf) and the *nikab* (black dress and head covering, showing just the eyes), and young men wearing Afghan-Pakistani-style clothes; and, especially around the time of Eid, after the fasting month of Ramadan, elderly Moroccan men can be spotted pottering down Golborne Road in their woollen *jelabas* (a long cloak with a pointed hood) and slippers.

Aisling Byrne
Former Co-ordinator of Al-Hasaniya Moroccan Women's Centre

By all accounts, Golborne Road in the 1960s was a friendly shopping street not dissimilar to Portobello Road. Both have retained their markets but lost all but a few of the family-owned butchers, bakers, grocers, confectioners and other shops that used to serve more or less all the needs of local people. The chief difference is that while Portobello catered for many different classes, including some left over from the grand old days of Chepstow Villas and Ladbroke Square, the absolute slum conditions of the surrounding housing meant that Golborne Road served mainly the very poor. This also meant that far fewer buildings survived the massive redevelopment of the 1960s and 70s, as symbolised by the fearsome presence of Trellick Tower.

Walk east along Golborne Road and you can't fail to notice the famous high-rise with its separate lift shaft; from Blur's *The Great Escape* to Nick Barlay's recent *Crumple Zone*, it has triggered nearly as much creative imagination as the Westway. Writing in *Crumple Zone*, the second in his 'urban trilogy', Barlay's narrator takes an uncompromising look out of his window in the sky:

One minute I'm standing in the middle of my place, the next face up to the corner window. Nothing's moved on. Below, far below, the alleys and narrow walkways that knot round Trellick suggest a million directions property could disappear. On one side the Grand Union Canal flows west towards Willesden Junction, away from yuppie balconies on the opposite bank laden with Ikea bullshit, window boxes, Japanese lanterns. On another side there's a scarred-up chicken-wired basketball court like something out of West Side Story. Which I guess it is, only without the fake knives. Inside, it's graffiti stand-off between Stanky Fly, Honk Fonk and some lone Nubian activist: My Bredrin, them that got beaten by police has got Staying Power.

Going the other way is Golborne Road. You can see right along it to where it hooks on to Portobello. Same crowd shifting. Or not. Slumming trustafarians in their Goa chic and blonde dreds. Slumming trustafarians in Gucci slingbacks and Versace wraps. Arab men, Portuguese men, drinking black coffee, smoking Marlboros. Ootie smoking and haggling in front of his store with his cousin Amil. Bicycle bobby O'Hara, the laughing lawman, squeaking his way through toytown till his batteries run out or till the last crime is solved. Whichever comes first. And shadows, the dark fugitive shadows of Burston and his crew that seem to fall everywhere, get in everywhere.

High above in the electric blue red sky is a Philips airship, glowing with its message: Let's make things better. One day Stanky'll tag that too.

Trellick Tower

Love it or hate it, Trellick Tower has become a symbol of the area for those who live here. Visible from the London Eye, it is the most easily recognisable landmark for miles around, dominating the skyline in the way that St John's Church once did in Ladbroke Grove. The tower is the pivotal element of Ernö Goldfinger's design for the Edenham Street housing scheme, one of two large projects he undertook for the Greater London Council, which replaced dilapidated Victorian terraces close to the Grand Union Canal. At the time, its 31 storeys made it the tallest high-rise in Britain and certainly the most uncompromising, with its bush-hammered external concrete and cantilevered gas-fired boiler house on top of the lift and stair tower.

It was begun in 1966 at a time of severe housing shortages, when the government was keen on high-rise developments and use of industrial-type building systems. The estate was organised as an integrated living unit, incorporating a central laundry, a nursery school, old people's club, doctor's surgery and so on. This was in keeping with Goldfinger's theories of urbanism and his belief in the notion of the concentrated city; communal facilities were intended to eliminate the need for individual domestic arrangements. If it had been up to him, London would have become a beautiful skyscraper city.

By the time the estate was finished in 1972, the tide had already turned against this school of urban planning in favour of low-rise schemes. However, Goldfinger's work was always exceptionally well built, using the best materials and meticulous in detail. In the secondary dwellings he also designed for the estate (which ranged from two-room flats to five-room, three-storey houses) he used marble in the entrance halls, provided high ceilings, ensured that the balconies faced south-west to catch as much sun as possible, and planned generously, often exceeding the minimum areas required by housing law.

Certainly, the inhabitants of Trellick Tower are always quick to defend it from criticism, and recent articles have appeared in the press suggesting, ironically enough, that what started life as an emergency response to a lack of housing is fast becoming one of the most sought-after addresses in the neighbourhood.

It's hard to say how much Trellick has influenced the rather bizarre transformation of this neighbourhood from urban ghetto to semi-chic hang-out for Notting Hillbillies. Outstanding views across London and proximity to Notting Hill have certainly made it ripe for exploitation as a luxury apartment block, in keeping with changes such as the metamorphosis of the Cobden Club in Kensal Road, from working men's club into the sumptuous Gothic-style watering hole frequented by Duncan Fallowell (see pp 229–31).

Close to Trellick Tower it's worth making a brief detour south to Meanwhile Gardens, a local-community success story currently under threat and so greatly in need of support. The gardens run along the canal and are accessible via a right-hand path just past Trellick. Established by a local sculptor in 1976 on a piece of council wasteland, this welcome green space houses London's first community skate bowl as well as environmental projects and numerous community-led activities and festivals. Thanks to the fundraising efforts of the Meanwhile Gardens Community Association, the gardens have recently undergone massive refurbishment, including the rebuilding of the skate bowl and introduction of new pathways, lighting, disabled access and general regeneration. This makes it all the more tragic that the council proposes to swallow up 100 square metres of space for a mix of private and public housing.

Returning to Golborne Road, you'll find some of the best opportunities for eating and shopping in all of Notting Hill. The sea of junk represented by the Friday and Saturday market can still turn up a genuine bargain, be it wrought-iron garden furniture, double-lined velvet curtains or the perfect butler's sink. The shops, too, offer an eclectic mix of furniture, fabrics, fireplaces and smaller household goods: Eighty-Eight Antiques (at No.88) sells a reasonably-priced selection of old pine chests of drawers, cupboards and tables; at No.82, Bazar stocks old kitchen and garden furniture, vases, door plaques and other knick-knacks, mainly from France; while both Ollies at No.69 and Les Couilles du Chien at No.65 sell a less predictable combination of antique leather chairs, animal skins, lighting and potted palms.

Market days are when the Moroccan community comes into its own and the Rai music of Cheb Khaled or more traditional Andalusian and Moroccan artists emanates from shops and stalls, and Berber rugs are hung out on the pavement. In between the shops and community advice and information centres, there are plenty of eating places to choose from. Coffee and cakes in the Portuguese Lisboa Pâtisserie are amazing value, equalled only by the similar but younger Oporto Pâtisserie over the road at No.62a. For more substantial Portuguese fare, try Casa Santana. Otherwise, the main alternatives are Lebanese at Baalbak, North African at the Moroccan Tagine, Pakistani at the Best Tandoori Khana takeaway and, on a more upmarket note, fish at the Poissonerie du Pêcheur allied to the exotic Golborne Fisheries shop over the road.

Foodshops further reflect the predominant Moroccan, Portuguese and West Indian communities. Just as Moses Aloetta proclaims in *The Lonely Londoners*, Sam Selvon's vivid novel of immigrant life in London in the 1950s, commercial interests rarely waste time before setting up shop to exploit new custom:

> *The grocery it had at the bottom of the street was like a shop in the West Indies. It had Brasso to shine brass, and you could get Blue for when you washing clothes, and the fellar selling pitchoil. He have the pitchoil in some big drum, in the back of the shop in the yard, and you carry your tin and ask for a gallon, to put in the cheap oil burner. The shop also have wick, in case the wick in your burner go bad, and it have wood cut up in little bundles to start coal fire. Before Jamaicans start to invade Brit'n, it was a hell of a thing to pick up a piece of saltfish anywhere, or to get thing like pepper sauce or dasheen or even garlic. It had a continental shop in one of the back streets in Soho, and that was the only place in the whole of London that you could have pick up a piece of fish. But now, papa! Shop all about start to take in stocks of foodstuffs what West Indians like, and today is no trouble at all to get saltfish and rice. This test*

who had the grocery, from the time spades start to settle in the district, he find out what sort of things they like to eat, and he stock up with a lot of things like blackeye peas and red beans and pepper sauce, and tinned breadfruit and ochro and smoke herring, and as long as the spades spending money he don't care, in fact is big encouragement, 'Good morning sir,' and 'What can I do for you today, sir,' and 'Do come again'.

Kensal Green Cemetery

Back on Ladbroke Grove, heading north across two roundabouts and over the canal will soon take you to Kensal Green Cemetery at the junction with Harrow Road. The canal towpath just beyond Kensal Road offers miles of peaceful walking in either direction. Otherwise, the way here is fairly bleak and best made by bus. Kensal Green station on the Bakerloo line is also nearby.

> *'Kensal Green may not have been typical in terms of its grand pretensions, fashionable associations or its wealthy clientèle, and its creation certainly did not solve the problems associated with the overcrowding of city burial grounds. But therein lies its singular fascination and its unique atmosphere. Furthermore, the Victorian cemetery ideal was that of 'sweet breathing places', set aside for contemplative recreation and the moral improvement, spiritual enlightenment and general education of the living. This is a role that Kensal Green Cemetery can fulfil even – and perhaps especially – in the present age.'* (Friends of Kensal Green Cemetery)

> *Pyramids and stone mansions whose original pomposity has been weathered by long indifference into something more democratic: a sanctuary for wild nature, a trysting place for work-experience vampires. Irrelevant memory doses. Boasts and titles and meaningless dates.* (Iain Sinclair, *Lights Out for the Territory*)

Kensal Green Cemetery is an extraordinary place – not only a vast walled burial ground peopled by stone sphinxes, angels and the ghosts of hundreds of remarkable characters, but a nature reserve where foxes prowl among the graves and bats are allocated special boxes attached to the trees. In addition, the monuments, many vandalised, robbed of their busts and decorations or simply demolished by time, provide a fascinating record of Victorian taste over the years.

History

The population of London increased so rapidly in the early nineteenth century that churchyards became dangerously overcrowded and there was soon a real shortage of places to bury the dead. In response to this crisis, commercial cemetery companies were set up, and it was the first of these, the General Cemetery Company, that established Kensal Green Cemetery, the city's biggest and in many ways greatest necropolis.

The General Cemetery Company was founded in 1830 by George Frederick Carden, a barrister, who visited Paris in 1821 and was very impressed by Père-Lachaise Cemetery. He dreamed of creating a similar burial ground in the region of London. The opportunity finally came over a decade later when Royal Assent was given to a Bill 'for establishing a general cemetery for the internment of the dead in the neighbourhood of the metropolis'. Carden spotted an ideal site in the expanse of fields just north of the Grand Junction Canal and, with the financial backing of Sir John Dean Paul, a governor of the Bank of England, 55 acres of land in Kensal Green were purchased in 1832 for £9,000; a further 22 acres were added in the 1860s.

Having established the site, Carden's company launched an architectural competition for the design of cemetery buildings. This was won by Henry Edward Kendall, but his florid Gothic plans were disliked by Sir John Dean Paul, who preferred Greek Revival styles and saw to it that the commission was given to his protégé, the architect John Griffith of Finsbury. By June 1837, Griffith had completed the Main Gate with its triumphal arch, the Dissenters' Chapel, the Anglican Chapel and the North Terrace Colonnade. The two chapels were constructed in Doric and Ionic styles over catacombs, a third set of which lies sealed beneath the Colonnade. The terrain was landscaped in the manner of a country park with thousands of specimen trees, creating an ideal habitat for the foxes, voles, kestrels, jays and many species of butterfly (half of those found in the British Isles) that now enjoy its protection.

In 1833, 48 acres were consecrated by the Bishop of London, the remaining seven acres being set aside for Dissenters. All kinds of burial – in catacombs, brick-lined vaults, earth graves and mausoleums – were possible at Kensal Green. From the beginning, plots of land were sold in perpetual freehold, a system retained by the General Cemetery Company, which still owns and manages the site. Although 18,000 funerals took place in the first 19 years, the cemetery's success was only firmly guaranteed when a plot was bought by Augustus Frederick, Duke of Sussex and sixth son of King George III. The excellent introductory guide by Paul Coones of the Friends of Kensal Green Cemetery notes that the Duke was 'a notable eccentric – his house was full of singing birds and chiming clocks, and during his final illness he subsisted on a diet of turtle soup and orange ices'. He also held progressive views and it was a wish to be buried with his wife, whom he married in contravention of the Royal Marriage Act, that led him to select a plot at Kensal Green.

In the early days there was a view over London to the Surrey hills and people could choose their vistas and buy plots wherever they wanted. It is said that you can still see the hills on a clear day, but, although there are still plots for sale, the choice of view is now strictly limited. The variety and scope of the tombs are remarkable – Gothic fantasies, Graeco-Egyptian mausoleums and classical-style monuments jostle with simpler structures. Among the graves of the famous are touching epitaphs of the lesser known: 'He burnt the candle at both ends – but oh what a lovely light'.

Notable names and monuments

Many legendary figures are buried here; more than 800 are listed in the *Dictionary of National Biography*, among them its first editor, Leslie Stephen, father of Vanessa Bell and Virginia Woolf. His wife, Harriet Stephen (1840–1875), was the daughter of William Makepeace Thackeray (1811–1863). She lies next to her husband's distinguished family, while Thackeray's grave occupies another plot marked by a York stone slab. Other novelists include Wilkie Collins (1824–1889), author of *The Woman in White*, said to be the first ever work of detective fiction, who is interred with both his wife and his mistress; and Anthony Trollope (1815–1882) whose remains rest beneath a red granite ledger with a cross in relief. The poems of poet and humorist Thomas Hood (1798–1845) were stolen from his monument, as were the bronze bust and decorations which once adorned the red granite stele designed by Noble. More recently, the ashes of playwright Terence Rattigan (1911–1977) were brought here from Bermuda to be placed in the family grave.

The names of two performers, Emile Blondin (1824–1897) and Andrew Ducrow (1793–1842), are well worth seeking out as much for their eccentric pursuits as the statuary that distinguishes their graves. Few can match the daring of Blondin, 'the most famous tightrope walker of all time', who not only crossed Niagara Falls on a rope but once paused halfway to cook and eat an omelette. He and his wife share a pink granite monument surmounted by a large angel. The flamboyant Ducrow was a circus performer and owner renowned for his equestrian stunts, hence the extravagant Egyptian sarcophagus complete with sphinxes, horses, angels, shells and other assorted ornaments which shield his remains. He even composed his own epitaph, beginning 'Within this tomb erected by genius for the reception of its own remains...'. Another extrovert performer, Freddy Mercury of Queen, was cremated at Kensal Green but his ashes were scattered in Bombay.

Others are distinguished for their achievements in design and engineering. Thomas Allom (1804–1872), architect of the Ladbroke estate and, among other buildings, St Peter's Church in Kensington Park Road, lies in a marble pillared chest tomb. Isambard Kingdom Brunel (1806–1859), chief engineer of the Great Western Railway, which runs past the cemetery, shares a plain rectangular block of marble with many members of his family, while the highly original clothes designer, Ossie Clark (1942–1996), is commemorated by a simple upright slab of Welsh slate, engraved 'with love from his two sons Albert and George'.

At least three notable doctors are buried here, the first of whom, James Barry (*circa* 1795–1865), Inspector General of the Army Medical Department, was revealed on 'his' death to be a woman. Dr George Birkbeck (1776–1841), the philanthopist and educationalist who founded Birkbeck College, is commemorated by a handsome mausoleum in Portland stone. The tomb of Dr John Elliotson (1791–1868), friend and doctor of Dickens and Thackeray and the first person to use a stethoscope for diagnosis, has partially collapsed. Less damaged are the monuments to William Whiteley (1831–1907), the tycoon who was shot in his own department store, in white Carrara marble, and to William Henry Smith (1792–1865), whose mother founded the successful stationery chain. A book adorns the pink and grey granite chest which serves as his tomb.

Among those of noble birth, the Duke of Portland (1800–1879) has the largest plot in the cemetery, where yuccas compete with English greenery. Princess Sophia, sister of the Duke of Sussex, also bought a plot here. Repressed by her father and blighted by scandal (she gave birth after a chance evening alone with a court equerry who turned out to be a rogue), she led a lonely life and eventually went blind. Her monument – a quattrocento sarcophagus in Carrara marble – was erected by public subscription and faces her brother's tomb across the way.

Marble cannot withstand the English climate and many such monuments are on the verge of collapse and would cost thousands of pounds to repair. On the other hand, the elaborate and fanciful Portland stone canopied tomb to Captain Charles Spencer Ricketts (1788–1867), which is made of artificial stone and granite designed by William Burges, will probably last hundreds of years.

The cemetery is open daily April–Sept until 6pm; Oct–March till 5pm. Walking round on your own turns up serendipitous discoveries, but there is also an excellent tour every Sunday. This starts at 2pm at the Anglican Chapel and on the first and third Sundays of the month includes a highly recommended visit to the catacombs.

EATING AND DRINKING

CAFÉS, SNACKS AND TAKEAWAYS

Baalbak

91 Golborne Road W10
020 8968 0136
Daily 12 noon–10pm
Despite recent price rises to accommodate escalating rent, this plain Lebanese café still offers good value as well as reliable, freshly cooked food. A plate of mixed *mezza* (around £5) is a meal in itself, while main dishes such as *shawarma* (marinaded lamb or chicken on the spit), *shish tark* (spicy boneless chicken) and a vegetarian moussaka wonít set you back more than about £6. Baalbak also does great sandwiches for £2.50, a range of coffees, including Turkish, and mint tea (currently 60p a glass).

The Garden Café

London Lighthouse
111–17 Lancaster Road W11
020 7792 1200
Mon–Fri 9am–7pm; Sat 10am–3pm; Sun (for registered members and carers) 1pm–3pm
The café sells a limited range of inexpensive sandwiches, salads and hot food but it's more the setting that you come for. Built as a pioneering support centre for people affected by HIV and AIDS (see p 73), the Lighthouse has won awards for its building but more specifically for its secluded garden, which is open to the public all year round. This wonderfully peaceful space incorporates a Tudor scented garden set around a small square camomile lawn, a healing garden and a fountain, as well as a paved area for sitting out next to the café. A perfect retreat from the noise and pollution of Ladbroke Grove.

Lisboa

57 Golborne Road W10
020 8968 5242
Daily 8am–8pm. No credit cards
This hugely popular café/pâtisserie has long been one of the highlights of Golborne Road, and deservedly so. The cakes – *pasteis de nata* (custard tarts), macaroons, apricot pastries and *millefeuilles*-type concoctions – all melt in the mouth, and the coffee and savouries, such as croissants filled with ham and cheese, are pretty good, too. Add the astoundingly cheap prices, a great atmosphere and incredibly hard-working staff, and it's easy to see why Lisboa is such a success story. The only problem is trying to get a table.

Taste of Punjab

Kerrington Courts
316b Ladbroke Grove W10
020 8960 9925
Tues–Sat 11.30am–11pm; Sun 1–11pm
Right on the roundabout where Barlby Road meets Ladbroke Grove, the family-run Taste of Punjab offers some of the best Indian food this side of Westbourne Grove. The straightforward menu includes a familiar range of balti and biryani dishes (£4.25–7.50), plus other seafood, lamb and chicken dishes from the ubiquitous chicken tikka masala (£3.50) to sag king prawn (£6.50) and a wide choice for vegetarians – all freshly cooked in the tiny open kitchen out the back. There are also plenty of snacks such as samosas, onion and spinach bhajis and pakoras, plus delicious mango lassi (£1.35).

Yum Yum

312 Ladbroke Grove W11
020 8968 1497
Mon–Thurs 10am–10pm; Fri & Sat till 11pm
This great Caribbean takeaway is tucked

Notting Hill in 1750

The Hippodrome racecourse, 1837–1841

Notting Hill tollgate looking east, circa 1835

Northwest corner of Kensington Church Street, 1879

Construction of the railway at Ladbroke Grove, circa 1863

Silchester Baths, Notting Dale, 1898

First Carnival, 1965

Ska style, Portobello Road north of the Westway, early 1970s

Taking a break, Portobello Road, late 1960s

Notting Hill Methodist Church, circa 1972

Gypsy man, Blenheim Crescent, 1970

Michael X and friends, circa 1970

The Tabernacle, Powis Square

Motorhead with Lemmy (centre), early 1970s

away on the same roundabout as Taste of Punjab. Choose from curry goat, chicken, steak or oxtail, plus several fish and vegetarian dishes, including a mouth-watering bean and dumpling stew – all served with either rice, boiled yam, dumpling or plantain. Owner Oakland Foster also makes some of the best patties in West London. Prices range from around £2.50 to £5.50.

Whoops!

103 Lancaster Road W11
020 7243 9000
Mon–Sat 7.30am–11pm; Sun 12 noon –6pm
Six sofas line the walls of this spacious café that makes a great meeting place on what has always been a rather desolate corner of Ladbroke Grove. It's a local enterprise: the owner Mark Williams lives in Cambridge Gardens, and all the food – mainly cakes, sandwiches and salads – is freshly cooked nearby. Drinks, starting at 80p for a filtered coffee and smoothies (£1.60), are especially good value.

RESTAURANTS

Modern European

Alastair Little

136a Lancaster Road W11
020 7243 2220
Mon–Fri 12 noon–2.30pm & 6.30–11pm; Sat 12 noon–3pm & 6.30–11pm
Excellent food and a delightfully mellow atmosphere in minimalist yet warm surroundings make this easily one of the best restaurants in Notting Hill. Lunch consists of a fixed-price menu (starter £6, pasta £8, main course £14 and dessert £5) with three to five choices in each category. Most dishes have a strong Italian slant, from the delicious *spaghetti al scoglio* (with mussels, squid, chilli, parsley and garlic) to wrapped corn-fed chicken breast with Parma ham and savoy cabbage; but you'll also find items like foie gras and roast chump of lamb with *pommes dauphinoises* on the menu. Portions are generous, but try to leave room for a pudding such as *Tarte Tatin* or bread and butter pudding made with panettone – unlikely to disappoint. Alastair Little's was the first upmarket business to colonise this corner of Notting Hill and it hasn't been easy. Both he and his restaurant partner, Kirsten, deserve every success.

Belgian

Belgo Zuid

124 Ladbroke Grove W10
020 8982 8400
Mon–Fri 12 noon–11pm; Sat 12 noon–11.30pm; Sun 12 noon–10.30pm
Judging by the difficulty of trying to book a table, admittedly on a Saturday night, the Ladbroke Grove branch of this global empire seems pretty much a success. A corridor lined with every kind of bottled beer opens out into a vast refectory-type dining room, the vaulted wooden ceiling of which creates the impression of an upturned boat. Friendly waiters dash about serving the Belgian standard of kilo-pots brimming over with steaming mussels (around £12), accompanied by frites and little bowls of mayonnaise. Other main dishes include half a spit-roast chicken with a cream and wild mushroom sauce (£8.95) and pan-fried cod fillet on a leek stoemp, served with curry oil and roasted garlic (£10.25), plus one or two options for vegetarians. The dazzling choice of beer, including apple, raspberry and mango, can also be enjoyed in the upstairs bar overlooking the restaurant.

Fish

Poissonerie du Pêcheur

46 Golborne Road W10
020 8968 2200
Lunch: Wed–Sun 12 noon–2.30pm
Dinner: Wed–Sat 6.30pm–11.30pm
Under the same ownership as the remarkable fish shop across the street, this new addition to Golborne Road is definitely recommended: the people are welcoming, the setting bright and there's a very good range of dishes. Try the squid in garlic and mustard, the blue crab or Japanese-style sushi as a starter; main courses include a mixture of grilled warm-water fish, whole fresh crab in a delicious sauce and very reasonably priced roast lobster, plus a few meat dishes for dedicated carnivores. The wine list is small and unambitious. You can eat well for £30 a head including puddings, which were not sampled, and wine. Try lunch on Saturday when the street is humming with traders.

Portuguese

Casa Santana

44 Golborne Road W10
020 8968 8764
Daily 12 noon–11pm
Authentic Portuguese fare accompanies the laid-back atmosphere of this simple restaurant-cum-bar which tends to come alive at night – and at Sunday lunch times when Portuguese families pack the cabin-like space. Soup, such as *caldo verde* (cabbage with sausage), is popular, as is fish, notably the traditional *bacalhau* (dried salt cod) in different variations. Prices, from £2.50 for starters and £6 for a main course, are fair. Take-away service also offered.

BARS AND PUBS

Chilled Eskimo

Corner of Southern Row
and Middle Row W10
020 8960 1777
Mon–Sat 5–11pm
The Chilled Eskimo arose from the profusion of creative industry workers in Canalot studios and on Conlan Street. Tucked away on the corner of East and Southern Rows, it has a pleasant wooden interior – nothing flashy – with comfy leather seats and lots of space on the main floor. A good local, popular for its no-nonsense attitude – £2 for a pint and 30p for a packet of crisps – if a bit tricky to find.

Golborne House

36 Golborne Road W10
020 8960 6260
Daily 12 noon–11pm; lunch 12.30–4pm; dinner Mon–Sat 6.30–10.15pm (Sun till 9.45pm)
Good food, unpretentious style and quality service are the mainstays of this increasingly popular gastropub on the corner of Golborne Road and Southam Street. The burnt orange walls display some great photos of neighbouring Trellick Tower taken by manager Tom Etridge. Otherwise, plain wood furniture makes up the décor, while the menu features an appetising list of globally influenced dishes. Starters such as smoked trout and mesclun salad (£6) or roast butternut and chestnut soup with garlic *crostini* (£4) can be followed by chargrilled monkfish with citrus cous cous, rocket and *chermoula* (£9.50) or imaginative versions of English staples, such as roast guinea fowl or calves liver with bubble and squeak. And be sure to leave a gap for the sticky toffee pudding.

ENTERTAINMENT

MUSIC AND CLUBBING

El Dorado

67 Wornington Road W10
020 8960 9669
Tues–Sat 8pm–12midnight, plus two Sundays a month
Described at www.mynottinghill.co.uk as 'a little kitsch, a little Moroccan, a little underground Portobello club not quite in the geographical arena of the "Hillite" social scene', El Dorado feels a bit like a speakeasy. The crowd is pretty much anything goes, from hairdressers to new media journos, who come to check out the new bands and DJs showcased, or just to lounge in the chill-out room with its animal-print chairs and sofas. Impossible to predict what you might find when you get here – a hot, sweaty dance floor crammed to busting or just a sprinkling of folk chatting at the bar – whatever the mood, it's always friendly and unpretentious, even if this is fast becoming one of the places to hangout in the area. Private rooms are also available for party hire.

The Ion Bar

161–65 Ladbroke Grove W10
020 8960 1702
www.meanfiddler.com
Mon-Fri 5pm–midnight; Sat 11am –12midnight; Sun 12 noon–11.45pm
Next door to Ladbroke Grove tube, with its vast plate glass windows allowing a nice view of the punters for passers-by, Ion is one of the busiest and funkiest bars in the area. DJs play soul, R'n'B, jazz and reggae for a smart, glamorous crowd, and there's live music on Wednesdays, and soul medicine on Sundays when in the summer an all-day barbecue adds to the Modern British menu available all week on the mezzanine floor. Go early at weekends to avoid a long queue.

Subterania

12 Acklam Road
(under the Westway) W10
0208 960 4590
www.meanfiddler.com
Ring first: Mon, Tues, Thurs 8pm–2am; Sun 7pm–12midnight; club nights Wed 10pm–2am; Fri, Sat 10pm–3am
Ladbroke Grove's only proper nightclub, the ever-popular Sub, tucked under the Westway just off Portobello Road, is best on a Friday night, when the long-running Rotation night provides hip-hop, R&B, soul and rare groove for a savvy, friendly crowd that packs out the main dance floor and the upper balcony. Wednesday reggae night with David Rodigan is more laid-back and it's always worth calling ahead to see if any live bands are booked.

William IV

786 Harrow Road NW10
0208 969 5944
Lunch Mon–Fri 12noon–3pm; Sat & Sun 12 noon–4pm; dinner Mon–Fri 6pm–10.45pm; Sat & Sun 7pm–11pm
Bar open 12noon–11pm
Frequented by music and media types (there's a lot of music industry based business around Kensal Green), this pub with a trad name isn't trad at all; big name DJs and opening hours until midnight Wednesdays to Saturdays ensure it's always packed, so come early if you want to be sure to get in. The menu is designed to line the stomach with such offerings as big chips with sweet chili sauce or cous cous and merguez sausages. Food prices range from £9 to £13.

STAYING IN

Channel Video Films

142 Ladbroke Grove W10
020 8960 2148
Mon–Sun 10am–10pm
The place to go if you can't get what you want at Notting Hill Gate's Video City. Higher prices and inflexibility over late returns are compensated for by extra multiple copies of all the latest releases. A large selection of old films is stocked in the basement.

CHILDREN

The Skate Bowl

Meanwhile Gardens W10
020 8960 4600
Open 24 hours
Colourful graffiti decorates this bowl which reopened after major refurbishment in the spring of 2000. Free access and its position, amid landscaped gardens beside the canal, make it a popular meeting place for young spectators, as well as those honing their skateboarding skills, especially in summer. The gardens also have a One O'clock Club for the under-fives currently open Mon–Fri 12.30–5pm, but due for extension.

Playstation Skatepark

Bay 65–66
Acklam Road W10
0795 7124 465
www.pssp.co.uk
Mon, Thurs & Fri 12 noon–4pm & 5–9pm; Tues–Wed 12 noon–4pm & 5–10pm; Sat–Sun 10am–12 noon (beginners); 12 noon–4pm & 5–9pm
Children – mainly boys – of all ages flock to this skateboarding park which opened under the Westway in 1997, with input from the team who designed the original bowl at Meanwhile Gardens. Users pay a £10 yearly membership fee, plus £4 for a four-hour session; non-members simply pay £6. Sponsored by Sony – hence the name.

SHOPPING

ANTIQUES

Arbon Interiors

80 Golborne Road W10
0208 960 9787
Mon–Sat 9am–5pm
Here you'll find everything to do with beautiful fireplaces, but also decorative antiques, great big chandeliers, crystal wall-lights, mirrors, pretty fabrics, curtains and bistro tables. Fireplace surrounds range from £70 to £16,500 (nineteenth-century Surina marble) and include antiques and reproductions in stone, wood and marble; gas effect fires are also in stock. Arbon has its own fireplace fitters for the installation of hearths, surrounds and grates. Valuations can be arranged for insurance purposes for fire surrounds. Also offers a prop hire service.

Bazar

82 Golborne Road W10
020 8969 6262
Tues & Wed 10am–5pm; Thurs 10am–6pm; Fri & Sat 9.30am–5.30pm. No credit cards
For more than 25 years, Bazar (formerly Decorative Parlour Pieces) has been selling a range of French furniture and items, from painted armoires, lovely made-to-order pine tables, sewing tables, country-kitchen shelves, and bamboo and wood coat racks. The shop has a light, sparkly feel about it and, as well as selling items in wood, stocks stylish armchairs, chandeliers, glasses, ceramics and properly made baskets – from £10 for an

egg basket or Red Riding Hood basket, upwards.

Les Couilles du Chien

65 Golborne Road W10
020 8968 0099
Mon–Thurs & Sat 9am–6pm; Fri 8am–5pm

Unless you're a dealer – and many visit this blindingly current shop – and can identify an Eames or Mies van der Rohe with mercurial speed, while being accosted by stuffed water buffalo, skeletons and looming arc lights, you had best take your time in Jerome Dodd's emporium. This is where to go to buy the most fantastic lighting at truly affordable prices. The ubiquitous arc light comes in various sizes and starts at £125, but more interesting is Jerome's stock of glass, metal and wooden chandeliers, and wall-lights, which range from the arborial to the celestial, in the guise of beautiful ferns, floral bouquets and crystal waterfalls. The word is that human beings have been comforted by the decorative arts ever since men first painted on their caves – minimalism is an unnatural state and will perish along with rare species. Taxidermy, framed entomological specimens (£22 for a scorpion, £45 for a large tarantula) and hide rugs peep out from between the unfaltering leather chairs (from £250). You'll find many buried treasures, from the stylishly practical to the ravishingly impractical, which rather describes Jerome and his eccentric assistant Oscar Darling. The 'dog's bollocks' also does prop hire.

Eighty-Eight Antiques

88 Golborne Road W10
0208 960 0827
Mon–Sat 9am–5pm

Victorian stripped pine and quality reproduction shelves and chests of drawers from £220 to £850, tables and blanket boxes from £120 to £180. Proper storage pieces for those who are tired of trying to arrange their linen and paper work into annoying piles of boxes and baskets. Also available to those in the know are one-off hand-crafted kitchens, but only for very local customers. No wood-stripping service.

Mac's

86 Golborne Road W10
020 8960 3736
Mon–Sat 9am–5pm (though erratic, so phone)

This is the place for grand architectural pieces; the term decorative antiques is not palatial enough to describe Mac's taste. Opulent gilded mirrors, unusual painted enamel sinks, vast gates, lead urns, and soaring horticulturally inspired light-fittings are just a few of the objects on offer. Stately, elegant and mysterious.

Mathews & Green

331 Portobello Road W10
020 8964 9738
Wed and Thurs 10am–5pm; Fri 8.30am–5pm; Sat 10am–6pm. No credit cards

Just around the corner from Golborne Road, Roger Matthews' is the sexiest antique shop in the area. The contents, often rare pieces, depend on what appeals to the owner or what mood he is in. From hand-crafted oriental statues to a big Sixties' white orb television, he stocks a curious and unusual arrangement of decorative arts, including spiral staircases, lighting, dinner services, paintings, French armoires, filigree gates and antique textiles. With Miles Davis playing on a Bang & Olufsen, an intelligent and inquisitive clientèle and the scent of lilies, it's a bit like shopping in a funky, petite version of the Victoria & Albert Museum, on opium.

FASHION

Asahi

110 Golborne Road W10
020 8960 7299
Mon, Tues 12 noon–6pm; Wed, Fri & Sat 10am–6pm; Thurs 11am–6pm
It's easy to overlook this Japanese shop, tucked away near the Portobello corner of Golborne Road. Asahi sells a great selection of kimonos, from vintage, heavily embroidered silk (up to £500) to modern cotton designs (from £10), as well as Obi sashes, fans and umbrellas. This is also a good place for fabrics and small gifts such as scented candles, ornaments and pretty silk-covered notebooks, all from Japan.

Jane Bourvis

89 Golborne Road W10
020 8964 5603
Mon 1–5pm; Tues–Sat 11am–5pm
Jane Bourvis's shop represents a pleasantly haphazard version of the lifestyle concept that dominates so many retail outlets, especially in Notting Hill. Prettily wrapped soaps, whimsical ornaments and flower-bedecked tea cosies mingle with exotic fabrics, throws, cushions, cashmere cardigans, silk wraparound skirts and wonderfully soft leather slippers and shoes for adults and children. At £60 for Italian driving shoes and £30 for sheepskin slippers (children's sizes around £15), these are a definite bargain. So, too, are the antique saris for £90.

Sportswear

The Sports Depot

335 Ladbroke Grove W10
020 8968 7101
us@sportsdep.freeserve.co.uk
Mon–Sat 9.30am–6pm
Situated on the left, just before the first roundabout running north past the Westway, the Depot specialises in US-imported footwear and clothing, including main brands Reebok, Fila and Nike. It's a small space so don't expect a huge selection but, with Reebok Classics at £25, puffa jackets for around £20 and plain tracksuit bottoms for less than £15, the prices are hard to beat.

Vintage

The Crazy Clothes Connection

134 Lancaster Road W11
020 7221 3989
Tues–Sat 11am–7pm
Derrick and his daughter Esther are said to have the best selection of 1920s–70s vintage clothes in London. They also offer costume hire, with prices starting at £50. Rave reviews in the press won't prepare you for the rather dingy appearance of the overcrowded shop, full of bulging clothes racks, reminiscent of a run-down charity shop, or the prices: £75–£100 or so for evening dresses, £50 upwards for men's coats, and so on.

Rellik

8 Golborne Road W10
020 8962 0089
Tues–Sat 10am–6pm
Notting Hill chic still sits rather incongruously at the bottom of Trellick Tower. Rellik offers a diverse selection of one-off designs from vintage Vivienne Westwood to hand-made customised designer wear that has been recycled using antique lace and fabric. Other exclusive labels include Identity, Laissez Faire and Affinity.

FLOWERS AND PLANTS

The Flowered Corner

110 Ladbroke Grove W11
020 7221 3320
Daily 8am–8pm
Grandfather Perring started up as a flower seller more than 20 years ago, after giving up work as a totter. He went on to build a thriving business, with another flower stall on Portobello Road (corner of Talbot Road), all still run by his extended family. Prices are very fair and the flowers always fresh, creating a welcome splash of colour at the busy junction with Lancaster Road.

FOOD AND WINE

L'Etoile

79 Golborne Road W10
020 8960 9769
Mon–Sat 8am–6pm. No credit cards
A mouth-watering array of North African pastries, packed with dates, almonds and honey, are sold alongside French baguettes, croissants and creamy concoctions. This friendly Moroccan bakery is enough to make anyone nostalgic for the Maghreb (or France).

Golborne Fisheries

77 Golborne Road W10
020 8960 3100
Mon 10am–4pm; Tues–Sat 8.30am–6pm. No credit cards
Those of you who think Chalmers & Gray is the Lidgate of the fishmongers' world should try this shop. Here you'll find a terrific array of fish and shellfish from all parts of the world, at prices that leave its upmarket competitor in the Gate at a distinct disadvantage.

Lisboa Delicatessen

54 Golborne Road W10
020 8969 1052
Mon–Sat 9.30am–7.30pm; Sun 10am–1pm
Almost directly opposite the famous pâtisserie/café of the same name, Lisboa stocks a comprehensive selection of Portuguese and Brazilian groceries. Packets of almond biscuits and tins of olives, anchovies, tuna, beans and vegetables fill the shelves, while the bread is displayed in wooden bins. Hams, sausages and cheeses are sold behind the gleaming counter at the back, where you will also find salt cod, pigs' trotters and other pork delicacies, as well as beer and wine.

Le Maroc

94 Golborne Road W10
020 8968 9783
Mon–Sat 9am–7pm
The most alluring of Golborne Road's Moroccan groceries combines household goods such as colourful tagines, ceramics, trays and wall hangings with traditional Moroccan food. Halal meat and delicious home-made merguez sausages are sold at the counter, surrounded by stacks of cous cous, nuts, olives, oil and honey as well as bundles of fresh mint, ladies' fingers, other vegetables and fruit – in short, everything you need to conjure a genuine taste of Morocco.

GIFTS, POSTERS AND STATIONERY

Portfolio

105 Golborne Road W10
020 8960 3051
Mon–Fri 9.30am–5.30pm; Sat 10am–5pm
A great place for greetings cards and posters, as well as odd gifts, Portfolio has the added prestige of having been transformed into a restaurant for a scene in *Notting Hill*. This is where Hugh Grant

and friends mull over his decision to reject the beautiful Julia Roberts, before setting off on a wild car chase to her hotel. Curious locals watched for hours as the actors repeatedly dashed out into the waiting vehicle, which merely shot down Bevington Road and back again.

HOME

Buyers & Sellers

120-22 Ladbroke Grove W10
020 7229 1947
Mon–Fri 9.30am–5.30pm (till 6.30pm Thurs); Sat 9.30am–4.30pm
Always one of the best places to buy large kitchen appliances in London, Buyers & Sellers has moved with the times and now stocks a wide selection of high-tech fridges, freezers and range cookers including brightly coloured designs and lots of stainless steel. These include American makes and lesser known brands such as Sub-Zero and Traulsen, as well as big names like Bosch and Zanussi. Friendly service and guaranteed discounts on certain items look set to ensure lasting success.

Fez

71 Golborne Road W10
020 8964 5573
Mon–Sat 10am–7pm
Tea glasses are one of the best buys in this authentic Moroccan houseware shop which also sells teapots, ceramics, rugs, rush mats, wall hangings, slippers and other items, with little if any concession to fashion. The main aim is serving the local community.

Lloyd Christie

103 Lancaster Road W11
020 7243 6466
www.lloydchristie.com
Mon–Sat 10am–6pm
An old carpet warehouse has provided the perfect-sized premises for this upmarket garden furniture emporium. While the original Lloyd Christie business still concentrates on designing and building conservatories, the shop is run in partnership with Joan Clifton's Avant Garden (formerly in Ledbury Road). The result is an inspired mix of wood and wrought-iron furniture, gifts, lanterns and plant containers, supplemented by Moroccan ceramics, baskets and other bits and pieces for inside as well as out. Favourites are Clifton's magical candle trees (£85–£380), plain zinc containers (£85–£800) and hand-blown glass ceiling lights, each in the shape of a bunch of grapes.

Ollies

69 Golborne Road W10
07768 790725 (Mobile)
Mon–Sat 9am–5pm
Ollies sells collectibles in a fashionable manner to the bright young Buffalo Bills on the Hill. The atmosphere is colonial cowboy hip, represented by a mix of zebra-skin rugs, leather sofas, bamboo, etc. and the stock moves along with the current fashions. Good buys are a pair of leather club chairs for £450, glamorous Venetian-style mirrors, Twenties' and Thirties' furniture, antique textiles, lamps (especially arc lamps) designed with a meeting of James Dean and Lawrence of Arabia in mind. The shop, visited by the likes of Damon Albarn, Richard E Grant and Wendy Richards, also stocks seasonal tropical plants, such as orange and lemon trees. Prop rental available.

Optime Lighting

156 Ladbroke Grove W10
020 8964 9711/8969 3103
Mon–Fri 8.30am–5.30pm; Sat 10am–3pm
Optime sells an increasingly imaginative

selection of modern lighting, including several Italian designs, as well as all the fittings you are likely to need for installing that cutting-edge chandelier.

Warris Vianni & Co

85 Golborne Road W10
020 8964 0019
Mon–Sat 10am–6pm
A combination of quality, originality and style make this one of the best fabric shops in London, but, of course, it doesn't come cheap. Rolls of organza, muslin, silk, cotton, linen, chenille and other hand-loomed materials originate from all over the world, with prices ranging from £10 to more than £50 a metre.

MUSIC

Dub Vendor Records

150 Ladbroke Grove W10
020 8969 3375
Mon–Sat 9.30am–7pm; Sun 12 noon–5pm
An enduring landmark that started out as a small shack beside the station, Dub Vendor specialises in reggae, soca, soul and the full panoply of remixes. Typical customers are a dense gaggle of 15-year-olds checking the latest beats, proving that, like all the music shops in this book, Dub Vendor is not just a place to buy CDs but a positive meeting point for local youth.

MIND AND BODY

Holmes Place

119–31 Lancaster Road W11
020 7243 4141
Mon–Fri 6.30am–10pm; Sat & Sun 8.30am–9pm
Converted from a former school, this spacious branch of Holmes Place has managed to create a feeling of light and space on every floor, topped by a lovely swimming pool, at the same time keeping the original Victorian façade. Exercise in the form of tai chi, pilates, chi ball and several variations of yoga, as well as less holistic body-conditioning classes, are complemented by a range of beauty treatments from facials to nail and hair repair. A crèche is available for up to two hours (Mon–Fri 9am–5pm; Sat 9am–3pm; Sun 9am–1pm). The joining fee is £250 (with occasional special offers), plus a monthly £69 (full membership) or £49 (off peak).

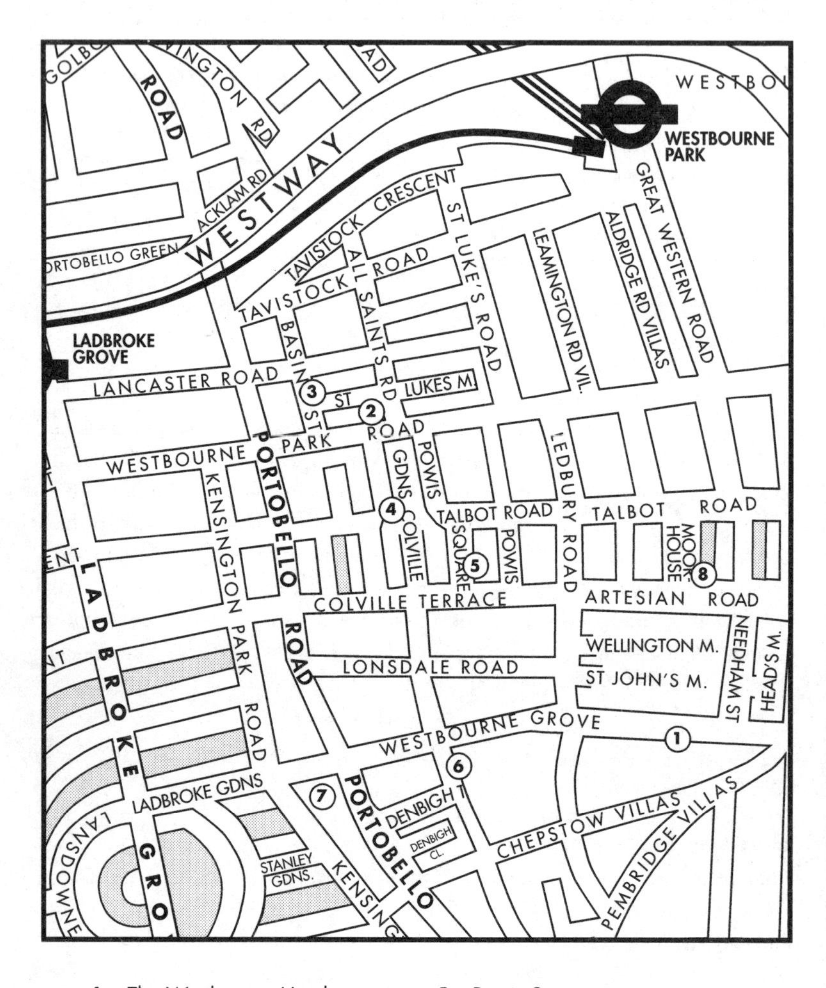

1 The Westbourne Hotel
2 The Mangrove
3 Sarm West Recording Studios
4 All Saints Church
5 Powis Square
6 Turquoise Island
7 20th Century Theatre
8 St Mary of the Angels Church

4. Westbourne Park and Westbourne Grove

One vivid contrast hung in his mind symbolical. On the one hand were the coalies of the Westbourne Park yards, on strike and gaunt and hungry, children begging in the black slush, and starving loungers outside a soup kitchen; and on the other, Westbourne Grove, two streets further, a blazing array of crowded shops, a stirring traffic of cabs and carriages, and such a spate of spending that a tired student in leaky boots and graceless clothes hurrying home was continually impeded in the whirl of skirts and parcels and sweetly pretty womanliness. (H G Wells, *Love and Mr Lewisham*)

This may not quite apply today, but the scale of municipal housing in this area, from Westbourne Park station on Great Western Road, in and around All Saints Road and Powis Square to Westbourne Grove, remains in stark contrast to the wave of Parisian-style boutiques that has invaded this modern version of the Grove since the early 1990s. After English, often with a North American twang, French and Italian are the languages spoken here. All Saints Road and Powis Square, with their heady memories from the 1960s and 70s, are equally cosmopolitan but in a quite different way. A large number of West Indian families occupied the tenement buildings of that time and, though many may have died or since moved on, many remain. It was no accident that this was one of the main hotspots of the 1958 race riots that so shook the fabric of Notting Hill.

Westbourne Park Road

Coming out of the tube station, a right turn takes you down the busy Great Western Road, past blocks of council flats to Westbourne Park Road. To the left, this unremarkable road soon shifts tone with the presence of the Cow 'Saloon Bar and Dining Rooms', followed by the equally popular Westbourne on the corner where the road takes on the grander name of Westbourne Park Villas. Despite being owned by Tom Conran of the Conran dynasty (also with his own nearby deli, see p 122), the Cow is a down-to-earth, not particularly stylish pub with a comfortable atmosphere and good food. The Westbourne, opposite a curve of interesting shops, tends to draw a younger crowd. Situated in the borough of Westminster (as opposed to Kensington & Chelsea), this is very much the outer edge of Notting Hill.

The main expanse of Westbourne Park Road lies in the other direction, westwards towards Portobello Road. Apart from the transformation of the grotty pub on the corner of Ledbury Road into the Liquid Lounge, the appearance of this stretch, past the junctions with Aldridge Road Villas, Leamington Road Villas and St Luke's Road, has changed relatively little in the past 20 years. The same cannot be said about the fourth street on the right, All Saints Road.

All Saints Road

Walking down this street of classy shops and restaurants it's hard to believe that for nearly three decades – the late 1960s to the early 1990s – All Saints Road epitomised the so-called 'frontline'. But it wasn't simply a no-go area controlled by drug dealers. With the Mangrove restaurant as its social centre, this short road represented an important focal point for many black people, both inside and outside Notting Hill. A popular West Indian takeaway, Philsen's Phil-Inn Station, occupied the site on the corner of St Luke's Mews West, now taken up by the Ripe Tomato restaurant. Shops displayed the Rastafarian colours, crowds chatted on the pavement, reggae music wafted or boomed from every other parked car, and, much to the frustration of residents, there was usually a shebeen close by. The Mangrove Steel Band practised for carnival out on the street, as it still does, but then it was for months rather than just weeks before the event. Apart from this seasonal burst of live music, only the presence of the Mangrove Information Centre, People's Sounds and the dilapidated offices of Mercury Radio Cars mini-cab service give any hint of All Saints Road as it used to be.

The Mangrove

The Mangrove restaurant was opened in the late 1960s by Frank Critchlow, who originally came from Trinidad. His previous venture, the Rio Café on Westbourne Park Road, had already combined being a black community centre and a slightly risqué meeting place for white adventurers such as Colin MacInnes and, later, Christine Keeler and friends (see History, pp 174–75). As Courtney Tulloch, a black activist at the time, put it: 'All kinds of people in high places used to go for their quaint cup of coffee down in the ghetto. Slumming.' But the Mangrove was a more ambitious project. Critchlow's aim was to create a smarter place, tastefully decorated, where a mixed crowd could meet over drinks and Caribbean and English food. And it worked. By day it was a popular hang-out for locals; by night it was packed with people from all over, among them academics, politicians, actors, musicians and other performers, black and white. In the words of Frank Critchlow, quoted in *Windrush*:

> *We had Sammy Davis there, we had a lot of stars there. Nina*

Simone, Vanessa Redgrave, Maurice Bishop, Walter Rodney, Darcus Howe. CLR James used to have a lot of people; he used to take over one side of the restaurant and talking to people because everybody wants to hear . . . very, very in-crowd.

But the police were never far away. Notting Hill was becoming an increasingly popular haunt of musicians, hippies and bohemian types, many of whom scored their dope in All Saints Road. The police response was to target the Mangrove and other Caribbean venues, raiding them again and again in a manner quite disproportionate to the level of crime at that time. Eventually, in exasperation, Critchlow led a protest march in 1970.When hordes of police tried to alter the direction of the march, trouble broke out and many were arrested, resulting in nine coming to trial in 'The Mangrove Nine' case. All were found innocent by the jury. Conflict continued well into the 1980s as drugs became an increasingly serious problem on the frontline, culminating in 1987 with the arrest of Frank Critchlow. Despite testimony against him from 36 police officers, it was proven to be a trumped-up drug charge and he was released. Within three years he was awarded compensation, but felt defeated. Unable to restrain the continuing conflict between youth and the law that would escalate around the August bank holiday Carnival, he decided to sell the restaurant. In no time the building reopened as the Portobello Dining Rooms, the street's first trendy restaurant, later replaced by the Mas Café. Nowadays 'the Mangrove' refers to the information centre opposite, which continues to serve the black community.

All Saints Road has other claims to fame besides its turbulent history and its current reputation for cutting-edge food and design. It was here, in August 1992, that Shaznay Lewis first met Mel Blatt, leading to the formation of the band All Saints. They were introduced in Metamorphosis recording studios (No.18, on the site of the old Apollo pub) where, joined by sisters Natalie and Nicole Appleton, they went on to record their first big hit *Never, Ever*. St Luke's Mews West, just around the corner from the Jackson sisters' colourful shop, (see p 118), also has strong musical associations. In the early 1970s, No.35 was squatted by Lemmy of heavy metal rock band, Motorhead. Ten years later, in Sarm West studios at the other end of the Mews, Band Aid recorded the famous hit *Do they Know it's Christmas*?, raising millions of pounds for charity. Sarm West continues to record a host of big names including Madonna, Blur, Radiohead, Boyzone, George Michael and M People, whose singer Heather Small was born and brought up off the Portobello Road.

Musicians also visit All Saints Road for its guitar and fiddle shop, run by a trio of enthusiasts at No.13. On the next block running north, cyclists will find another specialist haven – Ninon Asuni's Bicycle Workshop. As well as doing repairs, Ninon carries a huge amount of spares, plus publications and accessories, and will even order unusual new bikes (see Directory, p 160).

In and around Powis Square

Back on Westbourne Park Road, almost directly opposite the junction with All Saints Road, is Powis Gardens, leading to Powis Square. The square, with the handsome red-brick Tabernacle at one end, has an interesting history, as does All Saints Church and the old church hall which was demolished in the 1970s.

Towards the latter end of the nineteenth century, the large Victorian houses in and around Powis Square had become seriously dilapidated as investors were unable to fund the building work necessary for their upkeep. Many houses were divided into flats and single rooms, often occupied by students. One particular block on Powis Square provided the premises for Wren College, a coaching establishment run by a Mr Walter Wren who specialised in preparing young men for the Indian Civil Service. So many of these men took lodgings in the vicinity that according to Florence Gladstone, author of *Notting Hill in Bygone Days*, 'the neighbourhood acquired the name of "Little India"'. Unfortunately, this did little to halt its decline, which continued well into the 1950s when Peter Rachman came on the scene to make this the heart of his shady empire, later emulated, at least in part, by the highly controversial and erratic Michael X (see History, p 174 & John Michell, pp 198–201), who lived at various times in Colville Terrace, Powis Terrace and Powis Square.

This area was also a focus for part of the three days of violence that constituted the Notting Hill race riots in 1958, referred to by Peter Ackroyd in his recent biography of London:

> *. . . the worst rioting took place on Monday 1 September, in the central area of Notting Hill Gate. Mobs congregated in Colville Road, Powis Square and Portobello Road before going on a 'smashing rampage, chanting "Kill niggers!"'. . . One observer noted that 'Notting Hill had become like a looking-glass world, for all the most mundane objects which everyone takes for granted had suddenly assumed the most profound importance. Milk bottles were turned into missiles, dustbin lids into primitive shields'.*

In the wake of the riots, Powis Square remained in and out of the news throughout the 1960s, chiefly as a significant focus of community action. Among local people's many grievances was the lack of anywhere safe for children to play. Meanwhile, in their midst, behind metal fencing and firmly locked gates, lay a tantalising patch of green grass – the abandoned square. According to the late André Shervington, who lived nearby, it was so overgrown that at one point a goat was thrown in, presumably to fatten up for a good West Indian curry. Public protest came to a head with two separate occupations of the square, the second of which led to its permanent liberation when the Council was finally persuaded to capitulate and take the land out of private ownership to create a public play space for children. It took further years of campaigning by, among others, Rhaune Laslett, a great champion of children and a key figure in the history of Carnival, to obtain a play hut and equipment of the kind you see today.

In 1968, the year in which it was liberated, Powis Square attracted public attention of a very different kind with the filming of Nicolas Roeg and Donald Cammell's *Performance* at No.25. Only the exterior of the house was used, together with the square garden, which Cammell considered to be the ideal location for conveying 'kaleidoscopic moods in a strange and faded area of London'. Nicolas Roeg now lives nearby.

Many of the meetings held to plan community action took place in All Saints Church Hall, which was also used for socials and benefits connected to the London Free School, based at No. 26 Powis Terrace, opposite the former studio of David Hockney. Emily Young, a recruit from Holland Park Comprehensive, recalls the 'very curious double life' she led between home, Holland Park and the Free School:

> *Nothing was really taught but it was great fun. Local people could come in and play their instruments and it was a place for them to rehearse. John Michell had an interesting influence. He was knowledgeable, he did have these odd books – there were a lot of books – great enthusiasm for interesting old arcane knowledge, and a lot of talk about flying saucers, the measurements of Jerusalem and all this stuff.' (*Jonathon Green, *Days in the Life: Voices from the English Underground 1961–1971)*

The School lasted about two years, its precarious funding aided by several benefit concerts at All Saints Church Hall, the most memorable of which featured Pink Floyd in 1966 and virtually launched their career. The hall was also used for children's play groups and a number of theatrical events, including a production of Langston Hughes's *Shakespeare in Harlem*. Along with all the church's ancillary buildings, it was eventually redeveloped in the 1970s, in co-operation with the Notting Hill Housing Trust, to provide the flats now bordering Powis Gardens, as well as a new church hall, sacristy and vestry.

All Saints Church

All Saints Church was the project of the Reverend Walker, who planned it as the centrepiece of his housing development in and around what are now Powis and Colville Squares. It was also intended as a memorial to his parents, so it must have been doubly disappointing when, in 1855, final building work had to be abandoned due to lack of funds. The basic structure, designed by William White, was complete, but having no glass or furniture, the church couldn't be used. The doors and windows were boarded up and it remained abandoned for another six years, when it was popularly known as 'Walker's Folly' or 'All Sinners in the Mud'. Walker eventually managed to fund the remaining work, though in a more modest style than his original dream, and in 1861 the church was dedicated to All Saints and opened up to the community.

The church was badly bombed in the Second World War, after which it was again unused until 1951 when it reopened, resplendent with new shrines in honour of the saints, and gold leaf altarpieces by the famous designer of church furnishings, Sir Ninian Comper. These were symbols of the kind of ultra high Church worship for which All Saints had become renowned under its flamboyant vicar, Father John Twisaday (1931–1961). Entering All Saints, you will be immediately struck by the wide open sanctuary with its centrally placed stone altar, above which hangs the newly restored hanging rood, first installed in 1934. This was designed by Cecil Hare, as was the reredos beneath the east window with its figures of Our Lady, St Augustine, St Stephen and the prophet Isaiah. To the south, the small chapel dedicated to Our Lady of Walsingham reflects Father Twisaday's involvement in the restoration of pilgrimages to Walsingham in the 1930s. Halfway along the south side, the statue of St Mary Magdalene was designed and executed by M Dupon of Bruges, who also created the figures of St Joseph (on the north side) and St Anthony of Padua with its stone canopy. These, together with various other items such as sets of embroidered cottas, were brought back from Bruges bit by bit in the boot of Father Twisaday's car. In the south transept is the altar of St George, designed by Martin Travers as a memorial to the men of All Saints who gave their lives in the First World War. As with all the stained glass, the window above it was installed as part of the post-war restoration of the 1950s. Designed by GER Smith of Nicholson Studios, it depicts, among others, the patron saints of the four nations – England, Ireland, Scotland and Wales – and the Celtic missionary St Columba, marking the link with Reverend Walker's home town of St Columb Major in Cornwall.

(Walker was also responsible for the building of St Columb's Church in Lancaster Road, now the Serbian Church of St Sava, see pp 72–3.) On the north side, the church also has a chapel of St Columb with an altarpiece by Sir Ninian Comper who designed the two stained glass windows and the altarpiece in the Lady Chapel.

Further historical and architectural details are provided by the church's own excellent information sheet, *A Guided Tour Around All Saints*, from which much of the above is taken. Today, All Saints has a hugely active congregation, with as many as 300 people attending Mass on high days and holidays. The church has also developed a strong musical tradition and supports Carnival and, in particular, the Mangrove Steel Band. For more information, telephone 020 7727 5919.

Leaving Powis Square, with all its radical associations, a right turn into Colville Terrace, followed by a left into Colville Road leads to the glamorous world of Westbourne Grove.

Westbourne Grove

Coming from the direction of Powis Square, the first Westbourne Grove landmark is the famous 'Turquoise Island', featured on the cover of this book. Nearly ten years on from its opening, this space-age pagoda must still be London's most fashionable public lavatory. Commissioned by the Notting Hill Improvements Group (see p 4) and designed by Piers Gough, the building was opened on 28 June 1992 by Lucinda Lambton, author of *Temples of Convenience* (an illustrated history of the water closet). Following a ripple of outrage from local residents, most of whom were objecting to its failure to blend in with the surrounding architecture, it went on to win several awards and now, of course, seems a perfect match for the trendy outlets all around.

Origins of Westbourne Grove

The development of Westbourne Grove began in the 1840s. Up until then it had been a real 'grove', a lane flanked by tall trees and banks of wild flowers. To the east, around what is now Ossington Street, it was cut across by the River Westbourne (or Bays Water), running south towards the Thames and long since diverted underground.

The first building work was carried out by William Henry Jenkins who, in 1844, leased 28 acres from James Ladbroke on the agreement that all houses would be of good quality, with none of less value than £300. These were constructed at the far western end of Westbourne Grove, in and around what are now Pembridge and Chepstow Villas.

The Jenkins family also owned estates in Wales and Herefordshire, hence the naming of these streets and others, such as Denbigh and Ledbury Roads. The building on this section of Westbourne Grove, then known as Archer Street, was generally inferior, consisting mainly of shops which, though popular, were not in the same league as the fashionable businesses about to spring up further east. In 1863, the combined influences of the inauguration of the underground railway at Bishops Road (near Queensway) and the opening of William Whiteley's first shop, at No.31 Westbourne Grove, led to the stretch towards Paddington rivalling Oxford Street as London's most fashionable shopping centre. This lasted nearly half a century, until around the time of the Second World War when people's priorities changed and bomb damage, too, left its scars. Always the poorer end, Archer Street (renamed Westbourne Grove in 1938) became more run-down. Certainly, no one could have predicted that it would ever attain its current status as West London's answer to Beverly Hills, or that Whiteley's former patch of Westbourne Grove would be struggling to catch up.

Taking a short detour west towards Ladbroke Grove, the road leads you past red-brick council flats up to the junction with Portobello Road. This area was badly damaged in the Second World War. Among the casualties was Denbigh Road Methodist Church, which was rebuilt in 1957. Under a trilogy of ministers, assembled in the wake of the 1958 riots (see Notting Hill Methodist Church, pp 130–31), the church and its subsequent ecumenical centre became an important focus for the cohesion of the community. This was the case right up until the 1990s when the site was sold to the Westway Housing Association to provide accommodation for Caribbean families.

The next block takes in several antique shops and arcades, EJ Barnes's cycle shop (established in 1951 at No.285) and just a few doors down, the recently rediscovered 20th Century Theatre. Originally the Bijou Theatre, this building has housed performances by many famous names, from the early days of Marie Lloyd and Albert Chevalier to Laurence Olivier, who made his London stage début here in 1924. Soon afterwards, Westbourne Grove ends at the junction with Kensington Park Road and the route it follows becomes Ladbroke Gardens.

The 20th Century Theatre

The 20th Century Theatre started life as the Bijou Theatre in 1863. Since then it has had a varied and often illustrious history, as an auction house, a cinema, a theatre, a furniture showroom, a meeting place for amateur dramatic societies and, most recently, a venue for publishers' parties and launches for events such as London Fashion Week.

While Charles Dickens is only rumoured to have read from the stage of the Bijou, it is certain that Henry Irving, Herbert Beerbohm Tree and Marie Lloyd each appeared here. In 1893, the building was being used as an auction house and was badly damaged by fire. Alterations were made to the interior and in 1911 it became a cinema before reverting to a theatre in 1918 under the stewardship of Lena Ashwell, who called it the Century Theatre. She had made her stage debut at the original Bijou, appearing in a play called *Young Mrs Winthrop* alongside the celebrated character actor and stage manager, Sir Herbert Beerbohm Tree. Returning with her own repertory company, the Lena Ashwell Players, she performed in Archer Street as part of a special arrangement with several London boroughs, to produce entertainment affordable to the poor. At one time the Players were joined by none other than Laurence Olivier, who had also made his first appearance on the London stage here, as the Suliot Officer in Alice Law's play *Byron*. His family had lived nearby as his father, the Reverend Gerard Olivier, had been appointed to the slum district of Notting Hill in 1910. (The Reverend was attached to St James's but dismissed after two years for being too high church, having swung incense in the tin-roofed mission hut.)

From 1929, the theatre was used by amateur theatrical societies from Harrods and DH Evans department stores, and the BBC. It also provided an overflow for the local synagogue, as well as being a place for political meetings. The present name of 20th Century Theatre was bestowed by the Rudolph Steiner Association which took over in 1936 and started to stage Eurythmy, the Steiner art form which uses both colour and movement to convey music and speech. Around this time, right up to its closure as a theatre in 1963, it continued to be used by local amateur groups, including the Guild of Friendship and the Notting Hill Players. There followed several decades as a furniture showroom and warehouse. It is only now, under the new owners, Michael and Sandra Kamen, that it might once again become a serious theatre for plays, screenings and chamber music. They have so far obtained planning – but not yet licensing – permission to stage theatrical events in the building. Meanwhile it can be hired for parties, provided these are relatively peaceful and end well before midnight. For more information telephone, 020 7229 4179.

Heading back towards Queensway, marking the other end of Westbourne Grove, the atmosphere perhaps resembles Paris more than Beverly Hills. Hidden behind the bus stop opposite the 'Turquoise Island', Tom's café and deli provides delicious sandwiches, pastries and cappuccinos to take away, as well as groceries and a regularly changing menu. Above the shop are the offices of Karma Cabs, a taxi service with the ethos that 'it's the journey that counts, not the destination'. Inspired by his extensive travels in the Indian sub-continent, owner Tobias Moss runs a fleet of six Indian-built Ambassador cars, decked out in brightly coloured silk, with ragga music playing and incense burning on the dashboard. The cars, based on the design of the 40-year-old Morris Oxford, can be spotted by the garlands of plastic flowers wound around the bumpers (see Directory, p 163).

A few doors along from Tom's is the deservedly popular Italian Café 206. Virtually every other building is occupied by galleries, boutiques and designer furnishing shops, often European owned and invariably selling beautiful objects for beautiful people. One exception is the Oxfam shop, across the road from Tom's, which always stocks a great selection of second-hand books, as well as sometimes irresistible items of clothing. Beyond the Duke of Norfolk pub, the next junction is Ledbury Road, another shoppers' mecca, much featured in our listings below. On the corner is Westbourne Grove Baptist Church, whose strongly evangelical and charismatic services draw a loyal congregation from all backgrounds. A few minutes' away, down a left turn into Needham Road (entrance in Moorhouse Road), lies the interesting church of St Mary of the Angels. After a faltering start, the building was constructed to the designs of John Francis Bentley, best known for designing Westminster Cathedral (see also the Church of St Francis of Assisi, pp 139–40).

The Church of St Mary of the Angels

The construction of St Mary of the Angels began in the mid-nineteenth century with plans by the architect Thomas Meyer, but like so many projects of the time it foundered when the money ran out. The building remained unfinished and derelict for several years until Cardinal Wiseman began looking for a church in which to set up a community of the Oblates of St Charles Borromeo. The challenge was finally taken up by a priest called Father Manning. Once the order was approved in Rome, Manning moved in with his nephew and curate, and the church was consecrated and opened for worship in 1857. In keeping with his firm belief that that 'you should build a school before you build a church', St Mary's already had an adjoining school for which he recruited Mother Elizabeth Lockhart, who later moved with her community of sisters to the Franciscan Convent in Portobello Road (see pp 39–40). Manning wrote that 'The eight years I was at St Mary's were the happiest in my life. My name has always been over my door, and I never feel so much at home as when I am in that little room.' While at St Mary of the Angels, he preached a famous course of sermons to a packed congregation, and was much missed when, in 1865, he moved to Victoria, Australia, where he became Archbishop.

The church was completed in early French Gothic style by John Francis Bentley, who later added a second aisle in 1869. He also designed several stained-glass windows, including those in the Lady Chapel which portray Eve, Ruth, Judith and Esther. Others represent the English martyrs: Saints John Fisher, Thomas More, John Hale, Cuthbert Maine, John Houghton and John Forrest. Bentley later became a Catholic and was married in another church of his design – St Francis of Assisi in Pottery Lane. Manning showed his disdain for Gothic architecture by doing his best to transform the interior of St Mary's into the semblance of an Italian church. He hung thick curtains over the tracery of the Gothic windows and covered the stained-glass windows with paintings, all of which were removed when he left the parish. The High Altar in alabaster is in late Gothic style and was made by Messrs Jones and Willis. Manning brought back many relics of St Charles Borromeo from Italy, including a green chasuble. In 1978 Father Michael Hollings, who had previously been chaplain to Oxford University, became the parish priest at St Mary of the Angels. He was much loved by the local community and would often give up his bed for 'men of the road'. After he died in 1997 it was decided to open a centre for the homeless in his name in what had originally been the school building in Artesian Road. This is an ongoing project which is still short of funds. Further information is available from the parish office, telephone 020 7229 0487.

Our final stretch of Westbourne Grove leads to Chepstow Road on the fringes of Bayswater. The south side of the street has yet another row of groovy shops and restaurants, culminating in the ultimate chic of Solange Azagury-Partridge and the Westbourne Hotel. The first is a jewellers, whose secretive entrance and plush interior have had it mistaken for a high-class brothel, while the second, which only opened in October 2000, aims to provide 'elegant luxury' in 'familiar and comfortable' surroundings. Beyond the Westbourne, the buildings become scruffier up until the cheerful premises of Mandola, a friendly Sudanese restaurant which offers subtly spiced dishes at very reasonable prices.

The modern block opposite, on the corner of Chepstow Road, was once the site of Arthurs Stores, a high-class department store which at one time occupied the whole of Nos.114–20 Westbourne Grove. Writing in *Westbourne Grove in Wealth, Work and Welfare*, Eddie Adams describes how some people considered it to be a small equivalent of Fortnum & Mason. Besides having 'many departments including provisions, flowers, furnishings and ironmongery', it was noted for its 'attractive window displays and the big clock over the main entrance which used to be a meeting place for friends and lovers'. Upstairs, uniformed waiters served tea, coffee or meals on the balcony while a small orchestra played in the restaurant. As the prosperity of Westbourne Grove declined, so did Arthurs Stores, and it closed in 1937 to be eventually replaced by the Odeon Cinema, which opened in 1955. Unable to sustain enough custom, despite the addition of three screens, this in turn closed its doors in the early 1980s. The poet John Heath-Stubbs, though blind, was among those who mourned its destruction:

On the Demolition of the Odeon Cinema, Westbourne Grove

Never one for the flicks, I did not frequent the place:
Though I recall the *Voyage of the Argonauts*,
And a second feature – some twaddle about
A daughter of King Arthur, otherwise unrecorded
By history or tradition. Now, each day,
I pass it, and I hear the brutal noise
Of demolition: clatter of falling masonry,
Machines that seem to grit and grind their teeth,
And munch in gluttony of destruction.

Its soft innards, I guess, are gone already:
The screen, the lighting, the plush seats; the ghosts likewise –
Shadows of shadows, phantoms of phantoms,
The love goddesses, the butcher boy heroes,
The squawking cartoon-animals.

This Odeon – I should regret it? –
In which no ode has ever been recited.
Yet there's a pang – for I've lived long enough
To know that every house of dreams
Must be torn down at last.

ACCOMMODATION

HOTELS

The Westbourne Hotel

163–165 Westbourne Grove W11
020 7243 6008/Fax 020 7229 7201
enquiries@westbournehotel.com
www.westbournehotel.com
Considering all the hype that accompanied its opening late last year, this small 'designer' hotel is surprisingly friendly and unpretentious. The feel is Scandinavian, with lots of wood and leather, while contemporary Brit-art by the likes of Danny Chadwick, Sarah Lucas, Gavin Turk and Dan Macmillan adds a touch of glamour.

Each of the 20 rooms has a queen-size bed, shower, DVD player and internet access. Prices, from £175 for a portrait room to £255 for one facing the back garden, have risen steeply since the first guests checked in. All rates include coffee and a Danish, but exclude VAT.

YOUTH HOSTELS

The Leinster Hostel

7–12 Leinster Square W2
020 7229 9641/Fax 020 7221 8665
This former hotel is off the map for this book but only 20 minutes' walk from Portobello Road and a great find for budget travellers. Prices start at £10 per person for the cheapest room sharing with eight others, rising to £30 for a single room with shower.

EATING AND DRINKING

CAFÉS, SNACKS AND TAKEAWAYS

Café 206

206 Westbourne Grove W11
020 7221 1525
Mon–Sat 8am–6pm; Sun 9am–6pm
This was one of the earliest cafés to open in the area, long before the chain invasion, and it's still going strong, maybe because it's run by Italians so the coffee's decent, the staff don't change every five minutes and the food is made with good basic ingredients. 206 is always full, although not cheap. Another genuine Italian touch is that it doesn't pursue a no smoking policy, a relief for those social lepers among us who discovered they were being asked not to light up at a table on the pavement outside Fresh & Wild next door.

Dan's Bar and Grill

105–07 Talbot Road, W11
020 7221 8099
Tues–Sun 10am–4pm
Formerly a popular venue, especially for Sunday brunch, a huge furore broke out recently on mynottinghill.co.uk in response to changes, including a pricey fixed menu, made by the new owner. One local proclaimed that 'since the refurb, it has lost all atmosphere . . . The menu is limited at best, and if they aren't even prepared to try and make allowances for people who want something as simple as a bacon sandwich then what's the point?' The owner fought back, claiming these complaints were coming from the 'type of people who want to order a coffee and sit around all day'. If you feel like digging deep in your pocket, and are ready to brave the surly staff, you can judge for yourself. For what it's worth, the bacon sarnies (may they rest in peace) were probably the best in London.

Tom's (see Food and Drink, p 122)

RESTAURANTS AND BARS

Asian

Bali Sugar

33a All Saints Road W11
020 7221 4477
Mon–Sun 12.30–3pm; 6.30–11pm
Bali Sugar has held onto the original site of its sister restaurant, the famous Sugar Club (now in Soho), to become a truly special local restaurant in its own right. The upstairs setting is seductively glamorous, with French windows looking out onto a fairy-lit garden that provides a perfect dining hideaway for balmy nights. Downstairs, the pace, set off by the open kitchen, is busier, with olive and gold décor and comfortable chairs. But the food is the real work of art here. A good-sized menu presents Asian fusion at its best, using thoughtful combinations such as *soy-bonito* or ginger-*tosazu*. Fish lovers are urged to try seabass sashimi with shiso cress, or the classic grilled scallops with crème fraîche and sweet chilli sauce; and pan-roasted Trelough duck breast on *yaki-soba* noodle pancake, sake-flamed Asian greens and cucumber tamarind dressing is also delicious. Excellent food is matched by an imaginative wine list, plus friendly and knowledgeable service, both discreet and fast. Diners have included Madonna, Elvis Costello and Patrick Cox, to name but a few, so if you're looking for a relaxing time in a stylish space and the chance of George Michael sliding into the next table as you sip on your chilled glass of Cloudy Bay, then go for it. Average price per head £35 with wine.

Uli

16 All Saints Road W11
020 7727 7511
Daily 6.45pm–11pm
The first impression at this modern oriental restaurant is the friendliness. From the moment you walk in the door you are well looked after by informed staff who show a genuine love for the food that they are serving. The well-priced menu offers a huge selection combining Asian flavours such as Chinese and Thai, presented in very delicate and separate ways. The spicy calamari at £5.95 for a starter had a distinct but subtle taste, making you lick your lips for more. To follow, choose from dishes such as chicken with basil and chilli (£8.95) or Thai beef salad (£6.95), both of which had fresh clean flavours. Add to this a New World wine or a lovely Malbec, a dash of Bohemian Notting Hill locals, and you have a great evening, especially recommended if there are three or four of you. Average price with wine or beer £20.

English

Veronica's

3 Hereford Road W2
020 7229 5079/7221 1452
Mon–Fri 12 noon–2pm; Mon–Sat 6–11.30pm
Starting as a manageress in 1982, Veronica soon bought this slightly old-fashioned restaurant.. In the main restaurant – there is also a 'Victorian dining-room' – the few tables, with their welcoming red table cloths, are well spaced. An imaginative but slightly over-priced menu for what feels like a neighbourhood restaurant. Main courses of olde English food cost up to £17.50.

Fish

Livebait

175 Westbourne Grove W2
020 7727 4321
Mon–Fri 12 noon–3pm, 6–11pm; weekends 12 noon–10pm.
A recent branch of the expanding chain, Livebait, with its focus on fresh, quality seafood, is a welcome addition to an area already amply served by eateries of all

kinds. Vast platters of *fruits de mer* (£37–£57 for two) are ferried past at head height in this large open-plan restaurant which, with its distinctive black and white tiled décor, has more than a hint of the municipal baths. A little functional and chilly, it nevertheless does what it does extremely well. The seafood bar serves everything from three types of oysters (£7 per six), whole Dorset crab with mayonnaise (£8.95) to Nova Scotian lobster (£14 per half). The quality is consistently high and the prices reasonable. While the focus on fish remains constant throughout, there are always one or two options for the dedicated carnivore. Choose carefully and simply from the main menu with its rather cavalier attitude towards fusion cooking, as some dishes do disappoint. Simple combinations work best, such as roast cod, garlic herb mash and *sauce vierge* (£13.75) or the excellent catch-of-the-day choices cooked and accompanied as you wish (£13–£16).

Global

Nectar

The Tabernacle Arts Centre
Powis Square W11
020 7565 7890
Mon–Fri 8.30am–11pm; Sat 9.30am–11pm; Sun 10am–5pm

Friendly vibes, delicious, reasonably priced food and a great outside space away from the clamour of Portobello Road, make this one of the best additions to the area for a very long time. Local chef Maggie Mitchell turns out a truly international mix of dishes ranging from Caribbean rotis and chicken, peas and rice, to Mediterranean salads and *boeuf bourguignon*, all freshly cooked in the kitchen alongside the bar. Children are welcome and catered for with plainer staples like pasta and tomato sauce, and, as long as they're supervised, there's plenty of room for them to run around, inside and out. With breakfast, coffee and other drinks served all day, prices as low as £5.50 for a main course and the delightfully unpretentious attitude of all involved, Nectar is a real winner.

Italian

Assaggi

39 Chepstow Place W2
020 7792 5501
Mon–Sat 12.30–2.30pm & 7.30–11pm

Assaggi offers London Tuscan minimalism at its best. This large, airy room above the Chepstow pub makes a delightful setting for lunch, especially when the sun is out. If you can overlook the audacious prices, the food is simply very good and served with impressive understatement in truly Italian style. Good wine list. Expect to pay at least £30 a head without wine and book well in advance (up to six weeks), particularly for dinner.

Centonove

109 Westbourne Park Road W2
020 7221 1746
www.centonove.com
Daily 7–11pm; Sat & Sun till midnight; lunch planned for summer 2001

Recently bought out by its waiters, refitted and reopened, Centonove is a prime example of making a good thing better. Always a great local Italian, the new management has added a modern touch both to the menu and the interior. Subdued lighting, an open-plan kitchen and a great downstairs area with open fires and deep red walls make you feel instantly at home, enhanced by the gregarious nature of the head waiter. Food is good in a rustic, Italian kind of way. Go for the huge portions, fresh ingredients and reasonable prices and you will not be disappointed. The simple starters range from £5.90 to £7.20, with a *bruschetta al pomodoro* almost too big, comprising large slabs of grilled country bread smothered with ripe vine tomatoes, basil and olive oil (£5.90). *Linguine allo scoglio* (£12.90) turns out to be a gargantuan dish of pasta with a tomato and garlic based sauce stuffed with squid, clams and mussels. Order the salt-crusted seabass (£12.70) and a whole fish arrives, encased in rock hard-baked salt, to be theatrically waved under your nose before being taken away for filleting. Finish with a coffee and liqueur rather than the somewhat disappointing selection of puddings, and leave with a rosy glow.

Frattini

29 All Saints Road W1
020 7221 8585
Mon–Sat 7–11pm
Recently highly recommended for good Italian home cooking. Formerly Acqua Pazza.

The Wine Factory

294 Westbourne Grove W11
020 7229 1877
Mon–Fri 12 noon–3.15pm; Sat 12 noon –4pm (just pizzas later); Mon–Sat 6pm –10.50pm. Coffee from 11am daily.
Cheerful, minimally-decorated place spread over two floors and serving up tasty, no-nonsense Italian-style fare: king prawns in filo pastry or minestrone starters, pizza and pasta or daily meat and fish specials (around £8) for mains, and all the usual suspects for dessert. Pizza and pasta are discounted at lunchtime. As the name suggests, however, the real draw is the inexpensive but excellent selection of wine and champagne.

Zucca

188 Westbourne Grove W11
020 7727 0060
Daily 12 noon–3pm & 7–11pm
Zucca provides a convenient resting place after a morning's shopping; blond wood, dark blue banquettes and attentive service in the upstairs restaurant are echoed in a slightly subterranean bar downstairs. Zucca is the definition of 'modern Italian', as reflected in the menu, though always with an eye to the lettuce leaf and mineral-water brigade who seem to congregate here on a weekday lunch time. Starters such as grilled sardines with red pepper, tomato and coriander salsa (£6.50), Serrano ham with wood roasted peach, rocket and parmesan (£7.50) are a light lunch dish in themselves. Main courses reflect the kitchen's attention to quality and presentation. White onion and Gorgonzola risotto (£8.50), linguine with mussels, chilli and garlic (£9) or a heavier dish of roast rump of lamb with celeriac purée, wild mushrooms and *cavolo nero* (£12.75) all featured on a recent menu. A set lunch of £12.50 for two courses is a good way to sample the menu, and dinner is a more formal, expensive affair.

Modern European

Beach Blanket Babylon

45 Ledbury Road, W11
020 7229 2907
Restaurant 12 noon–3pm daily; Mon–Wed & Sun 7–10.30pm; Thurs–Sat 7–1.45pm
Bar daily 12 noon–11pm (Sun till 10.30pm)
Over-the-top theatrical décor make this more like a Gothic movie-set than a restaurant. The bar attracts a large crowd of young people who go to drink and obviously not for the tasteless, under-cooked food about which even the waiters are honest. At around £15 for a main course, attentive, friendly service is small compensation.

North American

Dakota

127 Ledbury Road W11

020 7792 9191
Daily 12 noon–3.30pm & 7–11pm; brunch at weekends 11am–3.30pm
Opening five or six years ago, Dakota was an instant success. Imaginative modern American fusion-cooking brightened up the jaded palates of restaurant-goers who probably thought they had tried everything. Unpronounceable menus, strange ingredients and explosive combinations of taste proved that they hadn't. The interior is grown-up but fun, with wooden walls allowing just a hint of the backwoods to permeate the otherwise sophisticated atmosphere. An outdoor terrace is cunningly hidden from a busy road by large box hedges, and provides a delightful setting for a lazy weekend brunch, something they do extremely well here (£4–£16). Recently, though, Dakota seems to have lost its way. Although there is less room for error now that the combinations have calmed down, starters in the past have disappointed. A salad of grilled squid, chorizo and almonds arrived dwarfed by the enormous plate on which it was presented on. The baby squid was fantastic, but the chorizo overcooked and rubbery, and the salad overdressed and not exactly in its first flush of youth (rather like a few fellow diners.) The mains are a better bet, and a recent dish of pan-fried king snapper, chilli spinach, ratte potatoes and sweet cured cherry tomatoes (£15) was a great combination of tastes and textures. Puddings (£4–£5) are also sublime, with home-made ice creams and sorbets featuring heavily.

Sudanese

Mandola

139–41 Westbourne Grove W11
020 7229 4734
Mon–Sat 12 noon–11pm; Sun 12 noon–10.30pm. No credit cards
Some say this Sudanese restaurant has become a victim of its own success, but it's well worth a visit – if only as an antidote to most of the smart watering holes in W11. The food is good and the prices reasonable. You can even take your own wine for a small corkage charge. Try the mixed salad bar which allows you to sample most of the starters on the menu, all of which are humming with flavour and zest. The main courses are mostly meat in various sauces, all good, but try the grilled cutlets or the fish, such as tilapia fried in flavoured batter. There is also a vegetarian selection including lentil stew with caramelised garlic. Good atmosphere and a mainly youngish crowd. Be sure to book for evenings.

Thai

See **Walmer Castle** (p 115)

BARS

Babushka

41 Tavistock Crescent W11
020 7727 9250
Mon–Fri 5–11pm; Sat 12 noon–11pm; Sun 12 noon–10.30pm
Slightly shabby Gothic décor, loud music and an open fire in winter give this place a clubby atmosphere, but strictly for the young and trendy. The staff are very friendly and the cocktails, expertly mixed, are delicious but expensive. The upstairs room can be hired out.

Jac's Bar

48 Lonsdale Road W11
0207 792 2838
Tues–Sat 6–11pm; Sun 7–10.30pm
One of the first pubby wine bars, or winebarry pubs to be done up, with squidgy chairs, cheerful antipodean staff, DJs on Thursday through to Sunday, and an upstairs balcony room you can use for private parties. A stylish but down-to-

earth refuge from the pretensions of the likes of Beach Blanket Babylon, full of Portobello residents who view it as their local.

Liquid Lounge

209 Westbourne Park Road W11
020 7243 0914
Mon–Tues 5–11pm; Wed–Fri 5–midnight; Sat 10am–midnight; Sun 10am–10.30pm
Small, stylish bar with modern all-blue décor following a liquid theme, plus leather sofas, dim lighting and mellow music. Aims for the 'chilled', sophisticated atmosphere which can tend towards cliquey. Age range approx 25 to 35 years. Monday night very quiet but busy on Friday and Saturdays. Drinks are normal London prices – just under £5 for a cocktail – but good.

GASTROPUBS

The Cow

89 Westbourne Park Road W2
020 7221 0021
Daily bar 12.30–3pm & 6.30–10.30pm; restaurant 12.30–3pm & 7–11pm
Eating on this corner has become a little like the battle of the gastropubs, for, like the Westbourne, the Cow, has its own style which it does extremely well. A cosy 'Irish' pub decorated in deep reds and old Guinness signs, it is owned by Tom Conran, son of Terence. The focus on food, as you might expect, is careful and concise. Downstairs serves a variety of seafood from a Parisian-style seafood bar, as well as daily specials such as ham and white-bean stew (£4.50) or linguine with squid, chilli and flat leaf parsley (£8.50). Upstairs, with its own entrance, is a small restaurant in its own right. Great chefs have passed through here on their way to larger venues, and a visit will never disappoint. A recent menu included rocket, walnut, pear and Parmesan salad (£6) or seared scallops, caviar, champ and butter sauce among the starters (£6–£12), as well as seared tuna, artichokes, white beans and tapenade (£15) as one of the well-executed main courses (£12–£16). Puddings such as hot chocolate mousse cake with ice cream and fudge sauce keep up the high standards, although at a fairly high price of £5.25.

Prince Bonaparte

80 Chepstow Road W2
020 7313 9491
Daily 12 noon–11pm; food served 12.30–3pm & 6.30–10pm
A fashionable pub to be seen in, the Bonaparte is nearly always packed with a youngish crowd of local residents and destination drinkers. Hard to imagine that only a decade or so ago, when still the Artesian, this was a sleazy dive notorious for its Friday afternoon striptease. Nowadays you're more likely to frequent it for the Friday and Saturday night DJs or one of the rocking Carnival parties. The food isn't bad either – modern British/European with a main course setting you back about £8.50, and a particularly enticing range of puds at £4-ish – and it has a good selection of bottled beers.

The Westbourne

101 Westbourne Park Villas W2
020 7221 1332
Tues–Sun 12.30–3.30pm; Mon–Sun 7–10.30pm
Increasingly popular since its conception in 1996, the Westbourne has become one of the premier gastropubs in Notting Hill. A table on a Friday or Saturday evening is virtually impossible to find or enjoy, due to the heaving mass of fashionable drinkers. Return at lunch time, or on a week night, and the scene will be

different. Dark wood floors, a mish-mash of old furniture and a relaxed atmosphere make this an easy place to be. The daily changing menu, reasonably priced at between £5 and £12, is imaginative and well executed. A focus on prime seasonal ingredients brings out the best in dishes such as venison carpaccio with celeriac remoulade (£7), pheasant and root-vegetable stew with barley (£11.50), and spiced pear, walnut and raisin tart (£4). A two-course set lunch at £8 is equally thoughtful and does not skimp on quality or quantity.

PUBS

Earl of Lonsdale

277–81 Westbourne Grove W11
020 7727 6335
Mon–Fri 12noon–11pm; Sat 10.30–11pm; Sun 12noon–10.30pm

Twenty years ago this was Henekys and definitely not the place to be on a Friday night, with fights breaking out regularly at closing time. Now it's been redone, with a decent terrace (parading as a 'garden' in summer) and, in spite of its location in the middle of the market, you'll still see the same barflys year in year out. The dartboard is popular and the back room pleasant enough, especially in winter.

Walmer Castle

58 Ledbury Road W2
020 7229 4620
Mon–Sat 12noon–11pm; Sun 12 noon–10.30pm

Everyone panicked when scaffolding went up a few years ago, but the Walmer emerged unscathed, still a good old pub only cleaner. On a summer's evening the pavement outside is thronged with drinkers, mainly locals, many of whom seem to know each other at least by sight. In fact, you wouldn't realise that it's now owned by a chain, Dragon Inns, which specialises in pubs downstairs and Thai restaurants above. Generous bar-snacks at £3–£5 with a Thai slant are on offer to go with standard pub drinks. The restaurant upstairs is also good, with a familiar Thai menu and pleasant service

ENTERTAINMENT

MUSIC AND CLUBBING

Woody's

41–43 Woodfield Road W9
020 7226 3030
www.woodysclub.com
Info@woodysclub.com
Open until 3am (last orders at 2am)
Mon–Wed £5; Thurs–Sun £10; reduced rates for cardholders

Despite being the focus of media frenzy when it first opened, Woody's (close to the canal) is, strictly speaking, not in Notting Hill at all, but is so much part of the scene that it can't be left out. Each of the four floors is dedicated to a different activity, from the dark sweaty dance cave in the basement where a catholic range of music is played, to the airy restaurant overlooking the canal. The chill-out rooms up top, à la Seventies' glam-rock star's pad, offer a chance to collapse on cushioned comfy seating and chat (the only club in London where you can hear yourself think). Available for private hire, it also has facilities for screenings.

MUSIC, THEATRE AND CHILDREN

The Tabernacle

Powis Square W11
020 7565 7800
Box office Mon 2–6pm; Tues–Sat 10am–6pm

In the last year the Tabernacle has hosted a variety of events from soca supremo Arrow to jazz, avant–garde theatre and a local children's musical. You never know what's coming next but it's a great venue. Latest details from the box office.

SHOPPING

ANTIQUES

Enshallah

24 All Saints Road W11
0207 727 8711
Mon–Sat 10.30am–6pm
Enshallah sells an eclectic mix of Morroccan and contemporary antiques. These embrace lighting, large pieces of carved, painted and limed furniture, black and white chequered bone boxes, chests, mirrors, mirrored dressing tables and unusual light fittings, such as large wrought-metal sunburst wall-lights with jewel-coloured centres, random chandeliers and crystal lamps. This shop is still an undiscovered gem, being off the main drag of the Portobello Road, and is utterly refreshing as a result, offering beautiful pieces that don't have the air of having been trawled over a hundred times, with polite, calm service and advice. Come here, too, for bright Morroccan slippers, felt bags, funky Tuareg saddle bags (from £100), nomadic jewellery and Berber textiles.

Revival Upholstery

22 All Saints Road W11
0207 727 9843
Mon–Sat 9am–6pm; and by appointment
Revival Upholstery makes, restores and sells antique and contemporary upholstered furniture. The best upholsterers in the area, attracting big-name interior designers who would prefer not to be mentioned, this is the place for re-covering all those chairs and sofas you've bought on the Golborne Road and don't know where to take. They also make properly sprung – not foam – sofas. The proprietor may seem a little grumpy, but persistence and a knowledge of Samuel Beckett is worth its weight in azure velvet, Mongolian sheepskin and tempered leather.

For stalls and arcades in Westbourne Grove see **Portobello Antiques Market** (pp 47–52).

CHARITY SHOPS

Oxfam

245 Westbourne Grove W11
020 7229 5000
Mon–Sat 9.30am–5.30pm;
Thurs 9.30am–7pm
Books are the best buy in this inevitably upmarket branch of the charity chain. Bargain clothes are harder to come by since anything with a designer label tends to be priced quite highly, even in faded condition. For instance, second-hand Ghost dresses are displayed for around £50, a Joseph trouser suit £120. Shoes, bric à brac, curtains, bedcovers and the occasional rug are also on sale. Much of the proceeds goes directly to Oxfam projects in the developing world, so at least any rash purchase funds a good cause.

FASHION

Agnès b

235 Westbourne Grove W11
020 7792 1947
Mon 10.30am–6pm; Tues–Sat 10am–6pm
First in the line of fashion shops to colonise Westbourne Grove, this 114th branch of Agnès b opened in 1995 and offers the French designer's whole collection of clothes for women, men and children. The overall style is simple, wearable chic, with a tendency towards tailoring for people of smaller build. Prices are reasonable, even for that

knockout evening dress for special occasions.

Aimé

32 Ledbury Road W11
020 7221 7070
Mon–Sat 10.30am–7pm
Owned by French-Cambodian sisters Val and Vanda Heng, Aimé introduces London to the cutting edge of Parisian creativity. Designer wear and home accessories represent high-quality French contemporary design, with established names such as Isabelle Marant and Christophe Lemaire sitting comfortably next to lesser-known up-and-coming talent from French fashion and art colleges. Revolving exhibitions of paintings and photography regularly transform the delightfully simple yet sophisticated décor.

APC Women

40 Ledbury Road W11
020 7229 4933

APC Men

43 All Saints Road W11
020 7221 0884
www.apc.fr
Mon–Sat 10.30am–7pm
This is French pared-down street/urban styling at its best, with the accent on simple clothes that let the fabric speak volumes. No extra frills and spills – just off-the-peg wearable clothes at reasonable prices. APC has also come up with some quirky home accessories such as vinyl record players, a collection of must-have CDs, beautiful scented pebbles and a quinquennial diary so you can plan your next five years.

Bill Amberg

10 Chepstow Road W2
020 7727 3560
Mon–Sat 10am–6pm; Wed till 7pm
Bill Amberg's name is synonymous with beautiful leather bags, wallets, briefcases and other simple but inventively styled accessories, even baby pouches. You will also find a selection of luxurious leather homeware from waste-paper bins, place mats and cowhide rugs to a zebra-skin ottoman. Everything exudes fine craftsmanship and an eye for detail, with prices to match.

Christa Davis

35 All Saints Road W11
020 7727 1998
Tues, Wed, Fri & Sat 10am–6pm;
Thurs till 7.30pm
An environmentalist at heart, Christa uses her passion for recycling and antique fabrics to create a highly original range of ultra-feminine creations. She and her team of dedicated seamstresses and dyers work with reconditioned cashmere, lovingly dyeing and recutting it into cardigans, while dresses, skirts and tops are made up in silk, silk crêpe and duchesse satin. The shop is a burst of luscious colours and extravagant textures, with the subtle smell of aromatherapy oils to relax and calm the most frazzled shopper's nerves.

Christina Bec

77 Westbourne Park Road W2
020 7727 3757
Tues–Sat 11am–6pm
This is where the well-hatted and gloved set come for imaginative yet wearable hats plus co-ordinating shoes and bags – and not just for Ascot. All merchandise is well displayed and, more often than not, Christina is on hand to give honest advice on the shapes and styles to suit you. She has broadened the appeal of the store by introducing a small focused line of knitwear. Well worth a visit .

Duchamp

75 Ledbury Road W11
020 72434708
Tues–Sat 10am–6pm
The black storefront offsets the riot of colour which characterises Mitchell Jacobs's inspired range of shirts, ties and accessories for men. Everything is immaculately displayed, including silk ties, Egyptian cotton dress shirts and the cufflinks for which he is renowned.

Ghost

36 Ledbury Road W11
020 7229 1057
www.ghost.co.uk
Mon–Fri 10.30am–6.30pm;
Sat 10am–6pm
In 17 years Tanya Sarne's Ghost label seems to have gone from strength to strength. What's more, she has barely wavered from the original flowing silhouette that made her name, winning support from such celebrity customers as Nicole Kidman and Madonna. The hallmark of the clothing is an exclusive fabric, which is woven from viscose yarns, derived from specially-grown soft woods. The result is a collection of sensuous garments in mouth-watering colours that are flattering to the figure, with the added bonus of being easy to wash and unnecessary to iron. Ghost jewellery and homeware, designed by Ericson Beamon, have recently been added to the collection, as has the recently launched Ghost perfume.

J & M Davidson

42 Ledbury Road W11
0207 313 9532
info@jandm-davidson.co.uk
Mon–Tues 10am–6pm; Wed–Sat
10am–7pm; Sun 12 noon–5pm
Famous originally for their fabric/canvas bags and leather belts, husband and wife team John and Monique now command a worldwide following, especially in the fashion capitals of New York and Tokyo. The look is understated elegance and luxury. Specialities include cashmere, Merino wool and silk mixes in cardigans and sweaters with the trademark belts. While the wood-panelled upstairs is devoted to clothes and accessories, downstairs houses the growing homeware line with 100 per-cent linen bed linen, throws, quilts and pyjamas. A range of crafted furniture is still to come.

The Jacksons

5 All Saints Road W11
020 7792 8336
www.thejacksons.co.uk
Mon–Sat 10am–6pm
The two Jackson sisters have come a long away since they started off selling trend-setting accessories from their studio. Today their creative spirit is evident in the wide range of fun, fashionable merchandise that fills this colourful shop on the corner of St Luke's Mews. Signature pieces include flower-bedecked flip flops and hair clips, unusual throws and wraps, wacky T-shirts and roomy bags with beaded handles.

Laundry Industry

186 Westbourne Grove W11
020 7792 7967
Uklon@laundryind.com
Mon–Sat 10.30am–6.30pm; Sun 12
noon–5pm
More like a tunnel than a shop, this Dutch company's European flagship store is certainly unusual. Subtle lighting, which changes colour during the day, softens the concrete interior and the clothes, simply displayed in two parallel lines – for women on one side and men and on the other – do not disappoint. Well-priced trousers, jackets and tops reveal an

eclectic use of fabrics and a lot of consideration to creative merchandising. Definitely worth checking out.

Lulu Guinness

66 Ledbury Road W11
020 7221 9686
Mon–Fri 10am–5.30pm; Sat 11am–6pm
The seductive, often whimsical window display will stop you in your tracks, but the true gems are to be found inside, for Lulu Guinness has turned handbag-making into an art form. Each item is created with originality, fine craftsmanship and an element of fun, as in the flower-embroidered baskets that helped make her name.

Paul & Joe

39 Ledbury Road W11
020 7243 5510
Mon–Fri 10am–6pm; Sat till 7pm
Following its runaway success in Selfridges department store, this Paris-based shop opened to great acclaim in 1999. This is chic power-dressing at its best. As you walk in you are treated in true French style to sugar-coated almonds. Clothing is beautifully cut and well presented, with the emphasis on opposing styles of ladylike glamour and glitz. A great place for that different item that will offset your wardrobe for years to come.

Ray Harris

73 Westbourne Park Road W2
020 7221 8052
Tues–Fri 11am–6pm; Sat 11am–6pm; private fittings by request
Situated on the quiet corner of Westbourne Park Road, this studio/shop caters for independent-spirited women who won't be dictated to by trends and figure-hugging garments. Clothes flow around the body in luscious colours, using natural fabrics with tribal designs in mind. Everything is designed and produced in-house, and Harris prides himself on the strong work ethic that pays seamstresses well for the skilled labour they perform.

Something

1–3 Chepstow Road W2
020 7229 9944
Mon–Sat 10.30am–6.30pm (Thurs till 8pm); Sun 12 noon–5pm
Something likens itself to a luxury department store cum art gallery with only the interesting bits left in. Accordingly, 300 square-metres of fashionable space are artistically arranged around every hipster's wish-list of designer gear. Clothes from Luella Bartlett and Alexander McQueen are displayed alongside cult CDs and photography, while furniture designers William Plunkett and Joe Colombo show their modern-day chairs that are strongly influenced by the Sixties. The changing rooms are almost too good to be true, with plush velvet curtains and pony-skin floors dyed to match. The layout and futuristic display units are filled with constantly changing merchandise. Strictly for gold card users.

Sweaty Betty

110 Westbourne Grove W2
020 7313 9793
www.sweatybetty.com
Mon–Fri 10am–7pm; Sat 10am–6pm; Sun 12 noon–5pm
Just across Chepstow Road, Tamara Hill Norton stocks athletic/casual sportswear and trainers for every activity, from tennis to pilates for women. Labels include Nike, Adidas, Danskin and Us Pro, but it's the smaller names such as Cassal of Spain and Australian Metalicus that make the shop special. Summer brings in an impressive range of beachwear, while in winter there's all the kit you're likely to

need for skiing.

Toby Pimlico

14 Powis Mews W11
020 7727 7244
Mon–Sat 10am–6pm
Slogans are the theme here – on everything from T-shirts and sexy underwear to cups and saucers. Models, ordinary mums and toddlers all sport Toby's upbeat words on urban living, printed in glitter in every shade from gold to pink, copper and turquoise. Old favourites are constantly updated to produce lines such as 'Yoga kills' and 'Scream to go faster'. When you are tired of reading, pull out a super-soft cashmere sweater, lie back on squashy new cushions and enjoy a drink from real china cups. Just off Westbourne Park Road, this lively shop is a contemporary space in an old mews building that still retains its character.

Tokïo

197 Westbourne Grove W11
020 7792 2515
Mon–Sat 10am–6pm; Sun 12 noon–5pm
Following on from the success of her Brompton Road store, Manami Slolely has opened a very feminine boutique filled with beautiful clothes from a wide variety of English and European designers. Newcomers include the current hot names in British fashion, Anthony Synods and Marcus Constable, as well as Japanese designer Mina. Manami also keeps a small but perfectly selected range of shoes, bags and accessories, from the likes of Miu Miu, Marc Jacobs and Hikara Noguchi.

Trudy Hanson

5 All Saints Road W11
020 7792 1300
By appointment only
Trudy specialises in hand-made traditional wedding gowns, plus outfits for bridesmaids and retinues. The dresses which hang in the front of her studio show exceptional embroidery and beadwork. If you don't find something to take your fancy on the sample rail, Trudy will come up with your own creation, inspiring confidence in even the most nervous bride-to-be. Complete exclusivity guaranteed.

Wall

1 Denbigh Road W11
020 7243 4623
Mon–Sat 10.30am–6.30pm
Wall specialises in plain, understated sweaters, jackets, long skirts and dresses in sombre colours, currently designed by graduates from the Royal College of Art. The company's emphasis on wearability and luxurious fabrics, such as alpaca and hand-picked pima cotton (owner Hernán Balcázar is from Peru), makes for a winning combination of blissful comfort laced with style. Smaller items include wonderfully soft socks and furry alpaca slippers. Mail order service.

Vintage and second-hand

Vent

178a Westbourne Grove W11
Fri & Sat 11am–5pm (no phone)
This tiny store is jammed full of vintage men's and woman's pieces (circa 1950-1980) from the likes of Christian Dior, Pucci and Missoni. There is also a good selection of used shoes, and the Seventies' and Eighties' glam look can be found for a snip. All items are in very good condition.

Shoes

Emma Hope

207 Westbourne Grove W11
020 7313 7493
Mon–Sat 10am–6pm; Thurs 10am–7pm
Unlike her busy shop in Sloane Square, Emma Hope's latest outlet provides the perfect calm space in which to contemplate her elegant creations. Beautiful soft ankle-boots in red and turquoise, brocade slippers and classy stilettos all carry her hallmark of exquisite detailing and style.

Issues

181 Westbourne Grove W11
020 7727 1122
Mon–Sat 10am–6.30pm
This branch of the Natural Shoe Store sells the usual comfortable range for women, men and children, plus a few extra styles to cater for fashion-conscious Notting Hillbillies. These include cowboy boots and cosy slip-ons in bright pink and purple suede.

Scorah Pattullo

193 Westbourne Grove W11
020 7792 0100
Johnnie@scorahpattullo.com
Mon–Fri 10.30am–6pm; Sat 10am–6pm; private fittings by appointment
Former model and actor Johnnie Pattullo has found the perfect site for his exclusive shoe boutique. Designers include Miu Miu, Bottega Venetta, Alberta Ferretti and Donna Karan, and the store caters for women and men. Also promoted are up-and-coming shoe names such as Eley Kaishimota, already well known for her avant-garde clothing, and Missoni. Soon to follow is Pattullo's own label designed by Rikke Hjelde and made in Italy.

Sigerson Morrison

184 Westbourne Grove W11
020 7229 8465
Mon–Fri 11am–7pm; Sat 10am–6pm
Kari Sigerson and Miranda Morrison design shoes for those they describe as 'smart stylish women who are fashionable yet not fashion victims'. A transparent plastic door leads you into the store's tiny space that is filled with beautifully crafted shoes, boots and leather bags.

FLOWERS AND PLANTS

Wild at Heart

49a Ledbury Road W11
020 7727 3095
Mon–Sat 8.30am–7pm
Also at the Turquoise Island
222 Westbourne Grove W11
Mon–Sat 8am–6.30pm
Nikki Tibbles's designer flower stall provides the perfect embellishment for Piers Gough's eau-de-nil creation on the triangle in Westbourne Grove. Having started up here, she now has headquarters and a shop in Ledbury Road, as well as a further outlet in Liverpool Street's Great Eastern Hotel. Thanks to Wild at Heart, and of course Tom on Clarendon Road, it's hard to remember the days before smart bouquets were wrapped up in raffia and brown paper.

FOOD AND WINE

Bradley's

63 Ledbury Road W11
020 7727 1121
charlie@charliebradley.com
Mon–Fri 8am–8pm; Sat 8am–6pm; Sun 10am–5pm
Delicious-looking cakes, pastries and take-away dishes – mainly with an Italian slant – are served upstairs, while the basement stocks a very select range of

foodstuffs such as muscatel raisins, preserved lemons, exotic vegetables and an impressive display of cheeses. Nearly everything comes from small producers, both here and abroad, and, apart from the breads, all cooked food is prepared on the premises. Prices are steep.

Ciarluzzo

56 Ledbury Road W11
020 7243 6037
Mon–Sat 10.30am–8pm
Yet another relatively recent arrival, Ciarluzzo is an Italian deli and coffee bar specialising in produce from various regions of Italy, including Puglia, where one of the co-owners grew up in the small village after which the business was named. Coffee, wines, organic olive oil, home-made pasta, cheeses, panettone and delicious-looking bread are all top quality, as are the filled panini for which increasing numbers customers flock at lunch time.

Fresh & Wild

210 Westbourne Grove W11
020 7229 1063
Mon–Sat 8am–8pm; Sun 11am–7pm
For many locals, the departure of Wild Oats has only been partly compensated for by this much flashier, more expensive but, admittedly, far more comprehensive organic supermarket.

Tom's

226 Westbourne Grove W11
020 7221 8818
Daily 8am–8pm
The upstairs of this friendly upmarket deli displays mainly bread, sandwiches and pâtisserie items, with an excellent café serving fresh food at the back. Downstairs, you'll find an even more tempting array of fine food, from the best of French, English and Italian cheeses to organic meats, salads, cooked dishes and a small range of good wines. The home-made pesto, rocket or basil, is especially hard to beat. Also stocks staples such as pasta, rice, oil and various preserves – usually high quality though you'll sometimes find the same item much cheaper elsewhere.

Vom Fass

187 Westbourne Grove W11
020 7792 4499
mosconi36@hotmail.com
Mon 12 noon–8pm; Tues–Sat 10.30am–8pm; Sun 12 noon–5pm
Vom fass means literally 'from the barrel' and this is what you get. Bring an empty bottle, or choose from all the attractive shapes and sizes on display, and owner Richard Mosconi or his friendly assistant, Laura Matthews, will fill it up from one of the many casks that line this delightful shop. The choice is dazzling – from wines, brandies, whiskies and liqueurs to oils and four different types of balsamic vinegar – with a selection of coloured-glass stoppers, and wrapping materials to compound your indecision. Yes, it's a great place for presents, as well as for high-quality produce at prices well below many specialist food and wine shops. As the first London outlet for what is a German company, Vom Fass looks set for success.

GALLERIES

Axia

21 Ledbury Road W11
020 7727 9724
Mon–Fri 10am–6pm; Sat by appointment
A sense of tranquillity descends as you walk through the immense dark red door into Axia, which specialises in Eastern Christian and Islamic art. The few well-chosen objects on display lend this gallery

an air of great sophistication and taste.

Caelt Gallery

182 Westbourne Grove W11
020 7229 9309
art@caeltgallery.com
www.caeltgallery.com
Mon–Sat 9.30am–6pm; Sun 10.30am–6pm
After starting with a stall in Portobello Road, Edward Crawshaw opened his gallery in 1969. This packed shop currently stocks around a thousand paintings, piled in heaps around the walls, with many other pictures in storage. Since 1993, Crawshaw has made 29 trips to the former Soviet Union and Central Asia where he mainly buys direct from artists' studios. He puts on the occasional exhibition here and in other venues, with prices starting at around £100, and supplies a lot of works to the designing and decorating trade.

Christopher Farr

212 Westbourne Grove W11
020 7792 5761
www.cfarr.co.uk
Mon–Sat 11am–6pm
That Christopher Farr trained as an artist is evident in his rugs, which are a synthesis of contemporary design and traditional craft skills. He also commissions designs for rugs and flatweaves from leading artists and designers, such as Rifat Ozbeck, Gillian Ayres, Romeo Gigli and Josef Herman, which are then made of the best Anatolian wool, handspun and handknotted.

England & Co

216 Westbourne Grove W11
020 7221 0417
Mon–Sat 11am–6pm
Jane England was born and grew up in Australia, coming to England via Italy. An art historian who had worked as a photographer, she opened her first gallery in nearby Needham Road in 1987. The gallery began with a programme of retrospective and contemporary exhibitions with accompanying catalogues. Having outgrown that space, England & Co moved to its present premises in September 1999, a large purpose-built gallery designed by Will White. It has sold works to many museums, public galleries and institutions and holds regular exhibitions here.

Flow

1–5 Needham Road W11
020 7243 0782
gallery.flow@ukgateway.net
Mon–Sat 11am–6pm
Yvonna Demczynska opened this gallery selling contemporary applied arts in October 1999. The wonderful space has a selection of craftwork in glass, felt, leather, wood and metal, as well as ceramics and jewellery. The emphasis is on young UK-based artists and Yvonna is always visiting studios in search of new talent. Flow currently houses two exhibitions a year, with a Japanese show planned for autumn 2001.

Hanina Fine Art

180 Westbourne Grove W11
020 7243 8877
www.hanina-gallery.com
hanina@globalnet.co.uk
After 15 years in New York, Hanina came to London in 1995 to set up this gallery specialising in the School of Paris 1900–1975. Every three months, it shows exhibitions of oils and sculptures on different themes, encouraged by a growing volume of passing trade.

Stern Art Dealers

46 Ledbury Road W11
020 7229 6187
www.stern-art.com
pissarro@ukgateway.com
Mon–Sat 10am–6pm
David Stern is the world's leading dealer in Camille Pissarro and his descendants, and holds regular exhibitions of their work. He has been in the area for 37 years and in his present premises, which were originally a café and restaurant, for 20. Realising the growing importance of presentation, Stern is planning major renovations to his gallery in 2001.

Themes & Variations

231 Westbourne Grove W11
020 727 5531
go@themesandvariations.co.uk
Mon–Fri 10am–1pm & 2–6pm; Sat 10am–6pm
This spacious gallery cum shop specialises in twentieth-century decorative arts and contemporary design from a range of mainly European countries. Artists represented include, from the 1950s, Gio Panti and Fornazetti, and contemporary names Tom Dixon and Mark Brazier-Jones.

Wolseley Fine Arts

12 Needham Road W11
020 7792 2788
www.wolseleyfinearts.com
info@wolseyfinearts.com
During exhibitions, Tues–Fri 11am–6pm; Sat till 5pm; otherwise by appointment
Founded in 1990 by Rupert Otten, Wolseley Fine Arts opened off Westbourne Grove in 1995. Otten and his partner, Hanneke van der Werf, now specialise in the works of Eric Gill, Edgar Holloway and David Jones. They have also held exhibitions by Edward Ardizzone and John Buckland Wright, and every June organise an exhibition of French art.

HOME

Big Table Furniture

56 Great Western Road W9
020 7221 5058
Mon–Sat 10am–6pm (Thurs till 10pm); Sun 12 noon–5pm
No one can remember exactly how Big Table came to specialise in beds, but if you want a good, solid wooden frame to sleep on, plus custom-made mattress, this is the place to come. There are five styles to choose from, including bunk beds and a plain four-poster, all hand-made in Scandinavian pine with care taken to preserve the forest by replacing every matured tree felled with four saplings. Run by a furniture co-operative, established here in 1984, the company has earned a strong reputation for friendly, efficient service, top quality and affordable prices – from around £100 to £330 without mattress (including assembly).

Celia Birtwell

71 Westbourne Park Road W2
020 7221 0877
Mon–Fri 10am–5pm
When Celia Birtwell opened her fabric shop 15 years ago, this corner of Westbourne Park Road was just a backwater. Now, sandwiched between two well-known gastropubs and a host of other designer shops, she's in just the right spot for selling her fine printed textiles, even if the bulk of sales does still come from trade. Sheers, silk, cotton and linen are designed mainly for use in curtains or upholstery, the latest coup being an order for velvet drapes patterned with stars and magic symbols for the forthcoming *Harry Potter* film. Ever since

her marriage to the late fashion designer Ossie Clark (see p 141), Birtwell has been associated with his world and that of her close friend, the painter David Hockney. However, she has long proved herself as a strong creative spirit in her own right and prefers to leave the past behind her.

Le Paul Bert

196 Westbourne Grove W11
020 7727 2159
Tue–Sat 10.30am–5pm
Jammed with every kind of light-fitting you can imagine, and some you wouldn't even begin to think of, all the pieces here are original and chosen with an eye for the decorative and fantastic. Prices reflect the shop's location and clientèle but are not too unreasonable. It also owns the Façade next door, specialisig in glass chandeliers.

Mattamondo

22 Powis Terrace W11
020 7229 5669
www.mattamondo.com
christina@mattamondo.co.uk
Mon–Sat 11am–6pm
Slightly off the beaten track, this is the sort of shop you stumble across by chance and then rush to tell your friends. Owner Christina Graham spent years travelling as a photographer in Africa, and during that time sourced an array of functional and decorative art, much of it brought to the UK for the first time. Simultaneously supporting community projects and ensuring the highest quality of work, she enthusiastically shares the stories behind such wonderful pieces as picture frames made from the planks of African river boats (around £40).

Ogier

177 Westbourne Grove W11
020 7229 0783
ogier@dircon.co.uk
Mon–Sat 11am–6pm
Devoted to 'complementary living' (a welcome change from the 'lifestyle' tag), this wonderfully innovative French-owned shop sells old and new objects, furniture and lighting from a variety of countries. Most popular are the interchangeable coloured DNA lights from modern French architects Studio 212, but items in stock are forever changing. Well worth checking out.

MUSIC

People's Sounds Record Shop

11 All Saints Road W11
020 7792 9321
Mon–Sat 10am–8pm
Specialising in reggae, ska and raga, People's Sounds was founded in 1988 and has survived to the present day thanks to the energies of Vigo, the proprietor, who sees music as essential to the well-being of the community. Perusal of his catalogue is an education in the past, present and future worlds of African-Carribbean music, of which he himself has an encyclopaedic knowledge.

Musical instruments

Portobello Music

13 All Saints Road W11
020 7221 4040
Neil@fiddles.demon.co.uk
Mon–Sat 10.30am–6pm
This is a music shop run by musicians for musicians. With an excellent range of guitars and basses, including some lovely vintage models, it's the picker's Aladdin's cave. Unusually, owners Neil, Andrew and Gervis also deal in violins, cellos and double basses – even more unusually, they understand them, too. The shop has existed in its present form for four years and brings a welcome hands-on resource

in a business that grows more corporate by the second. Offering an expert and comprehensive repair service, plus hire schemes, PM is also a networking resource for local musos.

MIND AND BODY

BEAUTY PRODUCTS

Miller Harris

14 Needham Road W11
020 7221 1545
www.millerharris.com
Mon–Sat 10.30am–6.30pm
Lyn Harris, who reputedly has the best 'nose' in Britain, and has worked for both Liberty and Conran as a consultant, opened this beautiful perfumery shop in July 2000 with her partner Christophe Michel. She's also studied in France for five years, so was well qualified to launch her own range of soaps, scents, candles, eau de toilette and eau de parfum. For £500 you can spend a day with Lyn and have your own scent created especially for you. Her range of three different smells starts with soap at £6.95. Miller Harris also sells a kit designed by Matthew Williamson and products by Bennison and The Cross.

Screen Face

20 & 24 Powis Terrace W11
020 7221 8289
info@screenface.co.uk
www.screenface.com
Mon–Sat 9am–6pm
Using products developed by make-up artists for make-up artists, Screen Face has been supplying the entertainment industry for nearly 20 years. Of these two shops (there's a third outlet in Covent Garden), No.20 focuses on natural glamour while No.24 is more geared towards the needs of film and theatre professionals. Both places are stacked with a staggering collection of pencils, mascaras, false eyelashes, foundations, concealers, powders and lipsticks, plus every imaginable kind of applicator, at well below big-name prices. In case you find so much choice bemusing, the friendly assistants are full of helpful advice – or you could invest £45 in an hour's make-up tutorial in the studio downstairs.

SPAce.NK

127–31 Westbourne Grove W2
020 7727 8063 (Shop)
020 7727 8002 (Spa)
www.spacenk.com
Mon–Wed & Sat 10am–7pm; Thurs & Fri 10am–8pm; Sun 11am–6pm (5pm spa)
Rows of enticingly labelled pots and jars of cream for skin and hair from all over the world are arranged on stylish shelves in this spacious shop, once the site of Bradley's Silk Mercers and Furriers. Its own label (which includes a fragrance, SPAce.NK. Woman) concentrates on bath products. This is the only branch of Nicky Kinnaird's ever-expanding empire to have a spa attached offering very pricey holistic treatments, eg aromatherapy £75 for 1½ hours, body balancing £75 for the initial 1½ hours, lymphatic drainage £50 for 1 hour and a variety of facials including Eve Lom £95 for 1½ hours, Samuel Par £65 for 1¼ hours, and Essential Rose £50 for 1 hour. It is hard to vouch for the therapy rooms when you are neither allowed to know how many there are nor see any of them.

NAILS

Nail 2000

215 Westbourne Park Road W11
020 7727 2704
Mon–Sat 10am–10pm; Sun 1–4pm

Florentine Ruks offers an infinite variety of nail treatments, from sculptured acrylic extensions to manicures, pedicures and natural nail repair, all done with her friendly personal touch. Prices are dependent on the exact procedure and the state of your nails, but are generally mid-range, with extensions starting at £30.

HAIRDRESSERS

Parson Skött

243 Westbourne Grove W11
020 7243 0939/0959
Mon 10am–7pm; Tues–Fri 9am–7pm; Sat 8.30am–5pm
Guy Parsons and his team have been cutting, colouring, perming and treating men's and women's hair for the last eight years. Determined to stay in the area, in spite of rumours about a possible rent-hike, this salon stocks hair accessories as well as hair and beauty products by MOP (Modern Organics Products), Kiehl and Phytology. Pricey.

10500

284 Westbourne Park Road W11
020 7229 3777
Mon–Sat 10am–7pm (Thurs 9pm)
Although owner Anthony Carenza and his team do the London, Paris, and Milan Fashion Weeks, the atmosphere is unpretentious and a wide cross-section of clients, ordinary mortals as well as the local fashion/designer/music crowd, trust the stylists to offer good advice, do great cuts, and excellent colouring. Prices from £25 (men) and £30 (women). In case you're wondering, it's 10,500 miles from Anthony's home town of Sydney.

HEALTH AND FITNESS

The Lambton Place Health Club

Lambton Place W11
020 7229 2291
enquiries@lambton.co.uk
www.hogarthgroup,co.uk
Mon–Fri 7am–11pm; Sat–Sun 9am–9pm
Hidden away in a mews, the Lambton Place Health Club opened in its present guise in 1988, having previously been a squash club. It has a fully equipped gym (and is constantly upgrading its machines), an exercise studio and a small but pretty swimming pool. Members can also indulge in a range of therapies, including aromatherapy, chiropody, physiotherapy, acupuncture, shiatsu, osteopathy, beauty treatments and reflexology. The pool area incorporates a steam room and jacuzzi, plus separate saunas for men and women.

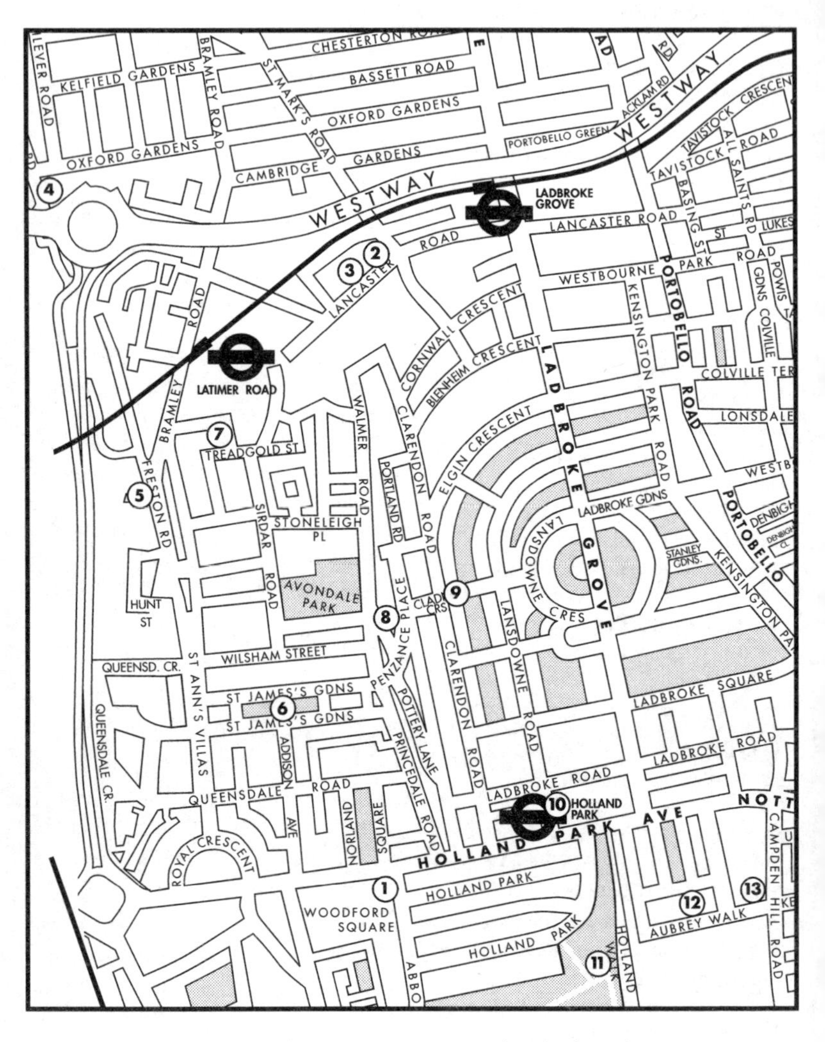

1 The Halcyon Hotel
2 10 Rillington Place (Site of)
3 The Notting Hill Methodist Church
4 Westway Stables
5 Frestonia
6 Church of St James
7 Church of St Clement
8 Church of St Francis of Assisi
9 Clarendon Cross
10 Lansdowne House
11 Holland Park
12 Aubrey House
13 Church of St George

5. Notting Dale and Holland Park

This chapter, more than any other, encapsulates the contrasts of extreme poverty and wealth that make up the history and fabric of Notting Hill: on the one side Notting Dale, with its nineteenth-century colonies of gypsies, brick-makers and pig-keepers, and on the other Holland Park and its grand society, centred around Holland House.

At first glance, Notting Dale today presents a confusing network of recently built streets and public housing, swathed by the Westway. But look closer and you'll discover, scattered among the tower blocks, quiet corners of terraced cottages, a historic park and three magnificent churches. This may not be the place for shopping, though it is beginning to gain its share of trendy eateries, but it's well worth exploring for its historical interest and as a less-trodden route to the fashionable reaches of Clarendon Cross and beyond. Many residents consider that Holland Park, even the north side of the Avenue, is simply not Notting Hill. In the past, however, the two areas were inextricably intertwined.

Lancaster Road

The boundaries of Notting Dale have never been totally clear, but for the purposes of this chapter we begin at the western end of Lancaster Road after the London Lighthouse, at the junction with St Mark's Road. It was near this intersection, at 10 Rillington Place, that, in 1943, John Christie carried out the first of a horrific spate of murders that were to shake Notting Hill for many years to come. An upstairs neighbour, Timothy Evans, was wrongfully hanged for the murders in 1950, after which the real killer went on to strangle his wife and three more women. Christie was finally caught, convicted and hanged in 1953. Evans was pardoned in 1966, largely due to the efforts of Ludovic Kennedy, whose book, *10 Rillington Place*, indirectly led to the abolition of the death penalty. The book opens with a description of this section of Notting Dale as it looked in the 1940s, before it was replaced by the neat private houses of Wesley and St Andrew's Squares:

> *You will not find Rillington Place in any street map of London now, for it has long been demolished. It was a mean shabby cul-de-sac of ten houses on either side. Although the houses had three floors, they were small, almost miniature houses, and their most striking characteristic was peeling paint and rotting stucco. The street was bounded at one end by St Mark's Road and at the other by the wall of Rickard's Transport Depot for*

> *Coaches and Vans. Originally Rickard's was Bartlett's Iron Foundry, and the foundry chimney still stands. It rises, as it were, from the centre of the boundary wall; and its squat pear-shaped form seemed to dominate the street.*
>
> *Just beyond the houses on the north side lay the Metropolitan Railway Line, and the sounds of the trains coming and going were part of the lives of the people who lived there. Many of them lived two and three to a room. On summer evenings the children played in the street and on the pavements, and the parents sat at the open windows watching the world go by. No. 10 was the last house on the south side.*

Past the junction with St Mark's Road, just before the corner where Lancaster becomes Silchester Road, stands Notting Hill Methodist Church. As well as providing a beautifully simple and serene place of worship, the church has a strong tradition of working towards peace in the neighbourhood, in particular the inclusion of the West Indian community. Part of the basement is currently used by the Kensington & Chelsea Community History Group, whose publications have provided much valuable material for this book.

Notting Hill Methodist Church

The site where the church now stands was originally occupied by the Anglican Church of St Andrew, which was destroyed by fire in 1865. The current church was built in 1878–79 by Jesse Chessure of Shoreditch as a two-storey structure with a hall in the semi-basement beneath.

Over the years, extensive alterations have been made to the building's interior to accommodate the congregation's changing needs, and today few of the original furnishings remain. Historically important as a social centre and as the site for a Sunday school, the church played an important role during the years following the riots of 1958 (see pp 100 & 173). Feeling the need for a stronger Methodist presence and for more inter-congregational activity to try and unite the different communities of Notting Dale, Donald (later Lord) Soper invited three young priests to work at the church in a Team Ministry, which would welcome all and attempt to break down barriers in a friendly multi-racial atmosphere. Drawing on their respective experiences in other inner cities, and in Jamaica and East Harlem, these three priests helped to bring the community together through informal meetings, and they became a key driving force behind the formation of the Notting Hill Social Council in 1962.

The church has remained very active and today the building is arranged over three floors: the area for worship at the top is also used for a range of classes, meetings and activities; the middle floor is devoted to meeting rooms and administrative offices; and the lower section is in constant use as a meeting place for various community and church groups. In addition to the Kensington & Chelsea Community History Group, a Day Project operates from here three times a week. The Project invites people who have been recently rehoused to use the space for classes, activities and as a centre to seek and be directed towards practical advice. The church also owns a hall on part of the site once occupied by another Methodist church in Denbigh Road as well as several other premises, including the Oxfam shop on Westbourne Grove. Typical of the area, this church combines the secular and the sacred in a way which both welcomes and serves the mixed community in which it is rooted. It is open to visitors during the day. For information on services and other activities, telephone 020 7229 7728.

Around the corner on the left was once the site of the Lancaster Road Baths and Wash House, opened in 1888 and later renamed Silchester Baths. As well as providing a desperately needed facility for all the hundreds of families who lived without running water, the buildings served as an important social meeting point for local women. The threat of closure in the early 1970s sparked off a vigorous campaign, which led to the provision of a public launderette under the Westway. The baths were demolished in 1975 to make way for the public housing you see now.

At this point, the sudden transformation of Lancaster into Silchester Road illustrates the extent to which so much of Notting Dale has been demolished, dissected and redesigned. Streets stop and start all over the place, making it hard to negotiate on foot, let alone by car. Beginning with a brief diversion to Latimer Road, the following route is a circuit taking in some key landmarks on the way to Holland Park.

Latimer Road via the St Quintin's Estate

Silchester Road passes under a railway bridge before reaching Bramley Road, where a left turn leads into the heart of Notting Dale and Holland Park beyond. A right deviation beneath the Westway takes in the Edwardian streets of the St Quintin's Estate. The area is named after Colonel St Quintin who owned much of this land, which remained largely undeveloped until early last century. Turn left again, into Oxford Gardens, and the road passes Oxford Gardens Primary School, alongside the low white studios of society photographer Patrick Lichfield, then on past rows of two-storey red-brick houses, to the desolate reaches of Latimer Road. Though primarily an industrial estate, Latimer Road is worth visiting for two unexpected attractions – ponies and pubs.

Facing the flyover, a lane on the right is marked Stable Way. This leads to one of North Kensington's most surprising finds – Westway Stables. As long ago as 1860, the patch of ground that now lies in the shadow of the A40 was a well-known site for gypsies, many of whom were gradually rehoused in the terraced cottages south of Latimer Road. Those who kept their horses and carts became totters or 'rag-and-bone-men', collecting scrap metal, old clothes and household implements from door to door. Their base was this yard, since transformed into a curiously picturesque oasis where brightly feathered cockerels pick among the dung, and pretty-faced ponies peer over wooden stable doors. For the last five years or so Westway Stables has been run as a riding school for inner-city children and the odd keen adult. Supported by the Amenity Trust, owner Sarah Tuvey has managed to build up a loyal following, including a fluctuating team of voluntary helpers, who come regularly to ride in the sandpit ring under the flyover or further afield on Wormwood Scrubs Common. Gypsies (now referred to as travellers) still have a site nearby.

Back on Latimer Road, heading north takes you past Latimer Place, a relatively new arrival in Notting Hill's growing list of gastropubs, with a noisy bar and a pleasant upstairs restaurant serving good, modern European dishes. A little further on, anyone needing breakfast need look no further than Sonia's Café, an unusually pretty greasy spoon with outside summer seating among the flowers. At the end stands the enduringly popular North Pole, another converted pub offering good-quality food.

The St Quintin's Estate is built on a grid system, so it should be quite easy to find your way back to St Helen's Gardens, which, running south, soon turns back into Bramley Road.

Bramley Road and Frestonia

Bramley Road unexpectedly branches off, while the route it was following takes on another name. After the junction with Silchester Road, a short walk takes you past the Irish Pig & Whistle pub, under the railway bridge at Latimer Road tube station, and alongside the Lancaster West Estate, a huge and notoriously deprived housing estate dating from the 1970s. Behind lies Treadgold Street, home to the Church of St Clement (see pp 135–36). Soon afterwards, Bramley Road appears to become St Ann's Road. In fact, it veers off to the right. Right again at the Laurel & Hardy Café lies a turning into Freston Road, birthplace of one of the most imaginative, spirited and successful projects to have come out of the 1970s: the Free Independent Republic of Frestonia.

Formerly Latimer Road, the street was renamed after the construction of the Westway effectively cut it in two. This disruption, exacerbated by the political squabbling and indecision that allowed the now derelict area around the flyover to lie abandoned, sparked off an upsurge in community action.

From the early 1970s, squatters had begun to occupy houses in and around the old Latimer Road. Many were artists, writers and musicians, and by the middle of the decade they had created a lively community, incorporating a communal garden and the Car Breakers' Art Gallery. In 1977, the Greater London Council announced that the whole area was to be leased out for industrial development and it was then that an alliance of locals was formed, declaring themselves 'The Free and Independent Republic of Frestonia'. They organised a series of protests, both provocative and crazy in spirit, and were successful; the original plans were ditched and the Bramley Housing Co-operative was formed. Working with the Notting Hill Housing Trust, the Co-op organised the erection of homes that were built on a human scale and managed on a co-operative basis, some of which border St Ann's Road. This movement marked a significant change, since when, it is hoped, harsh developments such as the Lancaster West Estate have become a thing of the past. (A first-hand account is provided by Nicholas Albery, Frestonia's erstwhile Minister of State for the Environment, see pp 211–14.)

The Parish of St Clement and St James

Returning to the main highway, St Ann's Road continues by Henry Dickens Court, a municipal housing development attributed to the good work of Henry, grandson of Charles Dickens. In her memoirs, *An Open Book,* the writer's great-granddaughter, Monica Dickens (herself a novelist), recalls her father's achievements as a councillor with the Royal Borough of Kensington in the 1950s:

> *In the desperate need for housing after the war, he caused some good blocks of council flats to be built on the far side of the curving Lansdowne streets that once were a race course. The estate is called Henry Dickens Court. The buildings are named after characters from Charles Dickens, but they stand as a memorial to the industry of his grandson, hammering against the fearful odds of bureaucracy. When the Queen Mother came for the official dedication of the estate, Henry was on the platform with her in his fur-lined Alderman's robe. And afterwards they had tea together in 4 Dombey House, with Mrs Langham pouring.*

Soon after Henry Dickens Court, as St Ann's Road becomes St Ann's Villas, the architecture takes on a sudden grandeur, albeit in the shadow of tower blocks, and continues east and south to Royal Crescent and Holland Park Avenue.

One of the most attractive landmarks here is St James's Gardens (originally

St James's Square) with its majestic church of St James Norlands. St James's and its sister church, St Clement Notting Dale, provide vivid illustrations of the two disparate worlds that existed side by side throughout the second half of the nineteenth century, and, to some extent, continue in their equivalent forms today.

Although united into the same parish since 1985, these two churches and their congregations could not be more contrasting. St James's stands imposingly at the centre of its elegant square, looking down Addison Avenue, one of the most exclusive stretches of housing in the area, while St Clement's merges into its humble surroundings – the artisan dwellings of Treadgold Street, directly adjacent to the grim blocks of the Lancaster West Estate. Both churches are of architectural merit, listed Grade II by the National Heritage Department, and, as we have already seen, the stroll through the streets between them provides a social history lesson in itself.

In true Notting Hill spirit, every effort is made to unite the two congregations and the parish runs a plethora of community activities, including English language classes, a study support group to help children with their homework, a steel band workshop, and dance, yoga, painting and drawing workshops. The parish also runs a community shop providing low-cost clothes, toys and household goods to people on benefits, as well as refugees and asylum seekers.

The Church of St James Norlands

St James's was designed as the centrepiece for the surrounding domestic development of the Norlands Estate. The architect was Lewis Vulliamy, son of the famous clock maker Benjamin Vulliamy, a previous owner of the estate. It was built between 1844 and 1850 in the Gothic revival style. However, lack of funds hindered the project's progress and Vulliamy's plans were never fully realised. The chancel was added in 1876 to a design by Robert Jewell Withers.

The church is built in white Suffolk brick and its exterior is notable for its fine tower, positioned so as to mark the north-south axis of the Estate. Had the money not run out, the tower would have been topped with a spire. Until 1948, most of the interior was coloured or decorated, and the columns and arcades (up to the stringcourse) embellished with printed patterns. Murals decorating the north and south aisles were removed in 1950. Today the effect is austere: the tall, wide arcades standing on their elegant monochrome quatrefoil iron piers are whitewashed and there is no flamboyance in the decoration, except for a recent candy-stripe detail on the west gallery underneath the organ. But the fine stained-glass windows (1880) remain *in situ*, along with a number of striking features. The wooden reredos of the main altar is finely and extravagantly carved with polychrome decoration depicting the Last Supper (made in 1880). The Lady Chapel contains a pleasing copy of a Raphael Madonna and child. The sturdy font features green marble and glazed tiles, and a fine brass eagle lectern is dated 1893. Perhaps most impressive is the wonderful organ, located since 1921 in the west gallery. A three-manual and pedal instrument, with prettily stencilled front pipes, it was made by Auguste Gern in 1878 and then rebuilt by JJ Binns of Leeds in 1895. It was restored in 1996 and is put to very good use: the church has excellent acoustics, and is the site of many musical events, including the highly rated W11 Children's Opera, which takes place every year in early December. (For information about auditions or tickets for the annual W11 Children's Opera, telephone 020 7371 4073.) For service times and other activities, the parish office can be contacted by telephone on 020 7221 3548 or e-mail at parish@clementjames.freeserve.co.uk

Leaving the Church of St James, it is simple to wend your way through pretty, affluent streets to Princedale Road and Clarendon Cross. The route described below takes in both these landmarks, only backtracking slightly via St Clement's, before moving on to Walmer Road and the heart of Notting Dale's poverty-stricken past.

In and around Treadgold Street

Back along St Ann's Road, past Henry Dickens Court, a right turn takes you into Stoneleigh Place. The next left into Stoneleigh Street leads directly into Treadgold Street and the church of St Clement – unprepossessing on the outside but well worth entering for its wonderfully harmonious decoration.

The Church of St Clement Notting Dale

It would be easy to pass this church without noticing it – small, squat and made of yellow brick with little embellishment. Yet it stands as an important memorial to its founder, the Reverend Arthur Dalgarno Robinson. An energetic humanitarian, Robinson came to Notting Dale in 1860 and founded one of the earliest schools for the children of the Potteries. He bought the land for the site of the church out of his own pocket and, prior to its completion in 1867, worked for seven years without pay. The church was designed by JP St Aubyn, inexpensively built, and consecrated in 1867.

As with St James's and so many other Victorian churches, the original richness of the decoration inside has been almost totally obliterated by later monochromatic over-painting. Yet the interior is still astonishing; here Victorian hi-tech meets traditional timber craftsmanship to very happy effect. A series of finely crafted cast-iron pillars rises to a vast wooden roof of oversized rafters supported by scissorblades. The impression is of an airy, unified space with no interruption between the nave and the aisles. Its treasures include the highly decorative painted wooden Renaissance-style reredos of the main altar, an elaborate crucifix made and signed by Ramsden in 1833, and a set of copper candlesticks made by Robe in 1855. The tessellated pradella incorporates *fleur de lis* motifs and those of the anchor of St Clement. The simple open benches are by St Aubyn and the south-east chapel contains an altar with a charming repoussé copper front. On the west wall there is a commemorative plaque to the Reverend Robinson. Standing here, you can readily believe that his spirit still lingers in this cheerful, busy, well-used space.

While St James's hosts the rather grand W11 Opera, St Clement's has become very much associated with the Carnival. Each year, the congregations help to organise a float and costumes, and all are invited to attend a special Carnival mass. For details of this, other activities and services, contact the parish office (see p 135).

The surrounding buildings are a mixture of relatively new housing developments and a few rows of terraced cottages that escaped war damage and have been allowed to remain. Compared to the East End of London, Notting Dale was relatively unscathed by the Second World War. The housing problems which made it such a troubled area in the 1950s and early 60s stemmed more from neglect than bomb damage. Those who could afford it moved out to the suburbs, leaving poor quality accommodation for the less fortunate, who were joined by a growing number of incomers from overseas.

In a seminal study into housing conditions and how to improve them, Pearl Jephcott provided a vivid snapshot of the local population in 1962:

> *The racial and social characteristics of Notting Dale are as heterogeneous as its housing. Saris and sandals, the Sikh's white turban and black beard, the carefully careless headscarf of the Nigerian, and the goffered guimp of the Italian nun lend a (slightly seedy) exoticism to the area . . . Habits and ménages are as bizarre as costumes and accents. Teddy boys hail taxis with assurance; a dignitary of some Eastern Church, purple cassocked, conducts his daily services in his council flat; and an elderly refugee landlady from Shanghai fights a losing battle*

> *with her smooth-tongued tenants from Cork. Cosmopolitanism on this scale means that even the officials whom it causes so much extra labour and anxiety agree that the place is oddly stimulating.* (Pearl Jephcott, *A Troubled Area: Notes on Notting Hill*)

Jephcott's report was commissioned in the wake of the 1958 race riots, which marked a turning point in Notting Hill's history (see p 172). They lasted over three days and were fuelled in large part by the Nationalist Union Movement of Sir Oswald Mosley. A self-proclaimed Fascist, Mosley was given to bringing out his soapbox on street corners throughout Notting Hill, where his small, but for a time influential, party was based. Although he was reputed to be a charismatic speaker, film-maker Kevin Brownlow had a very different impression. He went to hear Mosley speak only a few months before the riots, as part of his research for the film *It Happened Here* (see pp 142 & 144):

> *In April 1958 my co-director, Andrew Mollo, and I visited Porchester Hall in Westbourne Grove to attend one of Sir Oswald Mosley's meetings. We had always been told that however much of a villain he may have been, Mosley was a superb orator. We were disappointed. The speech he delivered was long-winded and absurd. He advocated the removal of blacks from the coasts of Africa – nobody would be forced to move – and their replacement by whites. This would simultaneously prevent Communist incursion and black emigration. Andrew stood up and asked him what would happen if Africans refused to move. Mosley said they would be given incentives. I stood up to make another point; Mosley denied being anti-Semitic but the current issue of his paper,* Action, *had an anti-Semitic headline. Mosley snapped, 'You've already asked a question', and turned to someone else.*

Mosley took advantage of people's insecurities over jobs and housing. In the months preceding the riots, he deliberately whipped up the tension, and gangs of white youths paraded the streets of Notting Dale, threatening black people and smashing up their property. When the tension finally erupted, the majority of people were determined that such an explosion of racism and violence would never happen again.

Among several positive initiatives to emerge after the riots were Pearl Jephcott's recommendations that people be given the opportunity to take control of their own living conditions. This new, enlightened attitude helped inspire many subsequent campaigns, including the laundry protests of 1973.

Walmer Road to Pottery Lane

Not far from the Church of St Clement, Treadgold Street becomes Grenfell Road. Follow the next right into Bomore Road and you'll come to Kensington Sports Centre, currently undergoing massive refurbishment. Another right turn takes you into Walmer Road, leading directly to Avondale Park, Pottery Lane, with its beautiful Church of St Francis of Assisi, and Clarendon Cross.

Not far into Walmer Road, one of the first buildings on the left is the Rugby Club, established in the late nineteenth century by Arthur Walrond, a former pupil of Rugby School. In 1889, with the support of the school, he managed to purchase an old bus yard in Walmer Road, and built a club for boys in search of warmth, light, amusement and comradeship. A fair amount of preaching went on here, but the centre was also noted for its swimming pool (one of the first private pools) and its many sporting activities, especially boxing. Theatrical productions were staged here too, providing funding for the club and activities such as summer camps every July and August.

Walmer Road continues between a mix of old terraced housing and modern developments up to Avondale Park, opposite which the old bottle kiln provides a reminder of the time when Potteries and Piggeries dominated Notting Dale (see History, pp 169–71). Wandering around Avondale Park, with its flowerbeds, bandstand and children's playground, it's hard to imagine the treacherous ocean of clay sludge and pig swill that lay over this site in the late 1840s right up to the time it was filled in to create the park in 1892. Living conditions and sanitation in the surrounding houses were so poor that when London's cholera epidemic of 1849 spread to Notting Dale, Charles Dickens was prompted to publish a piece about the area in the first issue of his journal *Household Words*. The article by WH Wills began:

> *In a neighbourhood studded thickly with elegant villas and mansions, viz Bayswater and Notting Hill, in the parish of Kensington, is a plague-spot, scarcely equalled for its insalubrity by any other in London; it is called the Potteries. It comprises some seven or eight acres with about 260 houses, if the term can be applied to such hovels, and a population of 900 to 1,000. The occupation of the inhabitants is principally pig-fattening; many hundreds of pigs, ducks and fowls are kept in an incredible state of filth. Dogs abound for the purpose of guarding the swine. The atmosphere is still further polluted by fat boiling. In these hovels discontent, dirt, filth and misery are unsurpassed by anything known even in Ireland. Water is supplied to only a small proportion of houses. There are foul ditches, open sewers, and defective drains, smelling most*

> *offensively and generating large quantities of poisonous gases; stagnant water is found at every turn.* (Quoted in *The Grove* by Tom Vague, an unpublished manuscript)

After the park, Walmer Road curves leftwards into Hippodrome Place (named after the racecourse, see pp 8–9), while straight ahead lies Pottery Lane and the delightful Roman Catholic Church of St Francis of Assisi. When it opened in 1860, the church provided a great source of comfort and celebration to the largely Irish community who first attended, and it continues to be hugely active today.

The Church of St Francis of Assisi

St Francis was built at the personal expense of the Reverend Henry Augustus Rawes. A member of the priestly community of the Oblates of St Charles Borromeo, he arrived at a time when the Potteries was described as suffering from a pestilent moral atmosphere. Rawes commissioned Henry Clutton (an associate of William Burges) to design the church on an awkwardly shaped plot of land situated on a north-south axis. The original building work was supervised in 1859–60 by Clutton's then assistant John Bentley. Very soon, enlargements were needed and Bentley, now in independent practice, was responsible for adding a baptistry, porch, presbytery and school to the original structure between 1861 and 1863.

The church's austere exterior is of stock brick relieved by bands of black bricks, and is entered via a small courtyard. The simple interior in French provincial style is notable for the graceful eastward curve of the Lady Chapel, a device to accommodate the awkward shape of the plot. This uncluttered architecture provides the perfect setting for a treasure chest of spectacular, exquisitely crafted church furniture, all made from the finest materials available. Bentley was particularly interested in metalwork and the decorative arts, and St Francis contains fine examples of his early work.

The alabaster altar of St John on the north wall of the Lady Chapel contains many elements of Bentley's creative genius, with its miniature columns, huge capitals, delicately inlaid marble and small painted panels by Nathaniel Hubert John Westlake. Bentley also designed the intricately made main altar and piscina for this chapel and the charming offertory box at its entrance. The chapel contains paintings by Westlake depicting the Seven Dolours of Our Lady.

The high altar and reredos, made in 1863 with inlays of marble and glass mosaics, are masterpieces of Victorian craftsmanship. The brass door of the tabernacle is particularly notable and set with enamels and precious stones. Also superb are the first and second super-altars, the latter ornamented by circular recessed panels, divided vertically by inlays of black foliate pattern with a distinctly art nouveau appearance. The reredos is set beneath a strongly carved leaf cornice. Above this a corbel projects and carries a throne on high. All of which is topped by a gilded canopy surmounted by a Pelican in Piety.

The paintings showing the Stations of the Cross are by Westlake, who claimed that these were the first Stations ever to be depicted in Britain. The bracket for the statue of St Francis by the west door was made by Bentley, as was the canopied niche for the statue of Our Lady, in 1870. The statue itself is by Theodore Phyffers, who had been brought from Antwerp by AWN Pugin to work on the Palace of Westminster.

Some of the objects that Bentley made for St Francis (including a monstrance) are no longer on display, but the church still contains a final small masterpiece intact and in all its glory: the baptistery. At the west end of the aisle, built in 1863, it was declared by *Building News* as having the promise to be one of the 'most complete little chapels in England'. It has two bays supported on marble columns with elaborately carved capitals. The huge font, of highly polished red granite on a marble and alabaster pedestal with an elaborately carved oak canopy, is integral to the design. Whether you love or hate all this ornamentation, there is no denying that this chapel stands as a magnificent expression of exuberant Victorian spirituality. While building the extensions to the church, Bentley converted to Catholicism. He took Francis as his baptismal name, was the first to be baptised here (by Cardinal Wiseman in 1862), and donated parts of the font to the church in thanksgiving for his conversion.

The church has been redecorated and restored several times, but has lost none of its charm. Together with the courtyard and cluster of small buildings containing the community centre (all built in the same French provincial style), it is a welcoming and tranquil corner of Notting Dale. The community centre runs a crèche and art gallery cum café (see Kiln Gallery, Listings, p 157), and it acts as the base for meetings of the local Eritrean and Filipino communities. Further information, including the times of church services, is available during office hours by telephoning 020 7727 7968 or e-mail parishoffice@stfrancis-nottinghill.org.uk. St Francis is usually open to visitors during the day.

Clarendon Cross and Princedale Road

Hippodrome Place leads directly to Clarendon Cross, a picturesque corner devoted to classy shopping. There is only a small cluster of shops but each is special in its own way. Of the 'old school', Myriad Antiques offers a labyrinth of rooms filled with furniture, old textiles and quirky objects for the home and garden, while Virginia's stocks an exquisite collection of vintage clothes. Equally tempting is The Cross, a girlie treasure trove of embroidered cashmere, saris, exquisite shoes, toys and accessories, much frequented by the stars. On a more down-to-earth note, Summerill & Bishop across the way sells an inspired mix of kitchen equipment from around the world, including some serious tools for professionals. When you've had enough of shopping, Julie's Wine Bar is the perfect place for refreshment. Opened circa 1970 by the same couple who own the Portobello Hotel, this was the hangout favoured by Notting Hill's original hip bohemians and still has its charm.

A note for drivers

The layout of this area is confusing, especially for drivers. The combination of one-way systems and streets blocked off for pedestrians can easily send you round in circles. For example, Pottery Lane and the Church of St Francis of Assisi are only accessible from Hippodrome Place on foot – drivers need to approach from the south side of Pottery Lane. Generally speaking, anyone visiting the church and Clarendon Cross by car is advised to park in one of the surrounding streets, such as Portland or Clarendon Road, and walk.

Just past Julie's, facing south towards Holland Park, the road forks on either side of Orsino's restaurant. Portland Road, on the left, leads directly to Holland Park Avenue, as does the more interesting Princedale Road, soon reached via the right-hand fork, Penzance Place.

Turning left from Penzance Place into Princedale Road, the first junction you pass is with Penzance Street, the last home of the fashion designer Ossie Clark, who was murdered here by his lover on 7 August 1996. Ossie had a long association with Notting Hill, starting in Linden Gardens where he lived during his marriage to Celia Birtwell, followed by a long spell in Cambridge Gardens and brief stays in Powis Terrace, better known for its association with David Hockney. The two men were once close friends and though they eventually fell out, Ossie Clark was immortalised in Hockney's celebrated painting *Mr and Mrs Clark and Percy*, in which he and Celia are depicted with their beloved white cat.

Gazing along the neat terraces of pastel-coloured Victorian houses that make up Princedale Road, it's odd trying to associate this peaceful, mainly residential street with its past political connections – first as home of Colin Jordan's Fascist

British National Socialist Movement (BNSM), then as the birthplace of Release, a help and advice centre for people in trouble with the law over drugs, and later for the offices of *OZ*, one of the most innovative and unruly publications to come out of the 1960s' underground press.

The film director and film historian, Kevin Brownlow, recalls the hazards of shooting not far from the BNSM's headquarters in the early 1960s. His film, *It Happened Here* (1963), was a drama about what might have happened if Britain hadn't won the Second World War and included a riot sequence.

> *The main prop in the riot sequence was a magnificent REO bus which Andrew [Mollo] and I had helped the owner restore. We painted it field grey, with Mosley's lightning flash on the side, and used it as a riot bus. It held 36 blackshirts. Early on the morning of the session, it passed by the headquarters of Colin Jordan's British National Socialist Movement in Princedale Road. Three members, one in breeches and jackboots, stood chatting on the pavement. Suddenly they spotted the riot bus and stared as though at an apparition. As soon as they had recovered from their surprise, they leaped on motorcycles and gave chase. But the bus doubled back into a parallel street and threw them off. Our location was uncomfortably close to the Nazi headquarters, but they never located it, even when the bus roared down Holland Park with its bell clanging. Local residents, however, decided that the worst had happened and telephoned the Special Branch: 'Colin Jordan has mobilised!'.*

Less than ten years later, in 1967, Caroline Coon and Rufus Jones set up Release at No.70 Princedale Road, now occupied by the Bow Wow gallery. Typical of the time, Release helped everyone from teenage runaways to rock stars and, according to a relatively recent interview with Caroline Coon, 'At one point, the organisation was handling one-third of all drug busts in Britain.' Coon stayed with Release until 1971 but it was a hard struggle, as Richard Neville, former editor of *OZ*, recalls in *Hippie Hippie Shake*:

> *Caroline Coon turned up at Release to find the door knocked down, the furniture burnt, phones ripped out and the files stolen. A message was scrawled on the wall, 'Give Release to the people.' At least fifteen 'people' were in court that morning, expecting Release to help. A solicitor offered the Release team a basement as emergency headquarters. Meanwhile, the invaders wanted Caroline Coon to face 'the people'.*
>
> *At a meeting in Princedale Road, I was hauled in to mediate.*

> *Despite her fabulous Forties' filmstar look from the Chelsea Antique Market, Caroline stood alone, blue-eyeshadowed and grim: an exotic outcast. Having fled home at sixteen, she never discussed her family background.*
>
> *Mick Farren, on behalf of the White Panthers, accused her of 'poncing around King's Road while the kids are being busted in the streets'.*
>
> *'If it wasn't for Caroline,' I said, 'most of you would be in jail.'*
>
> *Mick said Release was politically flabby: 'Why don't you bomb the police stations?'*
>
> *'You can bomb them if you want,' said Caroline. 'My work's in the courts.'*
>
> *A deal was hammered out. Caroline agreed that Release could be 'given to the people', if the files were brought back. 'See Caroline; that's the way it works,' commented Farren, 'continuous revolution.' His hands shook as he spoke, the legacy of a teenage splurge with amphetamines. I stood in the doorway, an arm around Caroline's waist, as Mick muttered to his mates, 'She doesn't even smoke pot.'*

A painter, Coon is currently trying to raise funding for an archivist to work on the Release papers, and still lives in what she describes as 'the heaven of Ladbroke Grove'.

When Release moved to larger premises in around 1968, *OZ* took over the offices. The brainchild of Australian Richard Neville, this was one of the most influential underground magazines of the 1960s, famous as much for its psychedelic graphics as for the extreme radicalism of its politics. It lasted only three years, culminating in the celebrated *OZ* trial which, though successful for its defendants, dissipated their energy. The magazine folded, Neville returned to Australia and everyone involved went their separate ways.

The rise and fall of OZ

By the time Richard Neville established *OZ* in London he had already been tried in Sydney for the Australian edition. This British version was originally conceived as a satirical magazine along the lines of a more outrageous *Private Eye* (still going strong). In Neville's own words on the publication of the first issue of the magazine in 1967: '*OZ* has it all – satire, sex, sharp and ideological perversity.' But it soon evolved into something even more adventurous. Driven by the increasingly psychedelic graphics of Martin Sharp, as well as the influence of journalists such as John Wilcock (see 'Summer in the City', pp 208–11) who imported radical ideas from the US underground press, it soon embraced the drug culture that so influenced the Sixties, led by people's growing experimentation with LSD. But it was the magazine's dedication to non-censorship and sexual liberation that caused its downfall. It wasn't long before *OZ* was attracting accusations of pornography from the establishment, and with them the attention of the police. Things came to a head in the spring of 1970 with the Schoolkids' issue, inspired by the following advertisement, placed in *OZ* 26:

> *Some of us at OZ are feeling old and boring. So we invite any of our readers under 18 to come and edit the April issue. Apply at the OZ office in Princedale Road W11 any time from 10am to 7pm on Friday March 13. We will choose one person, several, or accept collective applications from a group of friends. You will receive no money except expenses and you will enjoy almost complete editorial freedom.* (Quoted in Jonathon Green, *Days in the Life*)

Around 30 responded, many of them pupils from nearby Holland Park Comprehensive. The resulting fusion of sex, drugs, rock'n roll and schoolkids turned out to be the most outrageous edition that Neville and co-workers Jim Anderson and Felix Dennis had ever produced. The police pounced, the threesome were charged with 'conspiring to corrupt public morals' and the Old Bailey trial that ensued, though it happened in 1971, became one of the *causes célèbres* associated with the 1960s. In the end, the conspiracy charge was rejected by the jury but the magazine never revived.

Continuing along Princedale Road, you'll pass the Prince of Wales pub with its open courtyard backing on to Portland Road. The pub appears in *It Happened Here,* Kevin Brownlow's feature film, and was also a popular hangout for young people during the 1960s and 70s. A few minutes further on lies Holland Park Avenue.

Holland Park Avenue and the Park

Grand houses guarded by lines of statuesque lime trees give Holland Park Avenue the appearance of a European boulevard, an impression enhanced by the scattering of French pâtisseries and other specialist foodshops that border the near side. While the southern border is almost entirely residential, turning immediately left from Princedale Road into this long, straight thoroughfare takes you past a variety of small businesses. Several of the foodshops, most notably Lidgate the butchers and the Maison Blanc pâtisserie, are renowned for the high quality of their produce. After passing Lidgate and Clarendon Road, the next turning left by the tube station, is Lansdowne Road, leading almost immediately to the tall brick edifice of Lansdowne House. Nowadays it is a recording studio, used by both rock and classical musicians, the most notorious being the Sex Pistols, who recorded *Anarchy in the UK* here in 1976. Lansdowne House also has an interesting history through its association with art collectors Edmund and Mary Davis who, in 1900, commissioned its construction as a place where artists could enjoy the luxury of working and living under one roof.

Artists and Lansdowne House

In 1889 Sir Edmund Davis, who was born in Australia in 1862 and made a great deal of money from mining in South Africa, Australia and China, moved into No.9 Lansdowne Road. He and his wife Mary had the house enlarged and decorated by Charles Conder and Frank Brangwyn. At the same time they started a collection of old masters and began to patronise several contemporary artists, among them Auguste Rodin. In 1900, they started the building of Lansdowne House. It was designed by William Flockhart to have six flats for artists, each with a two-storey studio with good north light, communal bathrooms in the basement and a Real Tennis court. The first occupants were the sculptor Charles Ricketts and the painter Charles Shannon, who moved in here in 1902. Although not hugely successful as artists, they had a mass of successful friends including Diaghilev, Nijinsky, Leon Bakst, Isadora Duncan, WB Yeats and George Bernard Shaw. Other artists who lived in Lansdowne House included Glyn Philpot, Vivian Forbes, James Pryde and F Cayley Robinson; and Edmund Dulac lived close by at Studio House in Ladbroke Grove. Aston Webb, the architect of the Victoria & Albert Museum in South Kensington, also lived in Ladbroke Grove. Edmund and Mary Davis died in 1939 and 1942 respectively, leaving most of their collection to galleries in Paris and South Africa.

Not far after the junction with Lansdowne Road, the wide road on the other side of the Avenue is marked by the corner statue of St Volodymyr, ruler of Ukraine from 980 to 1015. As its plaque specifies, the statue was erected in 1988 by Ukrainians living in the UK, 'to celebrate the establishment of Christianity in Ukraine by St Volodymyr in 988'. The road is called Holland Park and soon traces the boundaries of the park itself.

One of London's most beautiful and secluded public spaces, Holland Park's long list of attractions include the Japanese Kyoto Garden, a wildlife reserve, excellent children's play facilities, tennis courts, and exhibition spaces in the Ice House and the Orangery of Holland House (also an upmarket restaurant). The east wing of what remains of this Jacobean mansion serves as a youth hostel (see p 150). You can enter Holland Park from the road of the same name through a door in the wall by the Greek embassy. (The main entrance with car park is in Abbotsbury Road.) Another way would be to continue a little further up the south side of Holland Park Avenue, past St Volodymyr and immediately right into the steep, narrow incline of Holland Walk, closed to cars. Running parallel, the next road is Aubrey Road, leading to Campden Hill Square and Aubrey Walk.

Holland House

Holland House was built circa 1607 for Sir Walter Cope, who lent it the original name of 'Cope's Castle'. Cope died in 1614 without a male heir, and the estate eventually came to his daughter Isabel. With the support of her husband, Sir Henry Rich (made the first Earl of Holland in 1624), Isabel initiated a number of improvements to the house, both inside and out, as did the succession of noblemen who lived here over the centuries following her death.

Isabel died in 1673, after which the family residence became known as Holland House. The house was inherited by her eldest son, Robert, who became the second Earl of Holland, but it later passed out of the hands of the immediate family to be leased by several tenants, one of whom, Henry Fox, bought Holland House in 1768. During this time, right up to its virtual destruction by fire in 1940, the building was a lively centre of social, literary and political life, entertaining such visitors as Byron, Macaulay, Disraeli, Dickens and Sir Walter Scott. The original Jacobean mansion was subjected to almost continuous renovation, including the addition of a garden ballroom in the former stables in around 1845. The last great social occasion here took place on 6 July 1939, when King George V1 and Queen Elizabeth came to a grand ball attended by the cream of society. Just over a year later, Holland House was struck by incendiary bombs during enemy action, never fully to rise again. There was much debate as to what to do with the building and its extensive grounds, until it was eventually bought by the London County Council in 1952. The grounds were transformed into a public park and the east wing reconstructed for use as a youth hostel, augmented by new buildings designed by architects Hugh Casson and Neville Conder. The Ice House, which once stored ice and later became a dairy, is now used for small art exhibitions, as is the surviving Orangery. (For information on the park's many activities, see Listings, p 154.)

Aubrey Road, Campden Hill Square and Aubrey Walk

Both Aubrey Road and Campden Hill Square, to the east of Holland Park were once part of the gardens of Aubrey House, a smaller mansion close to the park on Aubrey Walk. It was built in 1698 for use as a spa – hence its original name of Wells House – but soon became a private residence occupied by, among others, Lady Mary Coke. A wealthy divorcee, Lady Mary Coke combined a love of Court gossip with a passion for gardening, both of which are recorded in great detail in four volumes of her *Letters and Journals* (see extract, pp 180–82). Among some of the many inconveniences noted by her pen was the occasion, in 1774, when her usually peaceful garden overlooking Holland Park Avenue was invaded by a fox hunt in full cry:

> *I have had another vexation that never happen'd to me before, the having of a pack of hounds in my garden, & several men on Horseback broke into my grounds, leap'd into my North Walk, & from thence into Lord Holland's lane. These things are disagreeable, and so near London was not to be expected.*

In the years following Lady Mary Coke's departure in 1788, Aubrey House eventually came into the hands of the Alexander family with whom it remained for nearly two centuries. It is not known who lives there now and, hidden behind high walls, it retains an air of mystery.

The residents of Campden Hill Square are far less elusive, including as they do at least three literary figures: playwright Harold Pinter, historian and novelist Lady Antonia Fraser, and the crime writer Dame PD James – the last of whom has set at least one of her novels in and around Notting Hill. The following is an extract from *A Taste for Death*, in which Detective Kate Miskin contemplates the world outside her mansion flat in Holland Park:

> *She poured herself an inch of whisky, mixed it with water, then unlocked the security lock of the narrow door which led from the sitting room to the iron balcony. The air rushed in, fresh and clean. She closed the door then stood, glass in hand, leaning back against the brickwork and staring out eastward over London. A low bank of heavy cloud had absorbed the glare of the city's lights and lay, palely crimson, like a colour-wash carefully laid against the richer blue-black of night. There was a light breeze just strong enough to stir the branches of the great limes lining Holland Park Avenue, and to twitch the television aerials which sprouted like frail exotic fetishes from the patterned roofs fifty feet below. To the south the trees of Holland*

Park were a black curdle against the sky, and ahead the spire of St John's church gleamed like some distant mirage. It was one of the pleasures of these moments, seeing how the spire appeared to move, sometimes so close that she felt that she would only have to stretch out a hand to feel its harshly textured stones, sometimes, like tonight, as distant and insubstantial as a vision. Far below to her right under the high arc lights the avenue ran due west, greasy as a molten river, bearing its unending cargo of cars, trucks and red buses. This, she knew, had once been the old Roman road leading westward straight out of Londinium; its constant grinding roar came to her only faintly like the surge of a distant sea.

Aubrey Walk, with Aubrey House at one end and the Gothic-Italianate Church of St George at the other, can be reached via Campden Hill Square or else directly via Aubrey Road. Running between Holland Park and Campden Hill Road, it's a quaint, narrow street of old-brick houses, often covered with ivy. The novelist John Galsworthy lived here briefly in around 1903–1905. The atmosphere is peaceful, even rural, but all this is set to change with a large-scale private housing development beginning in early 2001 (see p 4).

The Church of St George

Consecrated on 23 November 1864, the building of this church was funded by John Bennett of Westbourne Park Villas, whose son George was its first incumbent. The site was originally part of the garden of Wycombe (Wickham) House and purchased by the Ecclesiastical Commissioners in 1863. Its new ecclesiastical district was carved out of those of St Mary Abbots (which stands at the bottom of Kensington Church Street) and St John's in Ladbroke Grove.

Building News at the time estimated that its construction cost around £9,000, and called the style 'continental Gothic, freely treated', understating the impact of the architect Basset Keeling's gloriously unrestrained *Hammer House of Horror* style, which would have been even more striking when the original striped blue-slate and red-tile roof was in place. Another notable change to the exterior is the replacement of the original spire with a pyramid copper cap in 1949 as a result of war damage. The tower was once one of three on Campden Hill, the others being the water tower and Tower Cressy, both now demolished.

A contemporary writer, William Pepperell, found it 'exceedingly beautiful and original' and went on to liken the gallery to 'a conventional ship's side with the ports complete'. The interior of the church, now sadly painted over, was by all accounts brave and colourful, with its use of blue, red and black bricks, yellow stocks, Bath and red Mansfield stone and rather exotic cast ironwork. In 1885 a richly sculptured reredos of the main altar by Forsyth was added, with cusped Gothic arches enclosing representations of the Crucifixion, St Michael and St George. Of Basset Keeling's wild interior, only the nave arcades, the jagged saw-tooth nave principals, and the west-gallery front remain untouched. For information on service times and other activities, telephone 020 7221 6546.

The top of Campden Hill Road brings us full circle to the favourite haunt of GK Chesterton, featured in the chapter 'Notting Hill Gate'. Many artists and writers have lived in this neighbourhood, especially on the south side of the hill, where you'll find quite a few houses dotted with blue plaques. One of the most renowned addresses is No.77 Bedford Gardens, where the Scottish painters Robert Colquhoun and Robert MacBryde shared a studio. In 1943, *The Listener* dubbed Colquhoun the 'most promising young painter to have appeared in Britain for some time', while writer Wyndham Lewis had already called MacBryde 'the wittiest man in the area'. John Minton joined the household of the Roberts (as they were known), and the studio's welcoming atmosphere drew a string of visitors. Joined by Lucian Freud, Dylan Thomas and the poet WS Graham, Sundays would often begin in the Windsor Castle in Campden Hill Road, where the smallest bar became their private domain. The merry group would then return to Bedford Gardens and embark on readings from Gogol, Cervantes and Burns, with Dylan Thomas playing the ham actor. A further resident of No.77 was Ronald Searle, who, in 1946, moved into one of the top studios while recovering from three-and-a-half years in Changi Gaol in Singapore. All the studios were looked after by Mrs Carrie Reynolds, who had moved into the porter's flat at the turn of the century with her eight children, and would cook the artists their breakfasts, clean their shoes and lend them money.

Finally, returning north to Holland Park Avenue on the fringes of Notting Hill Gate, another Scottish artist, the gifted etcher James McBey, lived at No.1 with his American wife Marguerite. At the beginning of the twentieth century they added a wonderful north-facing studio to the top of the building and after McBey died in the 1960s, Marguerite went on living there until her death at the age of 95 in 1999.

ACCOMMODATION

BED & BREAKFAST

Best Bed & Breakfast
PO Box 2070
London W12 8QW
020 8742 9123 (24 hrs)
Fax 020 8749 7084
Bestbandb@atlas.co.uk
www.bestband.co.uk
Best B&B offers good-quality accommodation at £40–£55 per person for a double and £40–£65 single. It currently has two Holland Park addresses on its books but none elsewhere in Notting Hill, though it's always worth checking for new additions. All rooms are personally inspected. Be sure to book well in advance, especially in summer.

HOTELS

The Halcyon
81 Holland Park W11
020 7727 7288/Fax 020 7229 8516
information@thehalcyon.com
www.thehalcyon.com
Two townhouses make up this upmarket private hotel, which has 43 generously-sized rooms, some overlooking gardens and all with air-conditioning and marble bathrooms. Each room is decorated in a different style, with its own selection of antiques. The hotel offers multi-lingual secretarial and conference facilities, plus 24-hour room service. Rates are high, from £175 for a standard single to suites at £660 (VAT and continental breakfast extra). The Halcyon restaurant is situated around the corner (see Aix en Provence, p 151).

YOUTH HOSTELS

YHA Holland House
Holland Walk W8
020 7937 0748/Fax 020 7376 0667
hollandhouse@yha.org.uk
www.yha.org.uk
Open 24 hours, all year round
Right at the other end of the spectrum, this youth hostel in the grounds of Holland Park has to be one of the most peaceful places to stay anywhere in London. The accommodation comprises 200 beds in single-sex dormitories. Facilities include a garden-terrace cafeteria, games and TV rooms, a self-catering kitchen and a luggage store. Prices per night are £20.50 (over-18s) and £18.50 (under-18s); bed linen is free. Full English breakfasts, packed lunches and three-course dinners are also available from £2.90 to £4.90.

EATING AND DRINKING

CAFÉS, SNACKS AND TAKEAWAYS

Chambéry Pâtisserie
108 Holland Park Avenue W11
020 7221 3598
Mon–Sat 8am–8pm; Sun 9am–7pm
Monsieur and Madame Chaufour opened their pâtisserie in 1991, and sitting inside over coffee and tarte aux pommes you could almost be in a Parisian café. The couple have built up a loyal and cosmopolitan clientèle – weekend breakfasts are especially popular, but they also sell sandwiches, salads, chocolates, quiches and pies, both to eat on the premises and to take away.

Chelsea Spice & Grill
126 Bramley Road W10
020 8969 0992

Wilf Walker, Stanley Gardens, 1977

Dummy with camera, Portobello market

Stallholder, Portobello market

Dolls for sale, Portobello market

Hanging out in 'the Grove', with Mustapha Matura (right)

A confluence of curves: Trellick Tower framed by trees, the Grand Union Canal and the Westway

A more picturesque view of the canal by Kensal Green Cemetery

Carnival

Moroccan women and children, Horniman's Pleasance playground, off Kensal Road

The Skateboard Bowl, Meanwhile Gardens

The Mangrove

Angels, Kensal Green Cemetery

Trellick Tower, viewed along Golborne Road

Westbourne Grove today

www.eats.co.uk
Sun–Thurs 5.30–11.30pm; Fri & Sat 5.30–midnight. No credit cards
Situated under the Westway, a few minutes' walk from Latimer Road tube station, it would be hard to find a grimmer location for this award-winning Indian takeaway, but for good food at very fair prices it's well worth making the journey. Both tandoori and curry dishes start at £3 for basic chicken or lamb, rising to £6.25 for a king prawn bhuna. Set meals also represent unbeatable value, augmented by free local home delivery.

Las Palmeras

55 St Helen's Gardens W10
020 8960 8947
Mon–Fri 9am–3pm
Long lunch-time queues testify to the popularity of this excellent neighbourhood sandwich bar/deli. As the name suggests, the food has a Spanish slant and includes several varieties of tortilla (£1.50 a slice or £15 for a whole round, ordered in advance), chorizo and breaded chicken fillets, delicious in a bap with salad and melted cheese. You can either buy to take away or, if the weather permits, there are plenty of tables on the broad pavement in front.

Sonia's Café

308 Latimer Road W10
020 7460 8956
Mon–Fri 7am–4pm; Sat 8am–1pm
With its tiny courtyard and cabin-like interior, Sonia's has an unexpectedly cosy atmosphere among the industrial buildings of Latimer Road. You could almost be in the country. The food is good standard greasy spoon, including excellent bacon rolls and refreshingly strong tea.

RESTAURANTS

Fish

Offshore

148 Holland Park Avenue W11
020 7221 6090
Mon–Sat 12 noon–3pm & 7–11pm
The only colour in this minimalist restaurant, with its bare wood floors and white walls, is provided by rather strange stripes on the back wall. Brash lighting and the absence of candles add to the room's cold feel – a pity, as the food, representing a mixture of cuisines, is delicious and original. Among the starters, we could have chosen from Thai fragrant green lip mussels (£5.25), parsnip and ginger soup (£3.95), or aromatic crispy duck salad (£6.25), but opted for pan-fried foie gras with toasted brioche (£8.50), perfectly done. The main courses included monkfish coconut curry (£14), asparagus cannelloni with plum tomato sauce and gruyère (£12), loin of venison (£16), and smoked haddock with wild mushroom risotto cake and hollandaise sauce (£14) – in which the mixture of consistencies worked perfectly. It does a Quick Lunch menu and the service is friendly and efficient.

French

Aix en Provence

129 Holland Park Avenue W11
020 7221 7288
Mon–Fri 12 noon–2.30pm; Sun brunch 12 noon–3pm; Mon–Sat 7–10.30pm (Sun 10pm)
There's a welcome feeling of spaciousness in this basement level restaurant with tables spread out, leaving no chance to eavesdrop. Dim muted light adds to the discreet atmosphere. The food is modern French with a Mediterranean influence. Most of the waiters seemed to have a problem with English and although

willing to help were quite slow and needed reminding about our orders. First courses start at about £7 and main courses range from £14 to £19. There is a two-course good value lunch menu for £10 which changes every three days.

The Belvedere

Holland House
Holland Park W11
020 7602 1238
Daily 12 noon–2.45pm & 7–10.45pm
Situated in the Jacobean splendour of Holland Park, with terrace seating on the first floor overlooking the landscape, this is a perfect location for lunch on a good summer's day. Under the influence of Marco Pierre White, the restaurant was recently made over in smart Euro style, serving smart Euro food. Expect to pay approximately £30 per head including wine, though you can spend lots more, especially on drink. The atmosphere is cool but relaxed, with attentive staff. Worth a visit, but bear in mind that food is only part of the experience.

Chez Moi

1 Addison Avenue W11
020 7603 8267
Tues–Fri 12.30pm–2pm; Mon–Sat 7–11pm
A long-established, comfortable, quiet and plush restaurant in Holland Park – ideal for romantic dining. It's also one of the few restaurants where the food is better than the menu. These qualities, coupled with unobtrusive service, ensure a faithful clientèle. Typical main dish £15.75.

---

6 Clarendon Road

6 Clarendon Road W11
020 7727 3330
six@restaurationco.demon.co.uk
Dinner only Tues–Sun 7–11.30pm
This second French neighbourhood restaurant opened only two years ago, since when it has had its fair share of ups and downs. At the time of writing, however, it appears to be on a winning streak. The accent is on traditional French cuisine with the odd contemporary touch, such as a starter of sautéed lamb sweetbreads with brandy sauce on warm lentils (£5.50), monkfish medallions and pan-fried chicken breast with preserved lemons (£14.75). The simpler dishes such as salmon soufflé (£5.75) and sirloin steak with mustard and tarragon sauce (£15.50) tend to be better executed. The décor is plain but warm and the wine list excellent.

Italian

Orsino

119 Portland Road W11
020 7221 3299
Daily 12 noon–3pm; 7–11.30pm; plus special early dinner and late supper menus 5.30–7pm & 10–11.30pm
A popular place with locals, including quite a few celebs, Orsino's offers reliable, fairly standard Italian dishes served up on rustic crockery in a smart location. It's better for lunch than dinner, with the bonus of welcoming children, despite the immaculately designed interior. The wine list is a bit esoteric if you're not into Italian wines but there's always Orvieto to fall back on. Expect to pay at least £25 a head before wine for two courses. The early, and late, evening special deals – two courses for £11.50 or three for £15.50 – are excellent value.

Modern European

Julie's Wine Bar & Restaurant

135 Portland Road W11
0207 727 7985
Restaurant 020 7229 8331
Bar daily 9am–10.30pm; restaurant Mon–Fri & Sun 12.30–2.30pm; daily

7–11pm
Julie's has been in the area for 30 years and still has a loyal following. The restaurant is a collection of small atmospheric rooms; we dined in the 'Garden of Love' with mirrors, plants and soft music, where the food was disappointingly bland although the steak was good. In other parts of the warren-like building there are bars and rooms where you can sink into cushions in a private nook and drink tea. Popular for illicit liaisons.

GASTROPUBS

Latimer Place

274 Latimer Road W10
020 8968 9118
Mon–Sat 12.30–3pm & 6.30–10.45pm; Sun 1–8pm
Opening in 1999, a couple of years after the North Pole had helped to establish this stretch of W10 as a feasible spot for wining and dining, Latimer Place quickly won local approval as a friendly neighbourhood bar serving good Mediterranean-style food in fairly basic surroundings. Since then its reputation has been a bit patchy, but it's a pleasant enough place for a drink, especially outside in summer, and the cooking by Ossie Clark's son Albert is well worth checking out.

North Pole

13–15 Latimer Road W10
020 8964 9384
Mon–Sat 11.30am–11pm, Sun 12 noon–10.30pm; lunch Mon–Sat 12.30–3pm, Sun 1–3.30pm; dinner Mon–Sat 6.30–10pm (Sun till 9.30pm)
Followed by Latimer Place, the North Pole has come to symbolise the gradual rise in status of this hitherto barren corner of North Kensington, now increasingly sought after by those who cannot quite afford to live in Notting Hill. It's a popular pub, perhaps more for the good-quality beer and friendly atmosphere than the food, which can be disappointing – especially for the price.

PUBS

The Castle

100 Holland Park Avenue W11
Mon–Sat 11am–11pm; food served 12 noon–3pm & 6.30–10pm
Modern, very spacious pub with a relaxed and comfortable atmosphere that hots up considerably at weekends with the addition of a DJ. Other days, the music is constant but not intrusive. The crowd, aged around 25–30, tends towards trendy, and the food, untried but looking good, is quite expensive and fancier than average pub fare.

The Prince of Wales

14a Princedale Road, W11
No phone
Daily 12 noon–11.30pm (Sun till 10.30pm)
More of an old-fashioned pub, the Prince of Wales attracts a good range of locals of all ages. Facilities include a pool table, juke box and a quaint beer garden which is a great summer retreat from the traffic and expensive trappings of Holland Park Avenue. Unless you're into football, keep away on match days when an excited crowd gathers around Sky TV. Food is a recent addition, not yet tried.

WINE BARS

Julie's (see p 152)

ENTERTAINMENT

CHILDREN

Bramley's Big Adventure

136 Bramley Road W10
020 8960 1515
Daily 10am–6.30pm
This indoor activity playground can be something of a godsend to parents, especially on a rainy winter's day. Play areas are divided in two, for the over- and under-fives, with a good choice of equipment from the more usual slides, balance beams and ball pools to monkey swings, an aerial runway and a 'spooky den'. Accompanying adults have to stay on the premises but there's a café where you can at least relax while your charges hopefully tire themselves out. Sessions are for 90 minutes and prices start at £2.75 for under-fives during school days; £3.25 weekends and holidays; for older children just add £1. Bramley's is also a popular place for parties, costing from £7 per child for 75 minutes' play, a party meal and a goody bag and balloon. Or you can simply hire the whole place, including experienced staff.

Holland Park

020 7602 9483
Open from sunrise to sunset all year round. **Adventure Playground** 020 7603 6956 *daily 10am–6pm*
One O'clock Club 020 7603 2838
Mon–Fri 1.30–4pm
Holland Park has something for everyone and children are especially well catered for. There are seven entrances altogether, but the main one (with car park) is on Abbotsbury Road, which runs directly off Holland Park Avenue, opposite Norland Square. The **Adventure Playground** offers a range of activities for five to 16-year-olds, including arts and crafts as well as a network of outdoor structures such as rope swings, poles and runways between the trees. However, it's currently under threat from Council budget cuts, so phone for the latest developments. Next door, the **One O'Clock Club** is for under-fives, with an indoor area for dressing up and construction games, while other toddlers play in the sand-pit or scoot around on trucks outside. Both places are supervised by experienced play leaders.

The park has an **Ecology Centre**, established in the refurbished stable block of Holland House, which holds displays and exhibitions based on the local and natural history of the park. It's also a starting point for nature trails, guided walks and pond exploration, usually organised for schools. For more information contact the main park telephone number, above.

Westway Stables

20 Stable Way (off Latimer Road) W10
020 8964 2140
Daily 9am–6pm
Stable Way is a narrow lane at the far south end of Latimer Road. It's a bit of a dumping ground for rubbish, but don't be put off – the stables are just around the corner. It's a friendly place, if a bit chaotic, and ponies come in all sizes and temperaments so you're almost sure to find one to suit you or your child. Prices for children range from £4 for a 15-minute pony ride, £9 for a half-hour group lesson to £18 for an hour's hack on Wormwood Scrubs Common. Adult prices start at £14 for a half-hour lesson. Hats can be hired for £2. It's a far cry from riding in the country but the sandpit ring is a good size and, for those with some experience, the Common offers a surprisingly picturesque open space.

SHOPPING

ANTIQUES

Myriad Antiques

131 Portland Road W11
020 7229 1709
Mon–Sat 11am–6pm
Sara Nickerson has a particular eye and fills her shop with a wonderfully eclectic mix of decorative antique objects and furniture for the house and garden. Generations of buyers return again and again to buy her latest acquisitions. Among the many objects crowding the two floors are 'shabby château-style' French painted furniture, rustic chandeliers, Victorian and Edwardian calico chairs and a mass of delightfully quirky objects.

Nine Clarendon Cross

9b Clarendon Cross W11
020 7792 0895
Tues–Sat 11am–6pm
Worth knowing about as a gallery which you can rent by the week. You pay a fee, organise your own opening and don't have to pay any commission.

D Sutherland

9 Bramley Road W10
020 7221 1443/ 07966 461 636 (Mobile)
Daily – but phone first
Debby Sutherland buys whatever catches her eye at auctions, clearance sales and the like. The result is an intriguing mix of anything from silk parachutes, beaded curtains, Fifties' crockery and crystal chandeliers to ornamental headboards and an ancient hand-made rocking chair made from willow branches. It's a delightful shop, located slightly off the beaten track, in the first block where Bramley Road branches off from St Ann's Road.

FASHION

Cath Kidston

8 Clarendon Cross W11
020 7221 4000
Mon–Fri 10am–6pm; Sat 11am–6pm
Kidston's distinctive style pervades this pretty shop, perfectly suited to the picturesque Cross. Her ultra-feminine, olde-worlde designs are transferred onto various materials to make a whole range of items, from floral trays, shower caps, furnishing fabrics, paisley quilts, pastoral wallpapers and cushions to handbags and T-shirts in crisp cotton for women and children. She also sells vintage items, sometimes hard to distinguish from the new, and runs an efficient mail-order service.

The Cross

141 Portland Road W11
020 7727 6760
www.thecrosscatalogue.com
Mon–Sat 10.30am–6pm
Few serious shoppers come to Notting Hill without visiting this quintessentially girlie boutique for the home and wardrobe. Nothing is cheap but much is quirky and desirable, especially if you go for the bohemian look. Cashmere, silk, velvet and brocade garments, throws and cushions come in a blinding selection of colours, while delicate pieces of jewellery and hair accessories glitter from the shelves. Look out especially for beautiful cardigans by Anna Louise Roswald and saris from Odi Green. Other items include shoes, bags, ceramics, T-shirts and a few children's toys at the back. The shop's clientèle reads like an A-list of models and movie stars, so don't be surprised if you bump into Kate Moss or Madonna.

Vintage and second-hand

Virginia's

98 Portland Road W11
020 7727 9908
Mon–Sat 11am–6pm
Established long ago, this magical shop is filled with exquisite vintage clothes: upstairs has evening dresses and coats covered with beads and lamé, while in the downstairs boudoir everything is pale grey or white. There is a feeling of decadence and temptation, and, as the stock changes constantly it is worth going regularly and thereby increasing the possibility of encountering celebs in the form of Nicole Kidman, Angelica Huston, Naomi Campbell or Liv Tyler, all of whom are customers.

FLOWERS

Tom's

73 Clarendon Road W11
020 7792 8510
Mon–Fri 9am–6pm
This tiny narrow space with its equally small basement is where Tom creates his wonderful floral arrangements for parties and other functions, as well as the individual bouquets. The shop has regular customers but most of the cut flowers are sold from his stall at the corner of Elgin Crescent and Kensington Park Road (see p 59).

FOOD AND WINE

Handford

12 Portland Road W11
020 7221 9614
james@handford-wine.demon.co.uk
www.handford-wine.demon.co.uk
Mon–Sat 10am–8.30pm
Owner James Handford is a Master of Wine and personally selects his fine bottles from all over the world, but with the emphasis on France and Spain. Much of the wine is kept in bond, but the shop has an interesting selection and provides wine for many launches and parties. Handford also runs a wine school which welcomes beginners and arranges a series of tastings throughout the year.

Jeroboams

196 Holland Park Avenue W11
020 7727 9359
Mon–Fri 9am–7.30pm; Sat 8.30am–7pm; Sun 10am–4pm
Cheese is the mainstay of this typically lavish Holland Park shop and the selection, including several unpasteurised varieties, is impressive. True connoisseurs will love to ruminate over which particular Parmesan, Stilton or Camembert to opt for, complemented by some delicious-looking breads. Jeroboams also stocks a few dried foodstuffs, preserves, puddings and a range of high-quality wines.

Lidgate

110 Holland Park Avenue W11
020 7727 8243
Mon–Fri 7am–6pm; Sat 7am–5pm
David Lidgate is the fourth generation of his family to run this 150-year-old business, possibly the oldest in the area. What makes this butcher unique is not just the excellence of the meat but also the quality of service and the advice. Lidgate deals direct with farmers, and personally selects organic and grass-fed beef, lamb and pork from, among others, Highgrove, Gatcombe Park and the Buccleuch estate. By only selecting the best, he aims to improve what he sells every year. Home-made sausages and pies vie for space with meat, game, cheese, jams and chutneys. An order received before 11am ensures same-day delivery, and although Lidgate is busy throughout the year, the queues at Christmas are almost a tourist attraction in themselves.

Maison Blanc

102 Holland Park Avenue W11
020 7221 2494
Mon–Thurs & Sat 8am–7pm; Fri 8am–7.30pm; Sun 8.30am–6pm
One of the best pâtisserie chains, Maison Blanc is a good match for all the other specialist foodshops gracing the Avenue. Succulent chocolate mousse gâteaux, creamy *millefeuilles* and wonderful tartes aux fruits (*cassis* is particularly recommended) are displayed alongside Belgian chocolates and other continental confectionery. All the breads on the back shelves are painstakingly baked in stone ovens, using authentic French ingredients, and it shows. Everything tastes as good as it looks, with prices to match.

Speck

2 Holland Park Terrace,
Portland Road W11
020 7229 7005
Mon–Fri 8.30am–8.30pm; Sat 8am–7pm
This Italian delicatessen, with its low ceiling and white-tiled floor, is filled with a wide range of dry pasta, Italian wine, liqueurs and panettone as well as a selection of home-made pasta sauces, soups and ready-made dishes. A good standby if your cupboards are suddenly bare.

GALLERIES

Bernard Shapero

80 Holland Park Avenue W11
020 7491 0330
gallery@shapero.com
www.shapero.com/gallery
Mon–Fri 9.30am–6.30pm; Sat 11am–5pm
Conveniently located right next to Holland Park tube station, two floors of antiquarian prints fill what was once a custom-built bookshop. The emphasis is on natural history, decorative arts, and travel, and it also does a range of nineteenth-century travel photographs.

Bow Wow

70 Princedale Road W11
020 7792 8532
Tues–Sat 10am–6pm
Ahmed Sidki's tiny gallery is a veritable temple to minimalism and good taste. A trained cabinet-maker in the Japanese tradition, he specialises in simple, technically perfect pieces of furniture in a basic range of designs, which can be tailored to customers' individual needs. Alongside his own work, for which this began as a showroom, Sidki displays ceramics, lamps, cushions and other accessories by up-and-coming designers such as Vivienne Foley, Abigail Simpson and Alev Saglam.

The Kiln Gallery

St Francis Community Centre
Pottery Lane W11
020 7792 8259
Mon–Fri & Sun 9.30am–3pm
Attached to the Church of St Francis of Assisi, the Kiln Gallery provides a pleasant space for local artists to display their work. Paintings and other artworks are selected by a gallery committee to which 30 per-cent commission is paid on any sale in order to cover costs and certain projects run by the St Francis Community Centre. The gallery doubles as a café (9am–3pm),which serves excellent lunches at reasonable prices between noon and 2.30pm.

One Three Nine

139 Portland Road W11
020 7221 5481/6959
Mon–Sat 10.30am–6pm; Sun 2.30–5.30pm
The Russian artists Valeri and Katya Gridnyev, who have a similar style and often use the same model simultaneously,

are the current stars of this new gallery, and their affordable paintings of ballet dancers are well worth seeing. The owner, Susie Watson, was an interior designer, and the rest of the space, over two floors, is filled with British and French hand-made pottery. Furniture can be painted to order and there is also a selection of unusual glass lamps filled with shells, oranges, rosebuds and dried seeds.

The Temple Gallery

6 Clarendon Cross W11
020 7727 3809
templegallery@cs.com
www.templegallery.com
Mon–Fri 10am–6pm (Sats during exhibitions)

For 40 years the Temple Gallery has specialised in icons from Byzantine and mediaeval Slavonic times through to the Revival Period in the nineteenth century. Prices vary enormously but everything sold comes with a guarantee of authenticity. The gallery gives valuations, provides a conservation and restoration service and produces splendid catalogues.

HOME

Arch 18

Arch 12
Kingsdown Close W10
020 7229 5391
www.arch18.co.uk
Mon–Fri 8am–6pm

Under the name of Arch 18 (but located in Arch 12), Michael Reed has been designing and manufacturing unique contemporary furniture for 25 years from a railway arch off St Mark's Road. His style is best described as 'high-tech William Morris', combining good old-fashioned craftsmanship, using wood from sustainable sources, with highly imaginative, often quirky ideas. The arch is a friendly place and Reed, who exports his one-off furniture designs world-wide, is nearly always happy to take on a new challenge.

David Black

96 Portland Road W11
020 7727 2566
www.david-black.com
davidblack@david-black.com
Mon–Fri 10am–6pm; Sat 11am–5.30pm

As another long-established business, David Black's gallery has been selling oriental carpets, kilims, tribal and village rugs, silk embroideries and Indian dhurries since 1965. The basement stocks an antique collection, while upstairs concentrates on modern designs – Black was one of the first specialists to introduce collectors to twentieth-century tribal rugs. An exciting new departure is that clients are now able to design their own carpets, using simple bold colours, on the internet.

Simon Harris Living

94 Holland Park Avenue W11
020 7727 8009
info@simonharrisliving.com
www.superstems.com
Mon–Fri 10am–8pm; Sat 10am–6pm Sun 11am–4pm

What makes this lifestyle store different from any other are the fresh flowers and plants that fill much of the shop. Simon Harris and his brother took over their parents' business, Flower Power, which had been in the area for many years, and they now mix candles, vases and furniture with the plants and flowers. The design is minimal without being clinical and there's a good selection of English-grown orchids.

Summerill & Bishop

100 Portland Road W11
020 7221 4566

Mon–Sat 10am–6pm
'We love our shop' say the owners and this is evident from the impeccably chosen mixture of old and new kitchen-ware on sale. Old French cafetières, linen and glasses are ranged side by side with new pottery, wooden chopping boards, ostrich-feather dusters, and storage baskets. This kind of elegance and quality does not come cheap, but everything in the shop is chosen because Summerill and Bishop would have it in their own houses, and there's not a plastic item in sight.

MIND AND BODY

HAIR AND BEAUTY

Hair & Tanning Rooms

53 St Helen's Gardens W10
020 8969 7582/8960 0344
Mon & Thurs 9am–6pm; Tues & Wed 8.30am–6pm; Fri 8.30am–7pm; Sat 8am–5pm; Sun 10am–2pm. No credit cards
Forget Nicky Clarke *et al.* Tony and Sandra Tahir have been running this recently refurbished salon and tanning rooms since 1979, and their team of friendly and experienced cutters are hard to beat. Prices start at £15 for a ladies' wash & cut (£10 for children; £12 men) up to £25 for a cut & blow dry, and £70 for a whole head of highlights. In addition to excellent sunbeds (£12 for a 20-minute session), the salon offers nail care and drinks from the downstairs bar, where you can also relax in the garden while waiting for your colour to take hold. A sister shop providing wider beauty treatments is planned for 2001.

HEALTH AND FITNESS

Holland Park (see p 154)

Westway Sports Centre

1 Crowthorne Road W10
020 8969 0992
Tennis Centre Mon & Tues 12 noon–10pm; Wed 12 noon–11pm; Thurs 9am–10pm; Sat 8am–6pm; Sun 10am–8pm. Phone for times of other activities
Established to encourage local children and young people to take up sport, this already impressive centre is currently undergoing extensive refurbishment, due for completion in September 2001. Indoor tennis courts will be joined by four astroturf pitches for football and hockey, as well as outside courts and a network of all-weather climbing walls. Despite being situated in the unwelcoming shadow of the A40 (near Westway Stables), the facilities are already more than adequate, and prices, from £2 per two-hour session, are very much geared to encouraging as many participants as possible.

Directory

BANKS/CHANGING MONEY

Thomas Cook Exchange
HSBC Bank
152 Portobello Road W11
Mon–Fri 9.30am–5pm; Sat 10am–4pm

Daychange
90 Notting Hill Gate W11
020 7792 3007
8am–10pm

BICYCLE REPAIRS AND SALES

EJ Barnes
285 Westbourne Grove W11
020 7727 5147
Mon–Wed & Fri 11am–7pm;
Thurs 11am–6.30pm; Sat 11am–6pm

Bicycle Workshop
27 All Saints Road W11
020 7229 4850
Tues–Sat 10am–6pm (closed 2–3pm)

CAR RENTAL

Portobello Car Hire
37 Bramley Road W10
020 7792 1133
Mon 8am–5.30pm; Tues–Thurs 8.30am–5.30pm; Fri 8.30am–6pm; Sat 8.30am–1pm & 2–5.30pm

---

CHILDCARE

Playgroups information
020 7361 3302
020 7598 4901

Services for under-eights
020 7361 2340/2422

Childminders (Council approved)
020 7361 2503

SCHOOLS

Schools Services
020 7361 3334
eduadmin@rbkc.gov.uk

DISABLED SERVICES

General
020 7361 2137

Transport
020 7361 2546

DRUGS ADVICE

The Blenheim Project
321 Portobello Road W10
020 8960 5599
Mon–Fri 1–4pm; Tues 6pm–9pm

EMERGENCIES

Accident and emergency departments

St Charles' Hospital
(minor injuries only)
Exmoor Street W10
020 8969 2488
Daily 9am–9pm

St Mary's Hospital (24 hour)
Praed Street W2
020 7886 6666

Dental Emergency Service
(Central London)
020 7935 4486

FAMILY PLANNING

Raymede Clinic
Exmoor Street W10
020 8962 4450
Mon–Fri 9.30am–12 noon, 2–3.30pm & 5.30–7pm

FINDING A FLAT

Faron Sutaria
020 7243 1352

Leslie Marsh & Co
020 7221 4805

Marsh & Parsons
020 7229 6960

FINDING A JOB

Manpower
2–6 Notting Hill Gate W11
020 7727 2784
Mon–Fri 8am–6pm

FURTHER EDUCATION

Kensington and Chelsea College
020 7573 5333

GAY AND LESBIAN INFORMATION

Gay and Lesbian Switchboard
020 7837 7324

GLASS, GLAZING AND MIRRORS

London West Ten Glass
485 Latimer Road
020 8969 5682/8960 3394
Mon–Fri 8am–5.30pm; Sat 9am–1pm

HOSPITALS

St Charles' and **St Mary's**
(see Emergencies)

LAUNDRY/DRY CLEANING

Crystal Clean
27 Kensington Park Road W11
020 7727 8235
Mon–Sat 8.30am–6pm

LEGAL HELP

Citizens Advice Bureau
Westway Information Centre
240 Ladbroke Grove W10
020 8960 3322
Mon–Wed & Fri 10am–12.30pm;
advice line Mon–Fri 12.30–2.30pm

North Kensington Neighbourhood Law Centre
74 Golborne Road W10
020 8969 7473
Mon–Fri 10am–1pm & 2–6pm
(closed Wed am)

LIBRARIES

Central Library
Phillimore Walk W8
020 7937 2542
Mon, Tues & Thurs 9.30am–8pm;
Wed 9.30am–1pm; Fri & Sat 9.30am–5pm

Kensal Library
20 Golborne Road W10
020 8969 7736
Mon, Tues, Thurs 1–6pm;
Fri 10am–12 noon & 1–6pm;
Sat 10am–1pm & 2–5pm

North Kensington Library
108 Ladbroke Road W11
020 7727 6583
Mon, Tues & Thurs 10am–8pm;
Wed 10am–1pm; Fri & Sat 10am–5pm

Notting Hill Gate Library
1 Pembridge Square W2
020 7229 8574
Mon, Tues, Thurs 10am–8pm;
Wed 10am–1pm; Fri & Sat 10am–5pm

Mobile Library
020 8968 6012

OPTICIANS

Shannon & Carton
102 Ladbroke Grove W11
020 7229 2218
Tues–Fri 9am–5.30pm; Sat 9am–4.30pm

PHARMACIES (LATE-NIGHT)

Bliss (Marble Arch)
020 7723 6116
Mon–Sun 9–midnight

Zafash (Old Brompton Road)
020 7373 2798
24 hour

POLICE

Notting Hill Police Station
101 Ladbroke Road W11
020 7221 1212

POST OFFICES

2 Ladbroke Grove W11
Mon–Fri 9am–5.30pm; Sat 9am–1pm

116 Ladbroke Grove W10
Mon–Fri 9am–5.30pm; Sat 9am–1pm

198 Kensington Church Street W8
Mon–Fri 9am–5.30pm; Sat 9am–12.30pm

222 Westbourne Grove W11
(opposite Turquoise Island)
Mon–Thurs 9am–5.30pm;
Fri 9.30am–5.30pm; Sat 9am–12.30pm

325 Golborne Road W10
Mon–Fri 9am–5.30pm; Sat 9am–1pm

PUBLIC LAVATORIES

Westbourne Grove
Turquoise Island, Westbourne Grove W11

Portobello Road
Portobello Road/
Talbot Road junction W11

Notting Hill Gate
Adjoining 94 bus stop in Notting Hill
(outside *Europa* supermarket) W11

PUBLIC TRANSPORT

Underground
Notting Hill Gate:
Central, District and Circle lines
Ladbroke Grove, Latimer Road and Westbourne Park:
Hammersmith & City line
Holland Park: Central line

Buses
Notting Hill Gate:
12, 27, 28, 31, 52, 70, 94, 328,
N12, N28, N31, N52, N94, N207
Westbourne Grove:
7, 23, 27, 28, 31,70, 328, N23, N28, N31
Westbourne Park Road:
7, 28, 31, 70, 328
Ladbroke Grove:
7, 23, 52, 70, 295, N23, N52
Bramley Road:
295
Holland Park Avenue:
94, N94, N207
Further information from
London Travel Information
020 7222 1234

National railway information
0845 748 4950 (24 hour)

SECURITY

Mario's Security Services and Locksmiths

132 Talbot Road W11

020 7727 5429

Mon–Sat 9am–6pm

TAXIS

Black cabs

020 7272 0272

Just Airports

0800 096 8096

Karma Cabs

0207 598 0132/8533

Tobias: 0370 693979

Minicabs

020 8968 3363

Part 2

HISTORY

A Brief History of Notting Hill

Annabel Hendry

Annabel Hendry studied social anthropology in London and specialised in the cultural effects of tourism. She has also worked and lived in Malta, Ireland and Brussels.

Notting Hill today still contains strong reminders of its recent history as one of the most grandiosely conceived suburbs in the country. The mansions and villas so characteristic of the area were mainly built during the middle of the nineteenth century to house the growing population of London, and they reflect the fanciful imaginations of enthusiastic Victorian speculators and architects. But the beauty of these façades sits uneasily amid a rather dislocated urban geography, reflecting the area's sometimes troubled social history. Notting Hill was both a beneficiary and a victim of the mid-Victorian spirit of entrepreneurship: by the end of the nineteenth century it contained some very grand suburban houses, cheek by jowl with areas of the most squalid living conditions in the country. During the twentieth, the area suffered some of the most brutal examples of urban redevelopment, and became a focal point for events in the period of turbulence and social upheaval in the 1950s and 60s, but emerged with new hope from the 1970s into the present. People speak of how the area 'resists gentrification'. Looking back, it seems that this has always been so.

Early history

The name Notting Hill probably derives from the Saxon 'sons of Cnotta (or Cnotingas)' who settled here around AD 700, near to the 'sons of Cynesige' who founded Kensington. The area's location, on a hill bounded by two streams, with a commanding position at the crossroads between London and the West, has always been significant, and throughout history has attracted the rich and the roguish in equal measure.

Notting Hill was originally part of the huge Kensington Estate given by William the Conqueror to Geoffrey, Bishop of Coutances, and then held by the De Vere family up until the reign of James I. In the twelfth century it was divided into four manorial estates: Abbot's Manor Kensington, Earl's Court, West Town (the fields west of Addison Road stretching between Kensington High Street and Holland Park Avenue) and Notting Barns (north-west of Notting Hill Gate). In circa 1100 the Abbot's Manor portion of the estate (between the present Church Street and Addison Road) was given by Aubrey de Vere to the Abbot of Abingdon in reward for curing his sick son. Later, during the fourteenth and fifteenth centuries, other portions of land were gradually leased off to a series of large estate holders, most of whom held on to their property until the end of the eighteenth century.

One of the most influential of these landowners was Walter Cope, a politician with influence at court who was knighted by James I in 1603. In eight years he acquired almost the whole area: West Town in 1591 and the Manors of Abbot's Kensington and Notting Barns in 1599. It was at Notting Barns in 1607 that he began building his Cope's Castle, later to become known as Holland House. This magnificent mansion, reflecting the extravagance of the times, was to become a social centre for the great and the good for centuries.

A second mansion was built in this period by another of James I's courtiers, Sir George Coppin. Originally called Sheffield House, this was to become Kensington Palace when William III bought it in 1689. Kensington had become a 'royal suburb of London' and a highly fashionable centre for aristocratic social life. Several more substantial mansions were built in this early period, including Aubrey House on Campden Hill.

With only a small cluster of houses, Notting Hill at this time was little more than a hamlet and remained so until the middle of the nineteenth century, when Portobello Lane (as the Road was then called) was still described as 'one of the most rural and pleasant walks in the summer in the vicinity of London'. However, there was some early industry in the form of the Kensington Gravel Pits which, for centuries, were worked on either side of what is now Bayswater Road and Notting Hill Gate. At one time, the desirability of the area was enhanced by the belief that emanations from the carts carrying the newly turned gravel from the pits to London were beneficial to health, and for a brief period the region was even extolled as a spa, when purgative springs were discovered on what is now Campden Hill.

From hamlet to suburb: the nineteenth-century building boom

In the first part of the nineteenth century, a series of building and development projects began to alter the rural character of the area. The earliest of these schemes were the cutting of the Paddington branch of the Grand Junction (now Grand Union) Canal, opened in 1801, and the allocation of land at Kensal Green in 1831 for the building of the first ever custom-built cemetery in London (see pp 82–85). But these developments were only foretastes of what was to come. Waterways were soon to be superseded in importance by railways and the dead outnumbered by the living. By the end of the 1820s the area was witnessing the beginning of one of the greatest, most ambitious and certainly most uneven building booms in the history of England.

The story of this upsurge in building begins in the early 1820s, when two of the largest local landowners, the third Lord Holland and James Ladbroke, began to develop their estates, building the first houses on Campden Hill and around the area now known as Ladbroke Square. Such speculations were a little premature, for the swell of population was yet to arrive, and both developers were severely hit by the financial crash of 1825. However, the enthusiasm of their original enterprises set the tone for a costly, fanciful and, for some, financially disastrous boom which lasted until the 1870s.

The original plans (there were many, but those for the Ladbroke Estate were the most impressive and extensive) amounted to a kind of collective Victorian dream, and employed some of the best architects of the time. Complex and ambitious, they incorporated every possible style, from Tudor Gothic (see St George's Church, Aubrey Walk) to classical-Italianate (the villas of Kensington Park Road). They also boasted the latest plumbing – not easy to achieve given all the clay and gravel in the area. The idea was to develop a series of estates providing spacious and stylish housing for the rising middle-class and professional population of London. Notting Hill was believed to be an ideal location, on the margins of fashionable Kensington and close to the flourishing West End. In spite of Lord Holland's and Ladbroke's hastiness, their planning soon proved fairly well-timed for, owing to decreasing mortality rates, in the first two decades of the nineteenth century the population of London had increased by 20 per cent. People wanted somewhere to move out to, and the most attractive magnets were the suburban areas close to the main highways.

A fair number of these newcomers did include the extremely well-heeled, such as those who moved to Campden Hill, which became nicknamed 'The Dukeries', and to Kensington Palace Gardens, known as 'Millionaires' Row'. Others were of the recently monied middle class who, during the 1850s and 60s, moved into the areas around Ladbroke Grove. However, as the century progressed, a growing working-class population began to settle here too, drawn by work opportunities offered by the construction of the railways. In 1863 the Metropolitan Railway, connecting Paddington and Farringdon Street, was inaugurated as the first underground railway in the world. A year later, the first feeder line was opened, extending from its western terminus at Hammersmith, through Shepherds Bush and Notting Dale (with a station at Ladbroke Grove) to Westbourne Park. The building of this line gave new life to the, until then, defunct Western London Railway, which was linked to the underground by a branch line from Latimer Road.

Despite all this development, the realisation of the original dream for the estates was thwarted from the start and things did not turn out as the speculators had hoped. The two problems were uncertain finance and uncertain takers for all the grandly conceived houses, as typified by architect Thomas Allason's plans to build a spectacular circus in the style of John Nash's work at Regent's Park.

More building and 'graveyards of buried hopes'

Following a failed venture to establish a racecourse on the slopes of Notting Hill during the slow-down in building after the crash of 1825, the land reverted to Ladbroke and was re-leased for the construction of the estate of villas with spacious communal gardens which, instead of Allason's circus, now occupy the region around Ladbroke Grove, Kensington Park Gardens and Stanley Crescent. Further financial crises afflicted the project, leaving several developers bankrupt and countless legacies of half-finished shells along the way. As late as 1861, Ladbroke Gardens was described by *Building News* as 'a graveyard of buried hopes . . . naked carcasses, crumbling decorations, fractured walls, slimy cement. Courageous builders have occasionally touched them and lost heart and money by the venture.'

Among the courageous builders who lost heart and a great deal of money was the Reverend Dr Stanley Walker. Described as a pious and very amicable man, he began building on both the Ladbroke and Portobello Estates, sadly to become bankrupt before he was able to finish what is now All Saints Church, intended as a monument to honour his parents. About the only survivor of all this activity was Charles Henry Blake, a retired Calcutta merchant and one of Walker's partners. Blake became responsible for constructing on most of the Portobello Estate much smaller, more modest houses for the growing working-class population – each now worth a cool one million pounds. He also bought up many of the leases elsewhere and completed the half-finished houses. By the time the building craze ended in 1880, 13,000 buildings, most of them houses, had been erected in 60 years.

Along with the problem of shaky finances, there was the growing difficulty of supply outstripping demand. The simple fact overlooked by the developers was that some of the land occupied by the estates was either too far from the West End or fashionable Kensington or too close to the working-class districts around the Potteries (described below) and the railways to attract the clients they were hoping for. Thus, houses built in the remoter areas, designed for single families and their servants, very soon became tenement blocks, leased off piecemeal at low rents. Others became overcrowded boarding houses. By the late 1860s, whole streets on the Norland Estate were crammed full of tenants very different from those for whom they had been designed, and squalor soon set in.

By the end of the nineteenth century, the area was marked by pockets of tremendous wealth, a good proportion of middle-class inhabitants, plus a massively growing working-class population hemmed into declining housing in areas away from the fashionable centres. A not dissimilar situation exists in several parts of Notting Hill today.

Notting Dale

Just to the west of Notting Hill, on land which formed part of the Norland Estate (originally part of Abbot's Manor Kensington), was an area known in the1800s as the Kensington Potteries, later absorbed by Notting Dale. From early days, gypsies settled here on a seasonal basis, arriving in late spring. The soil of the area is of yellow clay, ideal for making bricks to supply the rapidly expanding buildings of London. A large brick-field was established, as well as a pottery which made tiles, drains and pots, and the industry thrived until the clay was worked out by the 1860s. Over this period labourers flooded in, many driven from Ireland during the years of the potato famine, and by the middle of the century the area was already overcrowded with unregulated housing.

Alongside the brick-makers grew a population of pig-keepers. The colony was started in 1818 when Samuel Lake, scavenger, chimney sweep and pig-keeper, was forced to move from his previous premises in Tottenham Court Road. He leased land near to the brick-fields, with the idea that this isolated rural spot would cause less distress to the neighbours. Quite a colony developed – by the 1840s the settlement comprised 'a small village, where no less than 3,000 pigs shared 260 hovels with 1,000 inhabitants'. In an area of very poor drainage, there were no proper roads, let alone proper sewerage, and the need to boil down the fat and offal of the animals as part of the industry led to a horribly fetid and unhealthy atmosphere. Life expectancy was very low: in the years 1846-48 the average age of death was eleven years and seven months, compared to 37 years for the rest of London – and this was before the cholera epidemic of 1849.

Conditions continued to worsen. Cholera struck again in 1854, but in the next decade the population rapidly increased as people moved in from other parts of Kensington and from Paddington, driven out by slum clearances and the building of the railways. The plight of the inhabitants of Notting Dale finally came to national attention when the *Morning Post* published a shocking report, declaring it to be a 'West-End Avernus' (avernus meaning 'the mouth of hell').

Amid all this squalor, given the uncertain employment of the men as work in the brick-fields dried up, the women turned to laundering and ironing, by taking in washing from well-to-do households. By the end of the nineteenth century there were so many businesses that the area became known as 'Laundry Land'. Some of this work was extremely skilled, and a local saying went that 'to marry an ironer is as good as a fortune'.

Poverty, social problems and the birth of the housing trusts

Until the establishment of the London County Council (LCC) in 1898, local government, such as it was, was in the hands of the Kensington Vestry, which cared little about the growing social problems in the area. Following the famous 'Avernus' article in the *Morning Post*, on the urging of the parish priest of the church of St Francis of Assisi, the Vestry Works Committee undertook an inspection, only to report that any existing problems were merely 'brought about by the vicious proclivities and evil habits of the people themselves'.

The Vestry was a tight-fisted body. For instance, it delayed in allowing a public wash-house in Notting Dale on the grounds that, since so many families made their living from laundering, it might well be used for commercial purposes. They also did nothing to alleviate threats to public health from the particularly putrid expanse of clay sludge and pigswill known as 'the ocean'. Eventually, it was the parish priest of St Clement's who initiated a project to fill it in; he managed to raise £637 by publishing a letter of appeal in *The Times*, and the area was eventually covered over in 1892 to become what is still Avondale Park.

This initiative by a parish priest was, in many ways, typical of the plethora of philanthropic activities carried out by churches, private individuals, associations, trusts and clubs that arose to fill the vacuum left by a lack of concern from local government. It was part of the tradition of community self-help and direct action that has characterised the area for so long.

In spite of certain charitable efforts, the fundamental problem of inadequate housing remained unresolved, particularly in the region of Notting Dale. In 1898, the newly formed LCC instructed a medical officer to investigate the area, and accepted his recommendations that it should buy and renovate lodging-houses and also build more itself. By this time, Notting Dale had been nicknamed 'The Guilt Garden' and certain streets had been designated as constituting a 'Special Area'. The then mayor of Kensington made a large interest-free loan, and by 1906 had built 120 new tenements, housing 490 people.

Here again, the efforts of private individuals played an important part. Two pioneers in improving housing conditions for the poor, Octavia Hill and Amy Hayne, joined forces with other like-minded people, such as Octavia's cousin, Sir Reginald Rowe, to buy houses, renovate them and encourage the tenants to take an interest in maintenance and upkeep. They put a tremendous amount of energy into improving conditions and in working alongside the 'shiftless, the pauperised, the unemployed and the almost unemployable' as they described them and thus formed the first housing trust in the area: The Improved Tenements Association. In 1920, this trust amalgamated with the Wilsham Trust (which had been formed by ladies-in-waiting at Kensington Palace) to form the Rowe Housing Trust.

The Kensington Housing Trust followed in 1926, along with the Sutton Dwellings and the Peabody Trusts. By the 1930s, between them these three Trusts had built almost twice as many new dwellings as the borough council.

At last tenements actually designed for multiple occupation were erected. Something was being done, but it was never enough.

War and the roots of immigration from the Caribbean

As with the rest of the country, the First World War caused many casualties among young men. Left at home, the women became involved in the war effort by working in munitions factories and making canvas field tents for the front. Although bombing in the Second World War did not devastate the area, the local population was dislocated, and suffered its fair share of damage. In addition, one particular development at this time was to have an unprecedented impact on Notting Hill's history: the recruitment of people from the Caribbean into the armed forces.

The first group of recruits was made up of sons of professionals and administrators who came over as volunteers to join the RAF as officers at the start of the war. A second group was later actively enlisted to provide supply staff for maintenance of front-line fighters in the invasion of Europe. These ground crews came from a wide social spectrum, including farmers and agricultural labourers. As Mike and Trevor Phillips write in *Windrush*, 'this was an unprecedented opportunity for them to travel abroad and to change the entire course of their lives. This time recruitment was by invitation and, instead of in hundreds, they came in their thousands.' In spite of the grim circumstances, these recruits were welcomed with warmth. Many wanted to stay on at the end of the war, but were encouraged to repatriate.

Following repatriation, there was a general eagerness to return to the UK. Conditions in the Caribbean were very poor, the war having totally disrupted the sugar trade upon which many of the islands' economies depended. Also, the war had opened West Indian eyes to the fact that people did actually work in England – they weren't all of the 'governor' class to which the population had previously been exposed. Moreover, in a UK busy trying to reconstruct itself after the war, there were clearly plenty of opportunities for work.

Word soon got around that passages to England were available on a troop carrier, the *SS Empire Windrush*. A Jamaican newspaper, *The Gleaner*, declared the fare to be 28 pounds and ten shillings, and many got together to find the funds for the journey. Others boarded the ship as stowaways. On 24 May 1948, the *Windrush* left Jamaica with between 450 and 490 West Indians on board, the majority of them young men. They had a perfect right to return to the 'mother country' and as much right as any other citizen to live there: the 1948 British Nationality Act confirmed this. Stories of life on board during this journey reflect an exuberant group of people, buoyed up with hope, fully expecting work, roofs over their heads and a proper welcome as total citizens. By many accounts, these young men were not wanting to spend a lifetime in the UK; most hoped to earn some good money and return home after a few years.

Late 1940s and early 1950s England was drab, recovering from the war and still enduring the restrictions of rationing. Men returned from battle hoping for heroic futures to reflect their wartime experiences; they found instead depression, restriction and little space to live in. Although Notting Hill and Notting Dale had not been as badly bombed as the East End, housing conditions had worsened during the war, as even further decay set in. Overcrowded dwellings were, as ever, infested with bugs and rats; basements were frequently flooded. The piecemeal attempts to improve the situation over the previous decades had been insufficient, and the majority of the poor in Notting Hill and Dale were still living in three-storey terraced houses designed for one family.

This depressed area with its cheap housing was one of those to receive the steady flow of Caribbean arrivals from 1948 onwards. The immigrants did not receive the welcome they had expected. In fact the future looked grim for the unsuspecting passengers on the *Windrush* who, before setting foot on British soil, were already perceived as a problem. As the boat steamed towards England, anxious letters were being passed between Government Ministries questioning who had instigated and organised this regrettable movement. Inevitably, the press took up the story, with the *Daily Express* announcing the arrival of '500 unwanted passengers'.

On landing at Tilbury Docks, those classified as having 'no contacts in the UK' were placed in shelters. As soon as they found work, they moved out to join those already searching for somewhere to live. This proved difficult. Notting Hill was not the only place in England to begin displaying 'No Irish, No Blacks, No Dogs' signs in the windows of properties to let, but it was one of them. It was also an area where countless willing West Indian workers applied for posts (often below their qualifications) to be told that, for various spurious reasons (other workers wouldn't like it, the union would object etc), they couldn't be taken on.

In some ways, the decade from 1948 was one of the ugliest periods in the area's history in that it exposed a previously unmined vein of racism, culminating in the vicious riots of 1958 and the murder of an innocent man nine months later.

The 1950s–60s: shame, scandal and sleaze

Shame: riots and the killing of Kelso Cochrane

The immediate circumstances leading up to the riots of 1958 involved a spate of attacks on black immigrants by gangs of white youths throughout the summer. It was not an organised movement, but racist sentiments were already being whipped up by the activities of Oswald Mosley's neo-Fascist Union Movement (he was to stand as a parliamentary candidate for North Kensington in 1959 on a platform of 'Keep Britain White'). At the end of August, full-scale rioting broke out in Nottingham, to be followed a week later by three days of mayhem in Notting Hill. Large groups of youths stampeded through the streets, trashing any commercial premises known to be 'friendly' to blacks, and attacking any Caribbean immigrants they encountered. Although this was regarded as the worst race riot the country had ever seen, nobody was killed.

The wider circumstances of these events were, undoubtedly, far more significant than given credit for by the judge who condemned nine white youths after the disturbances as being 'a minute and insignificant section of the population'. One of the most shocking aspects of the riots is the way in which people apparently just stood by and let them happen.

It was not a simple case of xenophobia. The community was long used to absorbing immigrant populations. There was already a well-established Polish and Eastern European community in the area, along with many Spanish who came here during and after the Spanish Civil War. There were also quite a few Serbs and Portuguese. But with the West Indians, as with the Irish who arrived so much earlier, the reaction was different. The lack of a welcome was certainly connected with muddled ideas about Empire: people in the colonies were considered as inferior and belonging 'over there'. The fact that the West Indians were not foreign immigrants but newcomers taking up their rightful place as citizens was a cause of panic; they were feared as a threat to jobs and houses – a fear that intensified with the Rent Act of 1957 (see Rachman, pp 174–5) and the economic downturn in 1958.

An element of perverse moral panic or maybe collective sexual jealousy was also involved. Again, the prejudice ran deep and was widespread; there were plenty of examples of employers forbidding West Indian men from working alongside white female workers on the grounds that the former amounted to some kind of threat. In addition, Notting Hill represented a particular case: its proximity to the West End had resulted in the neighbourhood becoming an offshoot of the Soho vice empires and an overspill area for the prostitutes who lined up along the Bayswater Road. As Mike Phillips remarks in *Notting Hill in the Sixties*: 'whilst many immigrants deeply resented the propinquity with what they saw as vice and immorality, others plunged enthusiastically into the life they found here'. Some of the young men were determined to have a good time, which they organised with a style, glamour and openness quite new to Notting Hill. A network of clubs, 'blues' and shebeens was established – places to hang out and party.

The disaffected white youths who terrorised the streets for those three days of riots resented this gregarious, exotic scene which attracted a mixture of white people, including young women. It is no accident that accounts of both the Nottingham and Notting Hill riots record that they were sparked off by attacks on white women with black partners.

The following spring, a quiet-living carpenter from Antigua called Kelso Cochrane was stabbed to death in the street by six white youths. The killers were never identified. This murder sent a wave of shame and shock throughout the community. Cochrane's funeral at Kensal Green Cemetery was one of the biggest ever held in the area: the procession was joined by more than 1,200 people in a dignified public display of mourning. The event marked a turning point. Influenced by the Civil Rights and Black Power movements in the United States, with leaders such as Darcus Howe, Ben Bousquet, Stokely Carmichael, and Michael de Freitas (later known as Michael X, see pp 198–201), from this time onwards the black community became determined to assert itself.

Scandal: the Profumo Affair

Notting Hill again came to public notice in the early 1960s during the course of the Profumo Affair, one of the most sensational scandals in recent political history. At the core of the affair was beautiful good-time girl Christine Keeler, who divided her time between various flats in the West End and Notting Hill, and Spring Cottage on the luxurious Cliveden Estate, owned by Lord Astor. She also frequented cafés such as the Rio and Fiesta One in Notting Hill.

As well as her West Indian boyfriend, Johnny Edgecombe, Keeler's consorts included Lucky Gordon (another West Indian), Stephen Ward (society osteopath and friend to the rich), Jack Profumo (the Minister of War) and Captain Eugene Ivanov (a Russian military attaché). The national security risk and, hence, the national scandal centred on the Keeler–Profumo–Ivanov triangle. Rumours were already circulating during 1962, but the events leading up to the disclosures involved a series of violent misunderstandings between Keeler, Gordon and Edgecombe. At one point, Edgecombe needed to talk to Keeler, who was holed up with her friend and colleague Mandy Rice-Davies (mistress to Peter Rachman) in Stephen Ward's West End flat. When she refused to let him in, he tried to gain entry by firing gun shots at the door to break the lock. Edgecombe ended up being charged with attempted assault and possession of a firearm, and Gordon with assault. During their court case disclosures concerning Profumo and others emerged, leading to Profumo's resignation and Stephen Ward's suicide as he awaited trial.

The press had a field day and the copy made riveting reading, but the implications for Notting Hill were darker. Again the area was in the headlines, but associated with notoriety rather than fame, and the affair disclosed yet another unsavoury aspect in the underbelly of Notting Hill's history: the activities of Peter Rachman.

Sleaze: Peter Rachman's shady empire

Rachman died in 1962, a year before the Profumo scandal broke. His role in it was marginal, but his activities came under the public gaze owing to his close association with Mandy Rice-Davies and Christine Keeler. The extent of his slum empire and range of shady activities were well known locally, and the local press had long been on his case, but it was the Profumo Affair that raised his reputation to that of a national villain.

Born in Poland, the son of a Jewish dentist, Rachman fled to England after the war, in 1946. He fell in with property tycoons and began controlling a few flats in Bayswater, let out mainly to prostitutes, and soon became a property-owner. By 1955 he owned houses in and around Powis Square and Colville Terrace, the most notorious of the slums. At its height, his empire included more than a hundred buildings in West London. He also extended his activities to gambling and nightclubs. His method was to buy run-down properties at extremely low prices, divide them up into multiple tenements, and then let and sub-let them at extortionate rents. He had a network of agents, middle-men and rent-collectors running his empire, and was a very difficult man to pin down.

In 1957, a new Rent Act was passed, decontrolling the rents that could be charged on furnished properties once any sitting tenants had moved out. The idea was to increase the housing stock available. Instead, it led to landlords such as Rachman forcibly evicting sitting tenants and reletting properties at vastly inflated prices. In Notting Hill, many of those threatened or forced out of their flats were poor working-class white tenants, only to be replaced by the pool of homeless West Indians desperate for somewhere to live. A deeply ambiguous character, Rachman championed himself as a 'friend of the coloureds', and it was true that he was one of the few landlords who did not operate a 'No blacks' policy. Also, several who knew him speak of his kindness to old ladies. The whole truth of Rachman's activities was never established, but the word 'Rachmanism' entered the vernacular as synonymous with the exploitation of slum tenants by unscrupulous landlords.

The rest of the 1960s and 1970s: community action, redevelopment and Carnival

After the infamies of the previous years, the rest of the 1960s and 70s brought further new twists in the area's history. Changes during these decades laid the basis for much of what attracts contemporary visitors to the area: it became truly multicultural, the Carnival injected a large dose of excitement and joy, and Notting Hill began to be fashionable in an off-beat kind of way, as new waves of people moved in.

Community action

> *After you have finished beating each other up, you still have to live in the same area. People found eventually that they had to*

> *live together and love each other. It is a process that people knew should happen.* (Ben Bousquet, quoted in Sharon Whetlor, *The Story of Notting Dale*)

Following the riots, there was a considerable amount of rethinking and regrouping in the community. The Methodist Church in Lancaster Road took one of the first initiatives (see p 130). The church already had strong links with the West Indies and brought in young priests to help organise a truly mixed congregation, welcoming all. It was one of the main instigators of the Notting Hill Social Council, an informal forum involving a wide spectrum of community and social workers, who met to discuss and find solutions to housing problems, race conflicts and disaffected youth. These developments were part of a wider anti-racist movement which was sweeping the whole country.

Other voluntary organisations that began in the 1960s included the Notting Hill Housing Trust, set up in 1963 by Bruce Kenrick, a Presbyterian minister who went on to start Shelter, a national campaign for the homeless. Also, the Notting Hill Community Workshop developed in the mid-1960s into the Notting Hill Summer Project. Again involving a coalition of churches, local groups and volunteers, the Project organised a housing survey. Its findings provided depressing echoes of those of a century earlier: in some areas 70 per cent of households had either only shared or no access at all to a bath or shower. The Project also set up three neighbourhood centres and organised adventure playgrounds for children. Although it made a start at tackling social problems, it could not prevent some of the ugliest redevelopments taking place, such as the Lancaster West Estate – buildings epitomising poor planning and design. Two of the longest and most successful campaigns arising from the devastation caused by redevelopment plans in the building of the Westway were the achievement of low-cost housing for the former squatters of Frestonia (see p 132 & pp 211–14) and the establishment of the North Kensington Amenity Trust.

Part and parcel of all this community action was the diversifying population. The spirit of defiance and anarchic optimism which suffused most of these movements was catching and, throughout this time, students, writers, musicians, artists, hippies, social workers and political activists began to move in, further attracted by the cosmopolitan atmosphere. Notting Hill was finally becoming fashionable again.

Carnival: pageant, symbol, ritual of resistance?

The 1960s saw the hey-day of Caribbean street and night life, centred on the many local clubs and bars, such as Frank Critchlow's Rio Café, and on the many informal meeting places in the Hill, the Dale and the Grove. From the early Sixties onwards, for those less intimate with but attracted by the scene, the August bank holiday Carnival came to symbolise the *joie de vivre* embodied by

West Indian culture. From small beginnings, the Carnival had developed by the end of the Sixties into one of the largest outdoor celebrations on the calendar, attracting participants from far beyond the immediate community. Outsiders were largely made welcome and joined in the dance. (One of this writer's finest memories is that of sheltering under the Westway during Carnival 1972 and joining in with an impromptu calypso: 'Rain Won't Stop the Carnival!')

But, at the same time as outsiders were becoming attracted to all the fun of the Carnival, storm clouds were again beginning to gather around the community that originally developed it. During the late Sixties, many of the housing areas where the Caribbean population had been concentrated were being pulled down and rebuilt, involving dispersal of the population into more distant suburbs. Along with this, the latter-day sprawling street life began to shrink into a few islands. In this context, as Mike and Trevor Phillips point out in *Windrush*, for those who flocked in from the suburbs to take part in the processions, the Carnival became 'a symbol of the West Indians' continuing presence in the spot haunted by so many memories; and from all over West London they came to stage a re-creation of the legends of the Hill, the Dale and the Grove'.

Carnival had also become a symbol for the police, one of urban exuberance and disorder: something they did not control. Throughout the 1970s relations between the black community and the police went from bad to worse. In an example of policing gone mad, they launched a massive attack on inner-city crime, for which special units (the Special Patrol Groups) were deployed and equipped with knowledge of a particular power – to charge 'a suspected person loitering with intent to commit an offence'. This application of the Vagrancy Act of 1824 became know as the SUS laws,whereby black people and especially black youths were targeted in what amounted to a witch-hunt.

The Carnival provided the most dramatic example of over-policing. Until 1976, despite ever-growing crowds, it was a peaceful occasion; but the police wanted it banned. When this failed, they mobilised 1,500 to police the event, fighting broke out and 500 were injured. By the following August, the Carnival had become a 'Public Order' issue and listed under the category 'Demonstrations' in the Police Commissioner's report. Ensuing years saw the Carnival become a focus for provocation, counter-provocation and violence, until 1981 when the number of police officers deployed had risen to 13,000. That year marked a watershed, as riots in protest over police discrimination against black people erupted throughout the country. A wholesale reassessment of police practices was put in motion and, although it was never quite the same again, the Carnival was re-established as an occasion for fun.

Today it is a massive event, attracting close to two million people and, is not without crime. In the wake of two fatal stabbings during the celebrations of August 2000, policing tactics are yet again under scrutiny, as is the fate of the

Carnival itself. Yet, as Polly Thomas points out in her piece 'Growing up with Carnival' (see pp 223–27), it is hard to envisage such a happening anywhere but on the streets of W10 and W11.

Recent developments

> *Now it's THE place to live in I dread the future! Two tiny words that are worth millions: West Eleven . . . We have nothing against new residents and natural progress of evolution, but if people do not like to live among the working-class folk then please leave. We will not change for you nor alter our beloved Portobello.* (Rosalind Da Costa, *Notting Hill Revealed*)

Of course, much has changed since the heady days of the 1960s and 70s. In streets like All Saints Road and Westbourne Grove, 'blues' have given way to boutiques and upmarket restaurants, shebeens have been replaced by chi-chi cafés and delicatessens and a halfway house for the homeless has been turned into a fashionable hotel. Large impersonal chains are taking over quirky old shops and public houses, and mansion blocks in places like Powis Square are finally being occupied by the kind of people for which they were originally designed: the rich, the fashionable, the professionals. Carnival is now a massive and well-orchestrated event, further and further removed from its roots in Trinidad.

The ghosts of Reverend Walker and his colleagues might well welcome some of these changes, but many old-time locals resent such signs of gentrification. Perhaps they needn't fear so much. Even in the face of so many conflicting interests, the market appears to be thriving and community action is still a key element of the area. Many of the oldest-established secular and church organisations continue to flourish, and new ones are growing up to meet changing needs. Since the 1960s and 70s, a new population of Moroccans has arrived, centred around Golborne Road and the Muslim Cultural Heritage Centre in Acklam Road; the Gheez Rite Community Association has been set up at St Francis of Assisi Church in Pottery Lane, to provide a meeting place for Ethiopians and Eritreans; the London Lighthouse, once Europe's largest residential and support centre for those affected by AIDS and HIV, has successfully adapted in the face of threatened closure; the Tabernacle has a great restaurant, as well as providing a low-cost venue for wide-ranging cultural events. The list goes on. Notting Hill's rich, mixed, bumpy history looks well set to roller-coaster its way into the twenty-first century.

Part 3

WRITINGS 1767–2000

Days in the Life of Lady Mary Coke 1767–69

Lady Mary Coke was born on 2 February 1726, the youngest daughter of John, Duke of Argyll and Greenwich. In 1747 she married Edward, Viscount Coke, only son of Thomas, Earl of Leicester. After two years of constant disagreement they separated, and he died in 1753. A wealthy widow, Lady Mary moved to Notting Hill in 1767, where she took up residence at Aubrey House close to Holland Park. Nicknamed the 'White Cat' on account of her albino colouring and passion for gossip – the cattier the better – she remained here for 22 years. Apart from Court gossip and politics, Lady Mary dearly loved her garden, which in those days extended almost as far as Holland Park Avenue. These interests, together with such familiar topics as neighbour disputes, vandalism, the ill-health of royals, flooding and the inconveniences of having builders in the house, are reflected in these few extracts from her letters and journals. Lady Mary remained in Aubrey House until 1788 and died, still a widow, in the Manor House at Chiswick in 1811. She is buried in Henry VII's chapel in Westminster Abbey. The four volumes of her writings from which these extracts are taken were edited by the Hon JA Home and published in 1889–96.

1767

Saturday

The wind continues very high & there has been several showers of rain. I went at ten o'clock to my House. I had appointed a Gentleman that lives in the Neighbourhood, one Mr Phillimore, to come & speak to me. He has a field that comes close up to my garden, which wou'd be very convenient for me to have, & I offer'd him anything he pleased to ask, either to buy it or rent it. His answer was he had let it a long time ago, & he supposed all his estate that lies about here was worth the double what he let it for, but that he never raised his rents, that he was now old, & that everything shou'd go on in the way it had during his time, & that he cou'd not sell it as it was intailed upon his Son, who was under age. I then ask'd if he had any objection to my taking it of his tenant. To this he did not care to make me an answer, but in conclusion said he wou'd think of it & write me word, for he was going farther into the Country for a Month. I then told him I had another favour to beg, that he might Observe there was a tree in his ground that very much interrupted my view, & that I shou'd be much obliged to him if he wou'd cut it down. To this he agreed & said he wou'd order it to be done, & I am not out of hopes of getting the field. His Son that he mentioned had this year a fortune of a hundred thousand pounds left to him. I cou'd not help liking the Old Man, he seemed so disinterested.

1768

Friday

'Tis a very fine day, which makes me impatient to get back to my small retreat, & having no curiosity to learn the news of the Birthday, I am leaving Town without seeing a human being. No losses among my animals, but of one duck. This place looks in greater beauty than you have seen it, notwithstanding the malice of some unknown enemy, who has cut down all the roses & honeysuckles that were planted in my North Walk near the benches even with the ground, & done the same to all the flowers that were in bloom. I wonder they think I have too many pleasures, as they seem desirous of depriving me of all that is in their power. The Plasterers are still in my new rooms, & have fixt their Scaffolds in such a manner that I can't get in to see the situation they are in. I found employment in my garden till it was dark, & then writt & read. It wou'd seem as if I had been amused, for I set up till after one o'clock, not thinking it so late by above an hour. The Gentleman Dove is setting upon one egg, the perverseness of the Lady having occasion'd the breaking of the other; but She is now so ill treated, I forgive & pity her. She seem'd to desire (& I thought very reasonably) to hatch her own egg, but whenever She shew'd that inclination, her Husband used her so ruffly that he has not left her one feather in her tail, & has deprived her of several in her head. She has now very wisely given up the attempt, & I expect the Gentleman to hatch on Sunday or Monday.

1768

Wednesday

'Tis a very fine day. I have all sorts of Workmen about, & am very impatient for the fence in the North Walk being finished; the sheep have broke in again last night & done me more mischief. I hope for you I shall see somebody from Town before the week is ended, otherwise it will be a terrible dull journal. I've heard nothing from Lady Betty Mackenzie since She left Town, & as She did not tell me how to direct to her, I fancy She does not mean I shou'd write. In the Evening we walked on the outside of my grounds into some very pretty fields, which leads us to the back part of Kensington; 'twas warm & pleasant. Have you ever read Mademoiselle's Memoires? You must remember I recommended them to you before you went to Yorkshire, as I'm persuaded they will entertain you better than any other that was wrote at the same period of time. She mentions a circumstance relating to the death of the Queen Mother of England, her Aunt, that I don't recollect having met with anywhere else. She says She was always unhealthy, & that, after her last return to France, She was advised to take pills to make her sleep which succeeded so well that She never waked again. I suppose they put too great a quantity of opium by mistake, for there does not seem the least reason to believe it was intended. Tell Lord Strafford my Servants are very busy making sweetmeats that he may not be without a dessert when he is so good to dine with me, for I despair of ever seeing him at this time of the Year, when, if my garden had not been robbed, I cou'd have given him excellent plumbs of three different kinds; the poor remains are now making into sweetmeats, as they tell me they do mighty well. I have great plenty of apples, & some good pears, but as they are now ripe, I dread a second visit.

Thursday
At twelve o'clock it began raining, which continued one hour; 'tis now fair... It did not hold fair above a quarter of an hour, & after the rain began again it never ceased, & about eight o'clock it was with a violence I almost never heard. I don't suppose there cou'd ever fall a greater quantity of rain in the time. My Workmen, when they return'd to Town, could not go by Knightsbridge, the water lay too deep. It continued raining all night.

Friday
When I got up this morning I saw two Rivers, the grounds two or three miles off being all under water, & the Thames made a fine appearance. My Servants tell me two Houses at Knightsbridge have been washed away, & one of the Bridges on the King's road. It has almost carried away all my gravel walks, and my garden is the Picture of desolation.

1769
Friday
'Tis a very pleasant day: I did not pass it in Town. I was here very early & have worked very hard in my garden and have given up Lady Holland's Assembly to finish my journal, as you was so good to wish to hear from me before you left Boughton. I propose going to Sudbrook on Sunday & I shall call at Kew, tho' I think it is not probable I shall find Lady Charlotte, as I imagine the young Princes will go to Town that day. My best wishes attend Lord Strafford. Pray tell M' Hull, as Soon as it is convenient, I shall be glad to have my Cow.

Saturday
I sow'd a great many flowers before eleven o'clock. 'Till then it was a pleasant day: soon after it rain'd, & has continued ever since. 'Tis now one o'clock. My prospect is much enliven'd by a dozen Women gathering peas in the field joining to my garden: they are so merry, & laugh so excessively that it gave me spirits to hear them, but this abominable rain has drove them out of the field & me out of my garden . . . The rain is over, & I must go out. The evening made up for the rainy morning; it was quite clear, & I think I never saw the prospect in greater beauty.

Clarendon Road *circa* 1883: from the autobiography of Arthur Machen

Arthur Machen was a writer and specialist in the occult. In 1880, aged 17, he left his native Wales for London where he lodged for some 18 months in Clarendon Road near Holland Park. When he wasn't writing, much of his time was spent cataloguing diabolistic and occult books, through which he discovered various secret sects and societies, and joined the Order of the Golden Dawn. Machen is best remembered for his mystic, supernatural tales of evil and horror, among them *The Great God Pan* (1894), *The Hill of Dreams* (1907) and *The Three Imposters* (1895). The extracts below are taken from his autobiography, *Far Off Things*, published in 1922. He died in 1947.

At this time and for the next year and a half I was living in Clarendon Road, Notting Hill Gate – or Holland Park, to give the politer sub direction. I am sorry to say that I had not a garret, since the houses of that quarter, being comparatively modern, do not possess the sloping roofs which have seen the miseries of so many lettered men. Still, my room had its merits. It was, of course, at the top of the house, and it was much smaller than any monastic 'cell' that I have ever seen. From recollection I should estimate its dimensions as ten feet by five. It held a bed, a washstand, a small table, and one chair; and so it was very fortunate that I had few visitors. Outside, on the landing, I kept my big wooden box with all my possessions – and these not many – in it. And there was a very notable circumstance about this landing. On the wall was suspended, lengthwise, a step-ladder by which one could climb through a trap door to the roof in case of fire, and so between the rungs or steps of this ladder I disposed my library. For anything I know, the books tasted as well thus housed as they did at a later period when I kept them in an eighteenth-century bookcase of noble dark mahogany, behind glass doors. There was no fireplace in my room, and I was often very cold. I would sit in my shabby old great-coat, reading or writing, and if I were writing I would every now and then stand up and warm my hands over the gas-jet, to prevent my fingers getting numb. I remember envying a man very much indeed on a certain night in late winter or early spring. It was a very cold night; there was a bitter north-easter blowing, and the wind seemed to pierce right through my old coat and to set my very bones shivering and aching. I had gone abroad, because I was weary of my den, because I was sick with reading and in no humour for writing, because I felt I must have some change, however slight. But it was an evil and a bitter blast, so I turned back after a little while, coming down one of the steep streets that lead from Notting Hill Gate Station to Clarendon Road. And half-way home I came upon a man encamped on the road by the pavement. He was watching over some barrows and tools and other instruments of street repair, and he sat in a sort of canvas wigwam, well sheltered from the wind that was chilling me to the heart. His coat, too, looked thick and heavy, and he had a warm comforter round his neck, and before him was a glowing, ardent brazier of red-hot coals. He held his hands and his nose over the radiant heat, and smoked a black clay pipe; and I think he had a can of beer beside him. I envied that man with all my heart; I don't think I have ever envied any man so much.

Occasionally I had applications for the loan of a book from my step-ladder library. These came from the lodgers on the ground floor, an Armenian and his wife, who annoyed the landlady by sleeping in cushions piled about the carpet and hanging their blankets in front of the doors and windows. It was the Armenian lady who had literary tastes, and her desire was always for 'a story book'. I never saw her or her husband, but I often heard him calling Mary, the servant. He would stand at the top of the kitchen stairs and shout 'Marry! Marry!' and then, reflectively, and after a short interval, 'Damn that girl.' He gave a fine, oriental force to the common English 'damn'. Other lodgers that I remember were a young Greek and a chorus girl, mates for a single summer. They occupied the first floor and were succeeded by a family from Ireland. I have a confused notion that there was something a little queer about the head of this household. He was, I think, a major and I know he was Evangelical. As I went down the stairs I heard him more than once muttering in loud, earnest tones the words 'Let us pray.' This was startling; and one of his daughters would always shut the door of their room with a bang on these occasions, and that was startling, too.

The little table in my little room turned out to be a very useful piece of furniture. I not only read at it and wrote on it, but I used it as a larder. In the corner nearest the angle of the wall by the window I kept my provisions, that is to say, a loaf of bread and a canister of green tea. Morning and evening the landlady or 'Marry' would bring me up a tray on which were a plate, a knife, a teapot and a spirit lamp, which came, I think, from under that serviceable table – one may fairly say from the cellar – I made the hot water to boil and brewed a great pot of strong green tea . . . .

As the spring of 1883 advanced, and the weather improved and the evenings lengthened, I began the habit of rambling abroad in the hope of finding something that could be called country. I would sometimes pursue Clarendon Road northward and get into all sorts of regions of which I never had any clear notion. They are obscure to me now, and a sort of nightmare. I see myself getting terribly entangled with a canal which seemed to cross my path in a manner contrary to the laws of reason. I turn a corner and am confronted with an awful cemetery, a terrible city of white gravestones and shattered marble pillars and granite urns, and every sort of horrid heathenry. This, I suppose, must have been Kensal Green: it added new terror to death. I think I came upon Kensal Green again and again; it was like the Malay, an enemy for months. I would break off by way of Portobello Road and entangle myself in Notting Hill, and presently I would come upon the goblin city; I might wander into the Harrow Road, but at last the ghost-stones would appal me. Maida Vale was treacherous, Paddington false – inevitably, it seemed, my path led me to the detested habitation of the dead.

The Napoleon of Notting Hill
GK Chesterton

Gilbert Keith Chesterton became a professional writer in his twenties when he made his name in journalism, 'the easiest of all professions'. He was principally a reviewer and essayist. Among the newspapers he regularly contributed to was the *Daily News*, founded by Charles Dickens. *The Napoleon of Notting Hill* (1904), a bizarre fantasy set at the end of the twentieth century, was his first novel. The main protagonists are Auberon Quin (the King) and Adam Wayne, Provost of Notting Hill and the Napoleon of the title. Inspired by the waterworks tower that once dominated Campden Hill, it is a comic, bellicose and somewhat confusing tale of a small community resisting destruction by the march of progress and modernity. Chesterton went on to write many other novels, as well as verse, literary criticism and his *Autobiography* (1936) from which the first of these two passages is taken. He became a Roman Catholic in 1922 and died 12 years later at the age of 62.

I was one day wandering about the streets in part of North Kensington, telling myself stories of feudal sallies and sieges, in the manner of Walter Scott, and vaguely trying to apply them to the wilderness of bricks and mortar around me. I felt that London was already too large and loose a thing to be a city in the sense of a citadel. It seemed to me even larger and looser than the British Empire. And something irrationally arrested and pleased my eye about the look of one small block of little lighted shops, and I amused myself with the supposition that these alone were to be preserved and defended, like a hamlet in a desert. I found it quite exciting to count them and perceive that they contained the essentials of a civilisation, a chemist's shop, a bookshop, a provision merchant for food and a public house for drink. Lastly, to my great delight, there was also an old curiosity shop bristling with swords and halberds; manifestly intended to arm the guard that was to fight for the sacred street. I wondered vaguely what they would attack or whither they would advance. And looking up, I saw grey with distance, but still seemingly immense in altitude, the tower of the Waterworks close to the street where I was born. It suddenly occurred to me that capturing the Waterworks might really mean the military stroke of flooding the valley; and with that torrent and cataract of visionary waters, the first fantastic notion of a tale called *The Napoleon of Notting Hill* rushed over my mind.

Extract from *The Napoleon of Notting Hill*

'My God in Heaven!' he said; 'is it possible that there is within the four seas of Britain a man who takes Notting Hill seriously?'

'And my God in Heaven!' said Wayne passionately; 'is it possible that there is within the four seas of Britain a man who does not take it seriously?'

The King said nothing, but merely went back up the steps of the dais, like a man dazed. He fell back in his chair again and kicked his heels.

'If this sort of thing is to go on', he said weakly, 'I shall begin to doubt the superiority of art to life. In Heaven's name, do not play with me. Do you really mean that you are – God help me! – a Notting Hill patriot – that you are...'

Wayne made a violent gesture, and the King soothed him wildly.

'All right – all right – I see you are; but let me take it in.You do really propose to fight these modern improvers with their boards and inspectors and surveyors and all the rest of it -'

'Are they so terrible?' asked Wayne, scornfully.

The King continued to stare at him as if he were a human curiosity.

'And I suppose', he said, 'that you think that the dentists and small tradesmen and maiden ladies who inhabit Notting Hill will rally with war-hymns to your standard?'

'If they have blood they will,' said the Provost.

'And I suppose', said the King, with his head back among the cushions, 'that it never crossed your mind that' – his voice seemed to lose itself luxuriantly – 'never crossed your mind that anyone ever thought that the idea of a Notting Hill idealism was – er – slightly – slightly ridiculous.'

'Of course they think so,' said Wayne. 'What was the meaning of mocking the prophets?'

'Where?' asked the King, leaning forward. 'Where in Heaven's name did you get this miraculously inane idea?'

'You have been my tutor, Sire', said the Provost, 'in all that is high and honourable.'

'Eh?' said the King.

All Done from Memory

Osbert Lancaster

Sir Osbert Lancaster (1908–1986), artist and writer, was best known as a cartoonist on the *Daily Express* from 1939. He also designed stage sets for several theatrical productions and wrote many books, including two volumes of autobiography, *All Done from Memory* (1963) and *With an Eye to the Future* (1967). The following extract from the first volume tells of his childhood around Notting Hill.

In my subconscious eagerness to prolong my evening stroll, I must have walked right through the haunted district I had set out to explore and emerged into the once familiar playground of my childhood on the slopes of Notting Hill. The fact that I had done so all unawares, that I had passed the formerly so firmly established boundary line without for a moment realising it, spoke far more clearly of what had happened here in the last thirty years than could many volumes of social history. As I walked on up the hill, regardless for once of a flying-bomb now following the course of Ladbroke Grove seemingly only just above the chimney-pots, I noticed with a certain proprietary satisfaction that the progress of decay had not been halted at Elgin Crescent; that the squares and terraces that had once formed the very Acropolis of Edwardian propriety grouped round the church had suffered a hardly less severe decline. Some of the most obvious signs of degradation were certainly the result of five years of war and common to all parts of London, but here this enforced neglect was clearly but a temporary acceleration of a continuous process. The vast stucco palaces of Kensington Park Road and the adjoining streets had long ago been converted into self-contained flats where an ever-increasing stream of refugees from every part of the once civilised world had found improvised homes, like the dark-age troglodytes who sheltered in the galleries and boxes of the Colosseum. Long, long before the outbreak of war these classical facades had already ceased to bear any relevance to the life that was lived behind them; the eminent K.C.s and the Masters of City Companies had already given place to Viennese professors and Indian students and bed-sitter business girls years before the first siren sounded. And yet I who was only on the threshold of middle-age could clearly remember the days when they flourished in all their intended glory. At that house on the comer I used to go to dancing classes; outside that imposing front-door I had watched the carriages setting down for a reception; and in that now denuded garden I had once played hide and seek.

'Take me back to dear old Shepherd's Bush'

I was born in the eighth year of the reign of King Edward the Seventh in the parish of St John's, Notting Hill. At that time Elgin Crescent, the actual scene of this event, was situated on the Marches of respectability. Up the hill to the south, tree-shaded and freshly stuccoed, stretched the squares and terraces of the last great stronghold of Victorian propriety: below to the north lay the courts and alleys of Notting Dale, through which, so my nurse terrifyingly assured me, policemen could only proceed in pairs.

The Crescent, like all border districts, was distinguished by a certain colourful mixture in its inhabitants, lacking in the more securely sheltered central area, grouped in this case round the church. While residence there was socially approved and no traces of 'slumminess' were as yet apparent, there did cling to it a slight whiff of Bohemianism from which Kensington Park Road, for instance, was quite free. Of the residents, several were connected with the Stage, and some were foreign, but neither group carried these eccentricities to excessive lengths. Among the former were numbered a Mr Maskelyne (or was it a Mr Devant?) who lived on the corner, and, right next door to us, the talented authoress of *Where the Rainbow Ends*, whose daughter, a dashing hobble-skirted croquet-player, remains a vivid memory. The foreigners included some Japanese diplomats and a German family connected with the Embassy, whose son, a fair, chinless youth, was always at great pains to model his appearance on that of the Crown Prince Wilhelm, much to the delight of my father whom a long residence in Berlin had rendered expert in detecting the subtlest nuances of this elaborate masquerade. Fortunately my parents' arrival at Number 79 had done much to erase the principal blot on the fair name of the street, as our house had previously been the home of no less equivocal a figure than Madame Blavatsky.

Number 79 was a semi-detached stucco residence on three floors and a basement with a pillared porch, not differing stylistically in any way from the prevailing classicism of the neighbourhood. At the back was a small private garden opening into the large garden common to all the occupants of the south side of Elgin Crescent and the north side of Lansdowne Road. Such communal gardens, which are among the most attractive features of Victorian town-planning, are not uncommon in the residential districts of West London, but are carried to the highest point of their development in the Ladbroke estate. This area, which was laid out after the closure of the race-course that for a brief period encircled the summit of the hill, represents the last rational, unselfconscious piece of urban development in London. It was unfortunately dogged by misfortune, and the socially ambitious intention of Allom, the architect, and the promoters was largely defeated by the proximity of an existing pottery slum in Notting Dale, which received, just at the time the scheme was being launched, an enormous and deplorable influx of Irish labourers working on the Great Western Railway.

How different it all was in the years before 1914! Then the stucco, creamy and bright, gleamed softly beneath what seems in reminiscence to have been a perpetually cloudless sky. Geraniums in urns flanked each brass-enriched front door, while over the area railings moustachioed policemen made love to buxom cooks. And in every street there hung, all summer long, the heavy scent of limes.

Notting Hill in Wartime

Vere Hodgson

Winifred Vere Hodgson was born in 1901 and lived in Notting Hill – first at No.56, then 79 Ladbroke Road – during the Second World War, when she kept a daily record of events, primarily for her cousin Lucy in Rhodesia. She described herself as a diarist of 'ordinary rather than extraordinary people' and was a keen philanthropist, attached to a community known as the Sanctuary, at 3 Lansdowne Road. In the days before the welfare state, many Notting Hill families came here with their troubles. The following extracts are taken from Hodgson's published work, *Few Eggs and No Oranges* (1971). She died in 1979.

Thursday 26th September 1940

On investigation in the morning, we discovered a house in Lansdowne Rd., nine doors from us, was gone inside. The walls were standing, but it was burnt-out inside. Walked to Clarendon Cross. Every pane of glass had gone, and several houses down. A pretty bad night! It does not bear enquiring into too much! There seems no end to it. Our incendiary had put itself out against the Rockery.

Wednesday 9th October 1940

Quiet for the rest of the night. All clear at 6.45. But I heard the news of last night round here. Five houses were struck at the far end of Lansdowne Road. No wonder we felt it. Some people saved – others buried. All round Oxford and Cambridge Gardens, and Ladbroke Grove Station – houses and shops were down. Also Pembridge Place and Chepstow Villas. Mr Booker [owner of the Mercury café] told us the story of two men who were told by a policeman to take cover. They walked on – and were terribly injured. First Aid Parties had to turn out and face the bomb through their foolhardiness.

Thursday 10th October 1940

Went to see the houses in Lansdowne Road that caught it. Just heaps of rubble. . . . several people killed. It is nearer Auntie Nell's flat than this house . . . right on the corner of Ladbroke Grove – a stone throw from Stanley Gardens. It is 9 o'clock. A nasty sound is getting nearer . . . .

Tuesday 11th March 1941

Out early in Notting Hill this morning a little girl stopped me. She asked me to take her across the road. which I did. I enquired where she was going. It appeared to school – but had never been alone before. She did not know if it was this way – or, pointing in the opposite direction, the other. Here was a conundrum. She was about seven, the dearest little thing. It was her birthday, she said, and she was to have a party, and she had received five picture postcards. The School was called The Fox School, she explained. We went hand in hand to the ironmonger and consulted him. Yes, it was in Kensington Place and was probably bombed. With this information we set off for Church St. There we met a policeman and told him the story. He looked at me and I at him...we both had the same thoughts. She cheerfully set off hand in hand with him, doubtless explaining in fuller detail her birthday and why Mother was not able to take her to school as usual. I have never forgotten her.

At the Mercury arrived the Doctor's secretary whom Mr Booker had helped to dig out. We were amazed to see her. She said she still felt awful, but described to us her sensations as the first two bombs came down and knew in her bones that the third would strike her home. She had the presence of mind to turn off the gas. She was in a basement and it dropped in the garden. When she came to she found herself a prisoner. She could see a window, but both doors were jammed. She shouted for help, and a woman came out of the Mews near, and called all right. Then the wardens broke the windows and dragged her out. The others were buried deeper and it took some hours to release them. This woman was cold and I brought her down to the Sanctuary, found her a nice coat, suit and dress. We had no suitable underclothing, but I know others would help. She had a talk with Miss M and went away much cheered. It is considered a landmine exploded in the air over Holland Park on that awful night. That is why I thought the roof was off, and accounts for the terrible roaring. It is the only theory that accounts for the blast breaking so many windows in Shepherds Bush. Indeed we had a lucky escape.

Wednesday 12th

Miss Linde has taken refuge here with her two dogs! There were 38 bombs on Kensington last Saturday night, she says, during two hours . . . in addition to the landmine. No wonder we were kept diving under the table. Mr Major, head Warden on Campden Hill, is very badly injured. He fell into a bomb crater, broke his arm and is paralyzed from the waist. Saw the secretary again. She has worked twenty years for the same doctor, and mercifully had put all his records in the refrigerator. Hopes they are safe. She looked as if shock was beginning to tell.

Walked along to Kensington Place. It is a mess. All the little houses have been struck in one way or another. Kit Sauvary had lunch at the Mercury with me. They are nursing a casualty from Church St. They had terrible cases from Hendon. One man lay there for five days before he was claimed – he died eventually.

Thursday 25th June 1942

There was a bomb at 72 Ladbroke Road. I knew just the house. Mrs Beck had to find the bomb – which was said to be at the back. A very large house – eventually it was found in the basement. We got the pump going quickly, the Warden said. I was first on the nozzle, then went to fill buckets. I had seen a notice on a door: 'Baths full on first floor'. So I rushed there, but a pond had been found in the garden. Bomb extinguished and we reported back to Lansdowne House. A further fire was reported at 181 Ladbroke Road.

Sunday September 5th 1943

Walked back with a lady and daughter. The mother was a Florentine! Daughter on industrial welfare work but began the canteen at Holland Park Tube station during the blitz. Was there every night, and well remembers the occasion in October 1940, when the bomb skimmed our roof and nearly fell on the hundreds in the Tube station. Lots rushed into the street.

Sunday 6th February 1944

Oranges in N. Hill Gate, but so far have not achieved any. Long queues at the Old Pole's. He never knows when they are coming.

Wednesday 17th January 1945

Oranges in Notting Hill today. Not unpacked, but I could return. I spread the good news. We have a Disagreeable Greengrocer round here, and Barishnikov is always baiting him. He is determined to get some oranges out of him. He goes in every two hours to annoy him . . . B can see the cases of oranges in the shop. But at my shop I was served for three ration books . . . with five oranges. I looked doubtfully at these lovely Jaffas – but how do I divide five oranges among three people! I begged humbly for one more . . . he considered and caved in. I departed much elated.

John Gawsworth: King of Redonda

Roger Dobson

Roger Dobson is a freelance writer and editor who lives in Oxford. He helps run the Redondan Cultural Foundation, which publishes material on MP Shiel, John Gawsworth and the peers of the realm. He also writes the film-news column for *All Hallows*, the journal of the Ghost Story Society. Here Dobson tells of the eccentric life of John Gawsworth, one-time Notting Hill resident, and self-appointed ruler of the world's most literary kingdom.

Of all the bohemians who have dwelt in Notting Hill over the years none was more quixotically colourful than John Gawsworth, the bacchanalian King Juan I of Redonda. Gawsworth inherited the fantasy kingdom from the writer Matthew Phipps Shiel (1865–1947), who emigrated to Britain in 1885 from the Leeward Islands where he had been crowned King Felipe of Redonda, a mile-long volcanic rock, on his fifteenth birthday. Shiel had an erratically successful writing career, becoming friendly with Robert Louis Stevenson, Arthur Machen, Ernest Dowson and other literati of the day, and lived for a time in St Charles Square, off Ladbroke Grove.

King Juan, who possessed Irish, Scottish and French blood, was born Terence Ian Fytton Armstrong at 97 Gunterstone Road, Kensington, on 29 June 1912. Educated at Merchant Taylors' School, and living with his mother at Colville Gardens W11, and then at 40 Royal Crescent, Holland Park, Fytton Armstrong became a fanatical collector of literary memorabilia: autographs, letters, manuscripts, jottings and signed editions. After leaving school the 'Book Boy', as he was called, rented a basement room at 17 Sunderland Terrace W2 and embarked on a bohemian lifestyle as a scholar-poet. He worked at a Soho bookshop, then for the publisher Ernest Benn, and by his early twenties had published several pamphlets of poetry, compiled bibliographies of writers he admired, written a biography of Machen and edited a series of anthologies of horror and mystery fiction. He adopted John Gawsworth as a romantic pen-name in honour of his descent from the Fitton family of Gawsworth Old Hall in Cheshire. (Mary Fitton is reputedly the Dark Lady of Shakespeare's sonnets.)

In 1931 the 19-year-old Gawsworth, working as a clerk for a Fleet Street publisher, had written to Shiel, then in his mid-sixties, and became his foremost champion; he helped him gain a civil list pension and lobbied publishers about his books. Although Shiel reigned as King Felipe for 67 years, he regarded Redonda as a largely private concern; but the shrewd, promotionally-minded

Gawsworth, appointed the realm's Poet Laureate, soon assumed the role of *éminence grise*. In 1936, at Shiel's cottage near Horsham, Sussex, Felipe and Gawsworth cut their right wrists with a penknife and mingled blood. Through this rite, witnessed by the writer Edgar Jepson, Gawsworth became Shiel's heir apparent. When Shiel died on 17 February 1947, Gawsworth acceded to the throne as Juan I, arranged his own coronation and began a mercurial reign, holding his 'Court-in-Exile' in the taverns and bars of Soho and Fitzrovia. Later the Alma pub, at 175 Westbourne Grove W11, became Redonda HQ.

During Shiel's reign several writers, including Jepson, Lawrence Durrell and Henry Miller, had been ennobled, with Gawsworth acting as Regent. As King Juan he extended the practice, creating an Intellectual Aristocracy to perpetuate his predecessor's memory, issuing royal documents on antique Venetian paper. Arthur Machen, Rebecca West, Julian Maclaren-Ross, Arthur Ransome, Victor Gollancz and many other authors were awarded dukedoms or knighthoods in recognition of their services to Shiel or the realm.

In 1938 this slim, fox-faced, red-haired prodigy with his bent boxer's nose became the youngest Fellow of the Royal Society of Literature. He lived comfortably in a flat at 33 Great James Street, Bloomsbury, with his first wife, *Daily Mail* journalist Barbara Kentish, and mixed with writers such as TE Lawrence, Edith Sitwell and Dorothy L Sayers. Lawrence Durrell, four months his senior, was immediately attracted by Gawsworth's professional manner when they met in 1932. The obliging Gawsworth helped Durrell get his early poems into print. Paying tribute years later, Durrell wrote: 'I was a complete literary novice and a provincial and the meeting was an important one for me, for in John I found someone who burned with a hard gem-like flame – the very thing I wished to do myself . . . .'

Founding two literary magazines and helping neglected writers who fell on hard times, Gawsworth, afflicted by 'dipsobibliomania', became one of the capital's great characters. Known as 'the last of the Jacobites', he was an ardent Irish Republican and, after serving in India during the war, an Indian Nationalist who convert to Hinduism. The poet John Heath-Stubbs, appointed a Redondan duke in 1949, wrote: 'It was said that there was a superstition in Fleet Street that if you met Gawsworth twice in one morning you would die within the year and he would be your literary executor.'

Gawsworth's solid neo-Georgian verse, continuing the romantic lyric tradition of Ernest Dowson and Lionel Johnson, was the antithesis of the stark, socialistic modernism of the 1930s. Although anachronistic, his prolific output was admired in its day, but after his wartime service in the Royal Air Force he failed to fulfil the promise of his precocious youth. Although his *Collected Poems* appeared in 1949, and he was a catholic and able editor of the *Poetry Review* from 1948 to 1952, his subsequent career was marred by a prolonged descent into alcoholism. By the 1960s, when he was living at 35 Sutherland

Place, Notting Hill, he was headed downhill: his publications had diminished to a trickle of ephemera commemorating his dead mentors. The 'Inveterate old diabetic bookman, slipper-padding around my shelves and files', as he described himself, lived off the sales of manuscripts and books, and a good deal of the proceeds went on drink.

When feeling low, Gawsworth would visit the church of St Mary of the Angels opposite his home, and kiss the foot of the statue of St Joan: both he and Joan, he said, had been victims of English persecution. In 1968, after accepting a sum of money to leave Sutherland Place, Gawsworth effectively made himself homeless and was thrown on the charity of friends and his consort, Eleanor Brill of Peel Street W8, referred to as 'Queen SJ' – *sub judice* since the King never got around to marrying her.

Early in 1970, after an appeal was launched for the indigent poet, the BBC made a documentary about him for *Late Night Line-Up*. The portly, cane-wielding Gawsworth is shown visiting old literary friends and promenading the streets of Soho and Bloomsbury with great dignity. Near the end of the film, when he greets Durrell in a London pub, he is cheerfully drunk.

The same year, having managed to lay his hands on the collected funds of fourteen hundred pounds, Gawsworth enjoyed a binge at the Alma which lasted several days, followed by a sojourn near Florence, where he fell in love and ended up in hospital with haemorrhaging stomach ulcers. The years of riotous living took their inevitable toll and Gawsworth died three months after returning to Britain, at the Brompton Hospital on 23 September 1970. He was 58.

The Realm of Redonda was thrown into confusion at his death. In 1958 he had put the realm on the market, advertising it in *The Times* at a price of one thousand guineas. An avalanche of letters and telegrams poured in from around the world, and a member of the Swedish royal family sent fifty pounds as a deposit; but, feeling he was 'vulgarising a noble kingdom', Gawsworth withdrew the offer. In 1960 Gawsworth is believed to have passed on the kingship to Dominic Behan, brother of Brendan, but the Irish playwright was just one of a number of candidates selected as his heir.

Most Redondan scholars acknowledged the Sussex-based publisher and writer Jon Wynne-Tyson (King Juan II), the literary executor of Shiel and Gawsworth, as the most fitting successor. With some of his courtiers, including Shiel's biographer A Reynolds Morse, Juan II landed on Redonda on Good Friday in 1979 and they made the perilous ascent of its 971-foot peak. In 1997, at the age of 73, Mr Wynne-Tyson abdicated in favour of the eminent Spanish novelist Javier Marías. Among the distinguished writers and artists honoured by Señor Marías, known as King Xavier, are Francis Ford Coppola, appointed the Duke of Megalopolis, Spanish film-maker Pedro Almodóvar, the Duke of Trémula, AS Byatt, the Duchess of Morpho Eugenia, William Boyd, the Duke of Brazzaville, Cuban writer G Cabrera Infante, the Duke of Tigres and German novelist WG Sebald, the Duke of Vertigo. In addition, Señor Marías has founded an imprint to celebrate writers associated with the kingdom. Shiel and Gawsworth have gone, but the Realm of Redonda seems imperishable.

Sunny Napoli

Colin MacInnes

Colin MacInnes was born in 1914. He spent some of his childhood in Australia and on his return to England went to art school for a time before embarking on a career as a writer and journalist. He is best remembered for his novels of teenage and black immigrant culture, *City of Spades* (1957) and *Absolute Beginners* (1959), which ends with a vivid description of the Notting Hill riots of 1958. For many years MacInnes lived in the area he affectionately described as 'Napoli', and was a familiar figure in the club and coffee-bar life of the 1950s and 60s. He died in 1976. The following extract has been selected from *Absolute Beginners*.

I'd like to explain this district where I live, because it's quite a curiosity, being one of the few that's got left behind by the Welfare era and the Property-owning whatsit, both of them, and is, in fact, nothing more than a stagnating slum. It's dying, this bit of London, and that's the most important thing to remember about what goes on there. To the north of it, there run, in parallel, the Harrow road I've mentioned, which you'd hurry through even if you were in a car, and a canal, called the Grand Union, that nothing floats on except cats and contraceptives, and the main railway track that takes you from London to the swede counties of the West of England. These three escape routes, which are all at different heights and levels, cut across one another at different points, making crazy little islands of slum habitation shut off from the world by concrete precipices, and linked by metal bridges. I need hardly mention that on this north side there's a hospital, a gas-works with enough juice for the whole population of the kingdom to commit suicide, and a very ancient cemetery with the pretty country name of Kensal Green.

On the east side, still in the w.10 bit, there's another railway, and a park with a name only Satan in all his splendour could have thought up, namely Wormwood Scrubs, which has a prison near it, and another hospital, and a sports arena, and the new telly barracks of the BBC, and with a long, lean road called

Latimer road which I particularly want you to remember, because out of this road, like horrible tits dangling from a lean old sow, there hang a whole festoon of what I think must really be the sinisterest highways in our city, well, just listen to their names: 'Blechynden, Silchester, Walmer, Testerton and Bramley – can't you just smell them, as you hurry to get through the cats-cradle of these blocks? In this part, the houses are old Victorian lower-middle tumble-down, built I dare say for grocers and bank clerks and horse-omnibus inspectors who've died and gone and their descendants evacuated to the outer suburbs, but these houses live on like shells, and there's only one thing to do with them, absolutely one, which is to pull them down till not a one's left standing up.

On the south side of this area, down by the w.ll, things are a little different, but in a way that somehow makes them worse, and that is, owing to a freak of fortune, and some smart work by the estate agents too, I shouldn't be surprised, there are one or two sections that are positively posh: not *fashionable*, mind you, but quite graded, with their big back gardens and that absolute silence which in London is the top sign of a respectable location. You walk about in these bits, adjusting your tie and looking down to see if your shoes are shining, when-wham! suddenly you're back in the slum area again – honest, it's really startling, like where the river joins on to the shore, two quite different creations of dame nature, cheek by thing.

Over towards the west, the frontiers aren't quite as definite, and the whole area merges into a drab and shady and semi-respectable part called Bayswater, which I would rather lie in my coffin, please believe me, than spend a night in, were it not for Suze, who's shacked up there. No! Give me our London Napoli I've been describing, with its railway scenery, and crescents that were meant to twist elegantly but now look as if they're lurching high, and huge houses too tall for their width cut up into twenty flatlets, and front facades that it never pays anyone to paint, and broken milk bottles *everywhere* scattering the cracked asphalt roads like snow, and cars parked in the streets looking as if they're stolen or abandoned, and a strange number of male urinals tucked away such as you find nowhere else in London, and red curtains, somehow, in all the windows, and diarrhoea-coloured street lighting – man, I tell you, you've only got to be there for a minute to know there's something radically wrong.

Across this whole mess there cuts, diagonally, yet another railway, that rides high above this slum property like a scenic railway at a fair. Boy, if you want to admire our wonderful old capital city, you should take a ride on this track some time! And just where this railway is slung over the big central road that cuts across the area north to south, there's a hole, a dip, a pocket, a really unhappy valley which, according to my learned Dad, was formerly at one time a great non-agricultural marsh. A place of evil, mister. I bet witches lived around it, and a lot still do.

And what about the human population? The answer is, this is the residential doss-house of our city. In plain words, you'd not live in our Napoli if you could live anywhere else. And that is why there are, to the square yard, more boys fresh from the nick, and national refugee minorities, and out-of-business whores, than anywhere else, I should expect, in London town. The kids live in the streets – I mean they have *charge* of them, you have to ask permission to get along them even in a car – the teenage lot are mostly of the Ted variety, the chicks mature so quick there's scarcely such a thing there as a little girl, the men don't talk, glance at you hard, keep moving, and don't stand with their backs to anyone, their women are mostly out of sight, with dishcloths I expect for yashmaks, and there are piles and piles of these dreadful, wasted, negative, shop-soiled kind of *old people* that make you feel it really is a tragedy to grow grey.

You're probably saying well, if you're so cute, kiddo, why do you live in such an area? So now, as a certain evening paper writes it, 'I will tell you.'

One reason is that it's so cheap. I mean, I have a rooted objection to paying rent at all, it should be free like air, and parks, and water. I don't think I'm mean, in fact I know I'm not, but I just can't bear paying more than a bob or two to landlords. But the real reason, as I expect you'll have already guessed, is that, however horrible the area is, you're free there! No one, I repeat it, no one, has ever asked me there what I am, or what I do, or where I came from, or what my social group is, or whether I'm educated or not, and if there's one thing I cannot tolerate in this world, it's nosey questions. And what is more, once the local bandits see you're making out, can earn your living and so forth, they don't swing it on you in the slightest you're a teenage creation – if you have loot, and can look after yourself, they treat you as a man, which is what you are. For instance, *nobody* in the area would ever have treated me like that bank clerk tried to in Belgravia. If you go in anywhere, they take it for granted that you know the scene. If you don't, it's true, they throw you out in pieces, but if you do, they treat you just as one of them.

The room I inhabit in sunny Napoli, which overlooks *both* railways (*and* the foulest row of backyards to be found outside the municipal compost heaps), belongs to an Asian character called Omar, Pakistani, I believe, who's regular as clockwork – in fact, even more so, because clocks are known to stop – and turns up on Saturday mornings, accompanied by two countrymen who act as bodyguards, to collect the rents, and you'd better have yours ready. Because if you haven't, he simply grins his teeth and tells his *fellahin* to pile everything you possess neatly on the outside pavement, be it rain, or snow, or mulligatawny fog. And if you've locked the door, it means absolutely nothing to him to smash it down, and even if you're in bed, all injured innocence and indignation, he still comes in with his sickly don't mean-a-thing kind of smile. So if you're going to be away, it's best to leave the money with a friend, or better still, pay him, as I do, monthly in advance. And when you do, he takes out a plastic bag on a long chain from a very inner pocket, and tucks the notes away, and says you must have a drink with him some time, but even when I've once or twice met him in a pub, he's never offered it, of course. Also, if you make any complaint *whatever* – I mean, even that the roof's falling in, and the Water cut off – he smiles that same smile and does positively Sweet bugger-all about it. On the other hand, you could invite every whore and cut-throat in the city in for a pail of gin, or give a corpse accommodation for the night on the spare bed, or even set the bloody place on fire, and he wouldn't turn a hair – or turn one if anybody complained to him about you. Not if you paid your rent, that is. In fact, the perfect landlord.

Michael X: Views from the Grove

John Michell

John Michell was born in 1933 and, taking refuge from various failures and fiascos, in 1965 retreated to his imagination and to live in Notting Hill, where he is still. He has had writing published in *International Times*, 'underground' and small presses and has written more than 20 books, pamphlets and pieces of journalism, all in reaction against the narrow outlook of modern education and towards a more complete and satisfying world view. Here Michell writes about Michael X as he remembers him in the 1960s.

There are still many of us around who remember Michael. He was called Michael de Freitas, then took the name Michael Abdul Malik, and in between he became known as Michael X. His hey-day in Notting Hill was the 1960s, after which his life took a downward turn and in 1975 he was hanged for murder in Trinidad.

When you talk to his old friends around here, you hear very different accounts of Michael. Some of his fellow West Indians despise him as a fraud and a bully, who played the part of black man's champion simply for his own gain and glory. To others he was a great man and a great loss. Terry Radix, for example, who was once Michael's lieutenant (Terry X), speaks admiringly of what he did and tried to do. Another of his closest companions, Capitan, claims that Michael was totally non-violent: 'He was actually a coward; when faced with trouble he would back down.'

My own impression, and that of other friends I have spoken to, is similar to Capitan's. We liked Michael and were made easy by his mild, sympathetic manner. His admirers included William Burroughs, Alex Trocchi, Colin MacInnes, William Levy and other prominent writers of the time. In 1966 he discovered LSD and did his first acid trip. This exposed him to the hippy idealism of the period. Images of peaceful, loving communities entered his mind, competing with the fierce, radical doctrines that his militant followers expected of him.

Michael's life began in 1933 in Trinidad. His absentee father was Portuguese and his mother was a black witch in the voodoo tradition, though officially Roman Catholic. She wanted her son to be like a white boy and discouraged his black playmates. As soon as he could, aged 14, he ran away to sea and spent the next ten years or so voyaging on merchant ships to all parts of the world. He then came to Britain, first to the Tiger Bay area of Cardiff and then into our part of London. In 1959 he married Desiree de Souza, a beautiful young Guyanese woman who remained loyal to him through thick and thin, right up to the end. Their best man at their wedding was Roy Stewart, owner to this day of The Globe, Talbot Road.

The Grove, as it was then called, stretching from Ladbroke Grove eastwards towards Paddington, had never been a fashionable district, and by the end of the War it was partly derelict. Rooms and flats in its crumbling houses were among the cheapest in London. This made it attractive to West Indian immigrants, many of whom have made it their home ever since. In Michael's partly ghost-written autobiography, *From Michael de Freitas to Michael X* (1968), he describes how he settled among them and helped them in their troubles with racist thugs and grasping landlords. It is a fantastical book, full of good anecdotes, but as a record of Michael's career in the Grove it is somewhat unreliable.

In *False Messiah: the Story of Michael X* Derek Humphry and David Tindall tell a different story – of Michael's mean crimes and vicious cruelties, his deceptions and treacheries, his vain pretensions and ruthless exploitations. They expose the nature of his property dealings in the Grove; while posing as a protector of tenants' rights he betrayed his own people to the notorious landlord Peter Rachman, for whom he extorted rents. Michael's innate depravity, say the authors, was apparent in his childhood when a neighbour prophesied to his mother, 'That boy will end up on the gallows'.

A *Sunday Times* article in 1965 dubbed him Michael X and hailed him as the British successor to the American Black Muslim leader, Malcolm X. Michael accepted the set-up and the duties it imposed upon him, making himself host to black celebrities visiting England, including Martin Luther King, Muhammed Ali, Dick Gregory and Sammy Davis Junior. Fame and respect settled upon him. 'He is a writer of considerable distinction,' claimed William Burroughs. Literary journals published his thoughts and verses, he lectured to the Cambridge Union, and he represented Trinidad at a Commonwealth Poetry Conference in Cardiff.

Trouble came when, at a London symposium called Dialectics of Liberation, he shared the platform with Stokely Carmichael, the American Black Power agitator. Always impressionable, Michael was struck by Carmichael's violent, anti-white rhetoric, and he imitated it in a speech to a West Indian group in Reading. Arrested by the police, he became the first person to be convicted under the newly enacted Race Relations laws. After nine months in prison, he turned to community projects, setting up black people's libraries and social centres. This attracted the support of idealistic white people. An eccentric young millionaire, Nigel Samuel, contributed a large property in north London, which Michael named the Black House, and the Lennons, John and Yoko, donated their shorn hair to be auctioned for Michael's benefit.

From the time of his partnership with Nigel Samuel, I saw less of Michael. Exploits I heard of were his trips with Nigel, Trocchi and others to Africa and Asia for talks with third-world leaders. Much of this seemed crazy and there were signs that Michael was cracking up. On his last night in England he came to see me in Powis Terrace, worried and in a dark mood. Charges had been brought against him which compelled him to leave the country and go back to Trinidad. That was the last I saw of him, though we often corresponded, up to and throughout his agonising last months on Death Row. Michael wrote that he was living on a smallholding with Desiree, her four children and a few followers. Dick Gregory and Muhammed Ali both visited this rural commune, and John Lennon arrived with Yoko, staying two days with the Maliks and presenting their children with a piano.

Then came the murders. There is a detailed account of the whole thing in *False Messiah*, and it is gruesome, involving blood-drinking rites and the dark gods of voodoo. The horrors began with a visit from Hakim Jamal, a Black Muslim from Boston, and his doting girlfriend, Gale Benson, daughter of a Conservative MP. Jamal, a weak, excitable character, fell under Michael's spell. Even when Michael determined to sacrifice Gale (his assassins dug a pit in the garden, threw her into it, slashed her with knives and buried her half-alive) he made no move to save her.

The next person to be killed was a young Trinidadian who disobeyed one of Michael's commands. This time, according to the account, Michael himself carried out the execution, slicing up his victim with a cutlass. A few days later another of his followers died in what looked like a drowning accident. Michael disappeared to Guyana where, after seeking refuge in the jungle, he was arrested.

During his 32 months on Death Row in Trinidad's Royal Gaol, Michael always insisted that he was innocent. John and Yoko, faithful to the last, promoted a petition on his behalf, signed by many great names in entertainment, the arts and radical or sexual politics. All was in vain, and when his long wait was over, Michael walked quietly to the gallows. God rest his soul.

The Magical City
Jonathan Raban

Jonathan Raban's most recent book is *Passage to Juneau* (1999). He lives in Seattle with his daughter. He wrote *Soft City* while living in Earl's Court, from which Notting Hill was a nearby but distinctly foreign land. He lived in North Kensington from 1980 to 1985. The following extracts are taken from 'The Magical City' chapter of *Soft City* (1974).

In Notting Hill Gate in London, or it might be Greenwich Village in New York, the unreasonable city has come to the point where it cannot be ignored by even the civic authorities. The streets around Ladbroke Grove, with their architecture of white candy stucco, are warrens of eccentric privateness; they are occupied by people who have taken no part in the hypothetical consensus of urban life – the poor, the blacks, the more feckless young living on National Assistance or casual jobs on building sites or bedsitter industries like stringing beads or making candles. The district is notoriously difficult to police: it has a long, twenty-five-year-old record of race-riots, drug arrests, vicious disputes between slum landlords and their tenants, complaints about neighbours, and petty litigation. Like many impoverished areas in big cities, it is picturesque in the sun, and Americans walk the length of the street market in the Portobello Road snapping it with Kodaks; but on dull days one notices the litter, the scabby paint, the stretches of torn wire netting, and the faint smell of joss-sticks competing with the sickly sweet odour of rising damp and rotting plaster. Where the area shows signs of wealth, it is in the typically urban non-productive entrepreneurism of antique shops and stalls. Various hard-up community action groups have left their marks: a locked shack with FREE SHOP spraygunned on it, and old shoes and sofas piled in heaps around it; a makeshift playground under the arches of the motorway with huge crayon faces drawn on the concrete pillars; slogans in whitewash, from SMASH THE PIGS to KEEP BRITAIN WHITE. The streets are crowded with evident isolates: a pair of nuns in starched habits, a Sikh in a grubby turban, a gang of West Indian youths, all teeth and jawbones, a man in a fedora, greasy Jesus Christs in shiny green suede coats with Red Indian fringes at their hems, limp girls in flaky Moroccan fleeces, macrobiotic devotees with transparent parchment faces, mongrel dogs, bejeaned delivery men, young mothers in cardigans with second-hand prams. These are the urban spacemen, floating alone in capsules of privacy, defying the gravity of the city .

. . . Notting Hill Gate incorporates a central paradox of city life, in that its nature is as prolific and untameable as anywhere in London, yet for some at least of its inhabitants it has been accommodated to an order so benign as to be cosy.

The messy prolixity of the place makes it a perfect territory for the exercise of natural magic. Its unpredictability, its violent transitions from extreme wealth to extreme poverty, its atmosphere of being crowded out with disconnected loners, its physical characteristics as a maze of narrow streets and irregular crescents, combine to force the individual into a superstitious, speculative relationship with his environment. He cannot, merely by studying the arrangements and amenities of the district, deduce from them who he is, for the answers he would get would be impossibly various. Society in Notting Hill Gate reveals no rationale, no comprehensible structure. The sets of values embodied in it are almost as diverse as the number of people on the streets. If untutored man were to be set down on a tropical island and told to construct a pattern of beliefs and morals from what he saw around him, he could hardly have more difficulty than a newcomer to Notting Hill Gate. It is a place where anything is possible, a nightmare – or paradise, perhaps, for some – of chance and choice.

. . . Notting Hill Gate is a superstitious place because it seems to exceed rational prescriptions and explanations. On the Portobello Road, one feels oneself growing more insubstantial, less and less able to keep a sense of personal proportion in the crowd of people who all look so much poorer, or richer, or wilder, or more conventional than one is oneself. It is certainly hard to keep in touch with other people in the city; it may sometimes be almost as difficult to keep in touch with one's own self – that diminishing pink blob which rolls and slides like a lost coin in a gutter. The people who float on the tide of metaphysical junk – freaks of all kinds . . . into macrobiotics, yoga, astrology, illiterate mysticism, acid, terrible poetry by Leonard Cohen and tiny novels by Richard Brautigan – have managed, at a price. The new folk magic of the streets promises to have some unhappy political consequences but as a way of responding to the city it does reflect a truth about the nature of the place which we had better learn to confront.

The truth is one of an ultimate privacy, in which the self, cosseted and intensified, internalises the world outside and sees the city as a shadow-show of its own impulses and movements. Privacy and reality are profoundly equated, so that what is most real is located in the deepest recesses of the self. The external world turns into an epic movie, supplying details on which to feed one's fantasies; like Disney's *Fantasia* which, when shown in London three years ago, drew crowds of hippies who dosed themselves with acid at selected points in the film. Like Notting Hill Gate itself, it was perfect trip material and Disney's original intentions were as irrelevant as those of the civic architects who first laid out those streets and crescents.

In this search for the disappearing self, the physical body becomes a central symbol; the stomach intestines, and organs of reproduction are solemnly attended to, as vessels in which the precious self is contained. In Ceres, the macrobiotic shop on Portobello Road, I bought *Macrobiotics: An invitation to health and happiness* by George Ohsawa:

> *The kitchen is the studio where life is created. . .Knowing that no absolute rules exist, or can be followed forever, we start with principles that are as adaptable to the constantly changing world we inhabit as possible. Only you are the artist who draws the painting of your life . . . Strictly speaking, no one eats the same food and the same amount even from the same cooking pot. Such recognition of individuality leads us to the fact that we are living by ourselves and we are creating our life by ourselves.*

The girls who drift about the store, filling wire baskets with soya beans, miso and wakame seaweed have the dim inwardness of gaze of Elizabeth Siddall in Rossetti's 'Jenny'. In bedsitters in Ladbroke Grove, they create themselves over gas rings, feeding their immaculate insides on harmoniously balanced amounts of yin and yang foods. It is hard to tell whether their beatific expressions come from their convictions of inner virtue or from undernourishment. When they speak, their voices are misty, as if their words had to travel a long way from their inscrutable souls to the naughty outer world. Serious, narcissistic, terrifyingly provident, like all fanatics they brim with latent violence; when they exclude and condemn, they do so with a ringing stridency that smacks more of mothers in Romford and Hornchurch than of Oriental sages preaching doctrines of universal gentleness. 'Oh, man . . . ' withers its recipient as skilfully as any mean current of suburban disapproval. Their city is a pure and narrow one: they are miniaturists in their talented cultivation of themselves. In her scented room, Annette feeds herself on honey and grape juice and brown rice; she reads haiku by Basho. 'I think that's really beautiful,' she said . . . a vague poem, with a horseman and some bullrushes in it, a long way from the things you see at the Gate.

. . . Playing at being a Red Indian in a bandanna, or an Asian peasant in a tie-dyed sari, or a workman in a boiler suit, is a carefully stage-managed announcement. It trumpets a commonplace city freedom – the freedom to be who you want to be, without bonds of class, nationality, education, occupation, or even sex. It further expresses an allegiance to the irrational, mystical or magical values which the Red Indian, the peasant or the labourer are presumed to possess. The Mohawks and Cherokees of Notting Hill Gate belong among the lofty savages of Fenimore Cooper, not in the downtrodden reservations of the real USA. It is also a homage to 'dressing up'. Grown-ups don't dress up and indulge in make-believe; children do, and the boutique is the industrial equivalent to the Edwardian dressing up box, that grotto of old wedding dresses, turbans, yashmaks collected by a grandfather on furlough, and clumpy shoes all buckles and straps. There is something of the same coy, schmaltzily 'fetching' little-girlishness in the way the young rig themselves out in their incongruous costumes on the Portobello Road – elderly children smirking complacently under broad-brimmed hats. But they take childhood seriously, more seriously than politics, at least. The tradition of childhood represents their only real foray into history; they see themselves as terrible Blakean infants, or as Wordsworth's boy evading the growing shades of the prison house, or as Alice, wise in her naiveté. To be a child is to be in touch with dark, para-rational, para-urban forces, and to see the equivocations, arrangements and compromises of adulthood as a lunatic charade.

. . . These people at the Gate have clearly embraced the idea of a magical city. Their clothes, their language, their religious beliefs, their folk art belong to a synthetically reconstructed tribal culture ruled by superstition, totems and taboos. Most of what they have is borrowed affected and contrived; it reflects a sturdy unoriginality. But perhaps its very tawdriness is a measure of the urgency of the need which has created it. We live in a society in which magic is supposed to have been outlawed or outgrown, in which secular rationalism is presumed to be the standard by which everyone lives. Yet at the same time we have created an environment in which it is exceedingly hard to be rational, in which people are turning to magic as a natural first resort. Television clergymen fondly interpret the evidence of Notting Hill Gate or the box-office returns of *Jesus Christ Superstar* as the first twitches of a spiritual reawakening. That seems, to put it mildly, doubtful. The kind of magic I have been examining is profoundly solipsistic, self-bound inward. Its very ignorance of plan or creation is its most obvious strength. One would not deduce the existence of God from the Portobello Road; but one might register from it the force of the amoral, the relative, the anarchistic. One might also discover, with shock, one's own isolation, the space-suit of privacy and its attendant rituals, in which one travels in a state of continuous locomotion through the city. Leaning against the spiked railings of the Salvation Army Hall next door to a *Woolworth's* and a Wimpy bar, one could hardly be further away from Plato's city state and its supremely intelligible contractual relationships. The Gate opens not on to the gentle pot-smoking whimsy of *Gandalf's Garden*, but on a ruined Eden, tangled, exotic and overgrown, where people see signs in scraps of junk and motley. It may look like affectation, a boasting juvenile pretence, but perhaps it is real – a state of natural magic to which the fragmented industrial city unconsciously aspires.

Rocking under the Westway

Michael Moorcock

Michael Moorcock was one of the key figures of the counter culture that flourished in Notting Hill during the 1960s and 70s. A prolific writer, he started producing work about the area in 1965 in the first volume of *The Cornelius Quartet.* Since then he has written more than 70 works of fiction and non-fiction on various subjects. During his many years in Notting Hill Moorcock edited the seminal imaginative fiction magazine, *New Worlds,* which was based in Portobello Road, home of much of the underground press. As well as novels, he wrote lyrics and performed, as a guitarist, with several bands, including Hawkwind and the Blue Oyster Cult. The passage below, reprinted from his latest rollercoaster tale, *King of the City* (2000), is based on an actual gig that took place under the Westway in 1972. He currently lives with his wife Linda in the USA.

As it happened, I didn't meet Julie through Jack. She didn't know I was a relative. She just thought I was cool. I was performing under the motorway, doing a free Saturday lunchtime gig with Nick Lowe, Brinsley Schwarz and a scratch band made up of anyone we could find who could stand up before noon. Basing Street was only round the corner. Half the people we knew did session work there. Some hadn't gone to bed yet. Martin Stone hadn't been to bed for three years. His black beret was twitching on his scalp. He was beyond gaunt. His black little eyes were somewhere in the region of his cortex. He was so skinny you could use him to chop his own lines. He mumbled in a guarded, abstracted monotone. His guitar was getting edgier and edgier. He said warningly that it was all right, he was still warming up.

It was a benefit for Erin Pizzey's Women's Shelter. She was there with her journo husband. She'd only recently started it. Nice dope. Good vibes. Happy audience: youf, rastas, oldsters, hippies, proto-punks, all together. Naturally there were prune-faced ex-colonial protesters with lifted telephones at a couple of distant back windows. The first chord we played, they called the police and complained about the noise. The jollies were only too happy to respond. Call them out on a rape and see how long they took. We opened with a nice fast selection of Nick's best rock-and-roll songs and some ragged Chuck Berry stuff. Then we had to stop and sort ourselves out. As we tuned up, I looked into the audience. I'd never seen so many good-looking women. No-contest stunners. Swedish flower children. American yippies. French ippies. And Julie May, a Saxon virgin, with daisies in her yellow hair, serene and tall in her tie-dyes and a perfect image of the perfect day.

I should also mention the lust. I longed to have my camera with me. To record the moment. It was frustrating. Then Nick's disciplined, insistent rocking guitar put my mind back where it should be. But I played every note for her. Normally I never looked at the audience when I was on stage. My eyes were usually on the middle distance, listening to the others. It was the way I worked. And that day I was, needless to say, also whacked out on the nastiest speed money could find. Wired for sound. I was all over the stage in those days. It's a wonder I didn't spin myself up in the cables and vanish. There's a lot to be said for that really raw yellow Iranian whiz. While it lasted, it was our muse. Our inspiration. Don't say the Ayatollah's all bad. You could say he tried to silence one man, but actually he got an entire generation talking their heads off. The crowd had packed itself into the tiny theatre, made from a motorway bay, and spilled out over the whole of Portobello Green saturated in sunshine. Any time I looked forward I stared directly into her huge blue eyes. And got a godzilla power jolt. She was a Russian Earth Goddess.

Epic Hero *v.* the Beast! I turned into a spastic maniac. I was helpless. In the grip of a rock-and-roll orgasm, a holistic fit, I was flung back and forth like a Jack Russell's rat. And the way she kept moving closer in to the stage told me she was definitely there for the best reasons. Crouched over my instrument, I must have looked like I was being buggered by the Invisible Man.

If I'd been a pigeon I'd have had my chest puffed and my tail feathers flared. As it was, my hair seemed to be standing upright from my head. Which was blazing with copper fire. My eyebrows itched like scabs. There were suddenly thin red scars all over my fingers. I can remember the riffs, each one a rippling wall of colour, the way the set built and built. Every bone in my body was jumping to a different beat. I was hurting. Solid unrelenting pain. I found chords I never knew existed. My teeth screamed. But I couldn't and wouldn't stop. I never once lost control. My guitar was beginning to make Martin's seem mellow. I was electrocuted by love. Jazzed with the joo-joo juice. People still remember that gig.

The set lasted for over an hour. Then the jolly peelers muscled up with a dog in tow, armed with some garbled by-law to prove we shouldn't be irritating them by having fun for nothing. We dealt with the dogs in the usual way and they were soon running about whining to themselves, but finally the jollies turned off our power and we finished with the traditional chanting and drumming until we all got tired of it and the poor dogs sat down, their eyes and tongues lolling. They never could work out how we sorted their dogs. Always nice to leave a baffled bobby behind you.

Julie came over while we were packing up our gear. I felt her warmth against my cold sweaty back as I turned, pulling off my T-shirt. I winked at her. Friendly. Already intimate. She smiled uncertainly but had that familiar determined stance. This was her day for getting laid. She wasn't going home until it happened. I don't seek out female company just for the sake of it. I like being on my own. So I wasn't seeing anyone else.

I was still technically married to Germaine and living in Colville Terrace, but it was well over. I didn't yet have a drum of my own and Germaine's living room didn't seem the right place for the occasion. So I took Julie with us when we went up to the Princess Louise in Portobello Road. I thought she was foreign at first. The usual score. I thought she was a tourist. Her wide, pink face looked more Slavic than Surrey. Her father must have been that Polish Count she'd sometimes mentioned, who was a friend of her family's in Shepperton. I said she looked like some epic Northern heroine. She laughed and showed me the little bit of coke she'd bought at school. We did it all in the ladies' toilet before going on. It was getting cool and neither of us had much in the way of clothes.

After a while we went down to the Princess of Wales off Portland Road. I had a desperate idea. I was lucky. I scored a couple of half-an'-halfs off Little Ronny and an ounce off Geronimo and caught sight of Germaine who'd just come in with one of her friends. No need to tell her anything. She gave me the keys to the Pink Panther, her van. I didn't like to ask if the mattress was still in it.

The van was parked in a lock-up behind St James's School. A few minutes' hasty walk from the pub. And the mattress was still there, if a bit damp. Julie seemed perfectly happy with it all and took everything for granted. She told me later she'd no idea what was normal.

I apologised. I thought maybe she expected more from a rock-and-roll hero. But she was in heaven. She thought it was romantic. About as far from Shepperton as she could get without a spaceship. It made her gently randy.

It wasn't too much longer before I was engulfed in her slowly relished appetites. She enjoyed it from the first moment. And so did I. I was never a breast man, but those tits and buttocks were primeval. They took me back to the dawn of time, to the long slow pleasures of genesis, spending like mercury. At one point we did a bit of speed and then obsessively rolled enough joints to stone an army. We set the controls on cruise and didn't get up till Tuesday. You're dead right. We *were* having a better time than you.

Check it out. 10 October 1972. I was almost twenty. Maybe you weren't even here then. A golden age.

Summer in the City

Sally Moore

Sally Moore has been a frequent visitor to Notting Hill since the early 1970s and lived here briefly in the summer of 1974. She has since made her home in Bath where she writes novels. Here she recalls her life in the area.

Most people can look back and remember a time in their life when they felt really free. For me this time was the summer of 1974 when I shared a flat in a dilapidated tenement in Powis Square, in those days the heart of Notting Hill squalor. My flatmate was a young American, Martha Ellen Zenfell.

Martha and I had met through the ubiquitous John Wilcock, a prolific writer and founder of the New York *Village Voice*, who was then living in Talbot Road. That summer he had not only completed a book on the magic sites of England and Europe but decided on impulse to drive down to the Cannes Film Festival and produce a free magazine, *In the Cannes*. Martha and I had become instant reporters, wearing our press cards proudly as we sashayed into countless erotic movies and interviewed a smorgasbord of celebrities.

We soon discovered that not only were we born in the same year, but we were exactly the same dress, shoe and hat size. Back in London, we doubled our wardrobe in one swoop by moving into Martha's attic flat in Powis Square, where the only touch of glamour was a view of Donald Cammell's balcony, location for much of the cult movie, *Performance*. The flat was a nightmare: dark, dingy and smelling of cabbage. It lay at the top of five sinister flights of stairs, where dogs and the occasional down-and-out would sleep at the bottom. The front door to the building was always left open. Every Monday morning the council came to fix the lock and every Friday night the man downstairs kicked it off again.

My friend and I kept slightly different hours. I am basically a morning person; Martha likes to work and party at night, so often I would come in at lunch time to find her drifting around in her magenta silk Biba robe, running her hands through her tangle of black curls as she tried to wake up. We had adjacent rooms with long attractively shaped windows, and had we a little money to spend on No.8 it could have become a comfortable girlie apartment. But money was scant, as were our washing facilities, and the lack of a shower in the flat during this unusually hot English summer drove me to desperate measures.

'It's not a problem,' I assured our mutual friend Robert who was a constant visitor and enjoyed dressing up in the red Ossie Clark frock that my sister Jill's husband, Peter Gabriel, later wore on stage throughout his Genesis tour. 'I'm going to make a bathroom on the balcony.' Robert watched approvingly as I attached a rubber shower hose to the kitchen taps, stripped down to my underwear and clambered out of the window, hosing myself down with gusto. Perhaps I had hoped to be discovered by Donald Cammell and cast in a sequel to *Performance*, but I certainly provided entertainment for the barefoot children playing on the garbage-strewn pavement below, as well as getting the odd whistle from male passers by.

Saturday night was party night for John Wilcock around the corner in Talbot Road. Used to New York night life, where he had a list of parties he would visit in sequence for tiny spells of time, every week he'd invite an assortment of people. John would remain in his bed loft, built like a tree house with a ladder up which to lure pretty girls to his lair, while below him fascinating people circled around, talking loudly.

Among these stars of bohemia were Craig Sams who founded the Seed wholefood shop (now the Grain Shop in Portobello Road); Daniel and Tessa Topolski, writers and children of the famous sculptor, Felix; Jay Landesman and his poet wife Fran; odd actors and anyone who John might have happened to meet that week.

One night, John introduced me to a journalist from Pittsburgh, A Craig Copetas who was writing for *Rolling Stone* and wore archetypal English clothes bought from Harrods. We were instantly smitten with each other. As an indefatigable investigative journalist, he was particularly impressed by the fact that my father worked for the Queen. 'I've gotta interview Prince Charles,' he informed me. I was desperate to assist him and soon we were walking together from the seamy part of Notting Hill down Millionaire's Row to the barracks of Kensington Palace. I was hoping my mother would take to Craig as I ushered him into her beautifully appointed sitting room where he loudly proclaimed that he would interview the Prince informally, 'call him Chuck, take him to a real hamburger joint, make him feel at ease'. Sadly, it was soon apparent that my mother had not fallen for Craig in his stylish white suit, and it was a long time before I managed to introduce him to my father, let alone the Prince of Wales.

Craig held his own court in Julie's Wine Bar, and I loved to sit at his side while he and Richard Young (now a celebrity paparazzo) would eat expensive food, drink sparingly and lounge around beneath the palm trees. Julie's was a complete culture shock after Powis Square. I often felt I should take a bath before I entered, the shower situation having still not been resolved at the flat. One evening Paul Getty Jnr. came to meet Craig and Richard, bringing along his beautiful fiançée. He seemed rather subdued and I was too shy to talk much, and at all costs wanted to avoid the subject of his recent harrowing kidnap. I did, however, sneak several glances at his gingery hair to see if I could spot the missing ear beneath.

After a month or so, Martha and I decided that we had to return John Wilcock's continuously effortless Warhol-type hospitality and throw a party ourselves. Powis Square was smaller than the Talbot Road flat but that Saturday night I was delighted to see most of John's usual crowd, plus our own friends. The place was completely packed with talking, drinking, dancing people including the illustrious Heathcote Williams.

Poet, playwright, painter and actor, Heathcote was a true anarchist, renowned, among other things, for his graffiti. This often got him into trouble, as when he sprayed a huge 'NO' across the Talbot Road offices of the rock band Yes. Cheered on by two equally drunk companions, he then proceeded to blot out the window of the restaurant next door. As astonished diners watched their view recede behind a curtain of black paint, a group of enraged waiters marched out into the street and after a brief argument proceeded to beat the artist and his cronies to a pulp. Just as he was about to deal the final blow, one of them paused to snarl down at the dishevelled figure lying weakly on the pavement: 'And what do you do for a living?'. To the delight of Heathcote's gathering supporters, the reply was instantaneous: 'What makes you think I'm alive?'

Heathcote also liked to perform at parties. Once he burned real money, a gesture that had staggered me by its daring, and I couldn't wait to see what he would do to entertain us tonight. 'I'd like to be a writer,' I told him hopefully, wondering if genius could be contagious. 'When life fails, go to Wales,' was the response, after which he became very drunk and disappeared into the toilet. The party rollicked on, a huge success, but even Martha, the night owl, was wilting by the time everyone left. She had discovered she preferred parties in other people's houses.

In the morning I went to the lavatory to find Heathcote had written in indelible ink all over the walls. I forget the exact poems, although 'When life fails, etc.' featured prominently. I was thrilled – a real poet had used our toilet as his scroll. I couldn't wait for Martha to wake up and see this work of art in her own flat. Traumatised by the last night's invasion of her home, she rose earlier than usual. I soon heard a screech of fury from the confines of the toilet and went in to find her frantically trying to scrub out the spidery scrawl from every surface. I sought to console her by pointing out that he was a genius. 'I don't care,' she moaned, practically in tears. 'I have to live here, you know, and this is not going to come off.'

So a small division had appeared between my dear friend and myself. As the summer waned and autumn approached, the warmth of my parents' house drew me from my offbeat Notting Hill life with Martha and I spent more and more nights in the plush comfort of Kensington Barracks. John Wilcock set off on his travels, often with Martha as his assistant; Craig returned to New York, although we wrote to each other; and in the end I decided to sacrifice personal freedom and return to my mother and the pretty purple bedroom with the en-suite bathroom. I had traded dead cats on the stairs for endless hot water in the bath, David Hockney cycling past the window for Princess Margaret on the lawn.

The Free and Independent Republic of Frestonia

Nicholas Albery

As Frestonia's erstwhile Minister of State for the Environment, Nicholas Albery was a key figure in the community protest that followed the initial devastation caused by the building of the Westway (see pp 37–8). He has edited or co-edited several books, among them *Poem for the Day* (1994), an anthology of poems worth learning by heart, *The Time Out Book of Country Walks* (1997), *The New Natural Death Handbook* (2000) and *The Book of Visions* (1992). He also co-edits a number of websites, including www.globalideasbank.org (for socially innovatory schemes) and www.DoBe.org (for participatory events in cities throughout the world). Albery describes how Frestonia came to be a free and independent republic.

The Free and Independent Republic of Frestonia was founded on 27 October 1977. The residents in Freston Road, Notting Dale, London Wl0, threatened with eviction to make way for a giant factory estate, held a referendum. There was a 95 per cent majority in favour of independence from Great Britain and a 73 per cent majority in favour of joining the Common Market. An application for membership, complete with coat of arms, was sent to the United Nations, along with a warning that a peace-keeping force might be required. The application included the following statements:

Tribal Unity

Our national newspaper is called *The Tribal Messenger* and the motto of our country is '*Nos sumus omnes una familia*' ('We are all one family'). In celebration of this desire for unity, every citizen has been granted the honorary surname of 'Bramley'.

Geography of Frestonia

Frestonia is a very small nation, following the precedent of Luxembourg and

Monaco, and the precept of the late Dr Schumacher that 'Small is Beautiful'.

Frestonia is an area of approximately eight acres [later found to be one acre], a distinctly isolated island of near-dereliction surrounded by the West 10 and 11 sectors of London, England.

History

The first residents of the area were pig-keepers who settled here early in the nineteenth century. Later on, when the railways were built, they were joined by Irish brick-makers. The area also developed into a centre of laundry work.

The area was more recently acquired by the Greater London Council (GLC), an organ of the British Government, and by their own confession, the area was allowed by them to deteriorate over the years into a derelict site, with tenants moved out of their homes, the well-established community destroyed, and empty sites of demolished buildings fenced off with corrugated iron and used for dumping rubbish, with half-demolished houses next to people's homes.

The GLC and the British Government thereby demonstrated their lack of concern for the area and their unfitness to remain as its rulers and to plan for its future.

Over the last four years, the present inhabitants of Frestonia moved in and took over the empty houses as caretakers and pioneer homesteaders, and have renovated their homes to a remarkable extent, including putting roofs on houses which lacked roofs. Our architect's report confirms that, if the present period of uncertainty could be ended, it would be possible for the residents to give their buildings a long lease of life – and eventually of course to rebuild.

Two large areas of building rubble have been cleared for open space and horticulture. Greenhouses have been erected and a waterfall created.

Population

Presently the population of permanent residents has climbed to approximately 120, involved mainly in light industrial work within the Frestonian boundaries, although some work abroad. Examples of established and developing light industries in Frestonia include lute-making, weaving, sign-writing and pottery. With industries blossoming all the time, and with more derelict houses yet to renovate, the population will no doubt expand in the future.

Our population and land-mass are both relatively small. There is no international law which requires nations to be of a certain minimum size.

Frestonian Government

Our Frestonian Government is egalitarian and democratic. We have adopted as our National Bill of Rights the United Nations' own Declaration of Human Rights. All major proposals for action are submitted to referenda. All citizens have freedom to do whatever they wish, as long as it does not injuriously conflict with the freedom of another. There will be no conscription or involuntary service.

Frestonia's resources

We realise that for many years still Frestonia will be unable to attain self-sufficiency in food and other requirements – the same is however true of many existing small nations. We shall over the years concentrate on developing our own resources, and we hope that tourism will prove to be a major growth industry. We shall also endeavour to generate our own power supply.

Radio station

We shall also develop our own national radio station, which will in no way interfere with the broadcasts of neighbouring nations.

UN peace-keeping force

We appeal to the United Nations, in particular to other small, emerging and non-aligned nations, to treat our application with the utmost seriousness and urgency. If delay in processing our application occurs, an invasion into Frestonia and eviction by the GLC and other organs of the British Government may occur, in which case there will exist a crisis with international ramifications, and the necessity may arise for Frestonia to require the UN to send a token peace-keeping force. These are developments which we must at all costs avoid.

Referendum

If necessary, we would of course co-operate with a repeat referendum of Frestonian citizens, supervised by the United Nations, which would again reveal the desire of the overwhelming majority of inhabitants for self-determination and independence from Great Britain.

We await your swift reply.
Yours faithfully,

David Rappaport-Bramley
Minister of State for Foreign Affairs, on behalf of the Free Independent Republic of Frestonia, 113 St Ann's Road, Frestonia (via London W11, England)

There were 120 residents in Frestonia living in about 30 houses on one acre of land. Everyone who wanted to take part became a minister; there was no prime minister. The Minister of State for Education was a two-year-old, Francesco Bogina-Bramley, and the Minister of State for Foreign Affairs was a dwarf, the actor David Rappaport-Bramley (who wore a T-shirt saying 'Small is Beautiful').

The media descended on Frestonia from around the world. The *Daily Mail* printed a leader column and a report 'from our Foreign Correspondent in Frestonia'. Japanese television filmed New Zealand TV filming nothing much going on in our uneventful communal garden. Coach loads of young tourists, mainly from Denmark, arrived, and were shown round the borders in ten minutes or so, receiving their Frestonian passport stamps and leaving, rather dissatisfied.

A National Film Theatre of Frestonia opened in the People's Hall, with the first showing being *Passport to Pimlico* and films by the Sex Pistols. The theatre opened with the international première of *The Immortalist* by Heathcote Williams, preceded by no less than three national anthems. (The London *Evening Standard* had urged their readers to submit suitable anthems to us.) Frestonia applied to join the International Postal Union and printed its own postage stamps, with replies to our letters coming in from around the world.

It all worked like a dream. The GLC, who previously had refused to deal with us, now told the media that they would negotiate with us 'in New York or wherever' and their Tory leader, Sir Horace Cutler, sent us a letter saying 'If you did not exist it would be necessary to invent you'. We replied 'Since we do exist, why is it necessary to destroy us?'. Sir Geoffrey Howe MP wrote to us that as one who has 'a childhood enthusiasm for the Napoleon of Notting Hill Gate', he could hardly fail to be moved by our plight.

We were suddenly transformed in the GLC's eyes from a bunch of squatters, hobos and drug addicts into an international incident that was providing them with an opportunity to show how enlightened they were and threatening them with the prospect of negative media coverage if they carried on with their plans to evict us.

A public enquiry was ordered. The GLC had their QC, and I represented Frestonia as the Minister of State for the Environment. We proposed that Frestonia become a mixed-use site for houses and craft workshops. We won the enquiry.

Frestonia was eventually rebuilt to our design with several millions of pounds of foreign aid from Great Britain, channelled via the Notting Hill Housing Trust to our own co-operative. We used the superb *Pattern Language* book by Christopher Alexander (published by OUP) on timeless architecture, which is as simple as painting by numbers, to vote as a co-op on the various architectural patterns we wanted incorporated in our new development.

Today, I am immensely proud of the development that was built, complete with its overhanging roofs, enclosed communal gardens and decorated brickwork. Recently, there was a great party in a marquee in the communal garden to mark the twenty-first anniversary of independence. The spirit is still strong. Frestonia goes to show that with imagination and humour you can run rings round the establishment.

Working at the North Kensington Law Centre

Elisa Segrave

Elisa Segrave first used to visit Notting Hill and the Portobello Road as a teenager in 1966. In the early Seventies she worked at the North Kensington Law Centre in Golborne Road. She came to live in Notting Hill in 1978 and still does. Segrave has published several books, including the novel *Ten Men* (1997) and *The Diary of a Breast* (1995), an autobiographical account of her successful fight against breast cancer. Both are published by Faber & Faber.

In 1972 I became a volunteer at the North Kensington Law Centre, the first organisation of its kind in Britain. The Centre was at 74 Golborne Road W10, in an old butcher's shop, and had been started in July 1970 by, among others, Peter Kandler, a solicitor, and Lord Gifford, a barrister. It was intended to support the local community and encourage poorer people to seek legal help informally and without prohibitive costs. The City Parochial Foundation provided a grant of £2,500 and the Pilgrim Trust gave £1,500. The Royal Borough of Kensington and Chelsea agreed to make available, on a short-life basis, at low rent, the shop where the Law Centre is still based.

I had no legal training. At first I sat at Reception where I operated a small telephone switchboard. Our clients had to put their heads through a cubby hole to talk to me.

'Good afternoon, I'm Miss Franks.'

She had a very pale face and spots and was wheeling a pram. 'I've come for me dad. I've got a letter. Got to see the little bloke with the moustache.'

I took her letter. It was to do with car insurance. I buzzed the switchboard to James. 'Who?'

'Miss Franks. Her father's called Mr Harley.'

'Not my client,' said James, and banged down the phone.

'Will you wait here please with the pram,' I said.

James Saunders, slight, with a spiky beard like a goat's and horn-rimmed glasses, had started, when the Law Centre opened, as Peter Kandler's articled clerk after only three months' training. During the first three weeks, two hundred people had come. James had coped. I knew that he, Peter and the other solicitors could have been earning higher salaries in conventional law firms. There were other volunteers, but the regulars in the office with me in 1972 were Jim Peevey, an American solicitor, Paddy, in love with Jim, who'd been a journalist on a women's magazine, solicitor Pam Ditton, fresh-faced and cheerful, Walter, blond with big blue eyes, from a law centre in Canada, and Peter Kandler, the Director. Everyone was a bit frightened of Peter, who had a gruff manner and was overworked. A lovely older woman called Liz came to do the accounts. She had just left *Woolworths*. 'I thought, well, I'm taking home a measly fourteen pounds and the rest goes into Barbara Whats'ername's pocket. Much better do a job here and try to help.' Liz was motherly and was always offering us coffee and biscuits. She had a teenage son, Hubert, whom she was bringing up on her own.

After I'd been there about a week, I attended court, in South London. I had to escort one of our clients. A Mrs Griswold and her husband had been accused of stealing Coronation mugs from a Notting Hill neighbour. Mrs Griswold had grey skin and a mouth that was not like a mouth at all – just a slit in her face. Her hair was greasy and her right wrist was covered with a dirty bandage. She had just tried to kill herself. 'I'm all of a tremble,' she told me outside the court room. 'I'll ring the psychiatric hospital to see if they'll take you back,' I told her. Mrs Griswold explained that she had left the hospital early of her own accord because she was so nervous about the court case. Also, her husband, needed her support. He had just been bashed up by a crowbar in their basement flat. I watched him join her outside the court room. Both his eyes were nearly closed. He didn't want to talk. Mrs Griswold spoke for him. 'He wants to go to the toilet.'

In court she was surprisingly smooth. Although the neighbour, an elderly man, had made a list of his stolen mugs – 'Mrs Griswold told me she collected Coronation mugs' – and the couple had been in his flat the whole afternoon of the theft, there was not enough evidence to convict them.

Mrs Griswold was often in and out of the Law Centre for immoral earnings and petty thieving. A few weeks later, while I was at Reception, I saw her across the street. She was skipping and wearing light blue sandals, inappropriate for the time of year. She had dyed her dull hair the colour of a gold coin. I watched her stop at one of the stalls in the Golborne Road, by a shop called Pramwear, examine an old tea-pot, then skip across towards the Law Centre where she pushed the door open and put her face up to the cubby hole. She had painted a smoky star on her forehead.

'It's like a family, the Law Centre, isn't it? I've got my nightdress on under this!' she cried gaily.

I buzzed upstairs. 'Send her up!' said Peter Kandler.

That morning an old lady had come in about being re-housed. 'I never buy the food round here. Too many blacks. I'm used to a better area. I used to work in *Derry & Toms*. My son served in the Army. I think Mr Heath's a wonderful man. I sent him a letter the other day. I think it's a shame that hussey threw a bottle of ink over him. The young today don't know where they're at.'

She had a very white, thickly powdered face, a little rouge on her cheeks and she wore a pepper and salt tweed coat.

'You might think I'm well-dressed. Well, I can tell you, I've had this coat twenty years. I bought it with the money they gave me when I retired from *Derry & Toms*. It's scandalous how they treat old people today. Seven pounds ten a week I pay for my council flat and I've got bronchitis with the damp. Some boys threw a stone through the window and killed my budgie.'

I tried to be sympathetic in between operating the flashing lights on the switchboard. The old lady leaned forward: 'Excuse me dear, but I can see you're a country girl. I used to live in Surrey. It's so nice to talk to you young ladies. Especially living in an area full of blacks. I used to work in Kensington.'

In those first few years the majority of the Law Centre's cases involved tenant *v* landlord and 'loitering with intent'. There was a crisis between the police and the young males of the area, mostly black. You could be brought into a police station for 'being a suspicious person loitering with intent', charged and put in prison without a solicitor to represent you. Beatings in the local police station were common. Only in the Eighties were these infamous SUS laws abolished.

The housing situation was bad. In the Sixties Rachman had used Alsatian dogs to terrorise his tenants. Stephen Sedley, a barrister (now a judge) who often worked for us, once drove a judge to North Kensington to show him some of the conditions in which people lived. The judge was so horrified that Sedley won his case.

Mr Giles, one of our clients, had trouble with his landlord. It was raining. Mr Giles nearly fell. The Centre's windows were steamy. Mr Giles had a grey film over his eyes. Mr Giles was nearly blind. He came and sat by our electric fire, nodding his head.

'I have to take my pills. Otherwise I get blackouts. They all know me; the grocer knows me, the butcher knows me. They've had to pick me up off the street. Sometimes I think to myself, 'I won't take my pill today'. But if I don't, I get another blackout.'

Outside, a hearse went by. The man in charge of the fruit stall crossed himself. Mr Giles didn't see the hearse. His head was bent very low. He couldn't see me at Reception either. He was waiting to talk to a solicitor.

'My brother, he's paralysed. The landlord knows this. He's not a civilised man. He bothers us all the time. We pay the rent. But he's not just.'

'Why do you get blackouts?'

'I was pushed off a bridge in Jamaica.'

In July 2000, invited by Brian Nicholls, a long-time adviser at the Law

Centre, I went to its thirtieth birthday party where Peter Kandler made a speech. He said he was a socialist, 'which means a commitment to the poor and deprived'. He now runs a criminal law office a few yards away from the old butcher's shop. Jim Peevey left. He married Paddy and they had three children, then divorced. James Saunders practises criminal law and left North Kensington a few years ago. Pam Ditton champions the rights of aborigines in Alice Springs. Liz, the book-keeper, died. The Law Centre continues, but now it focuses on immigration, welfare benefits, mental health advocacy, discrimination, employment and education. I'm proud to have worked there.

The names of clients and their circumstances have been changed in order to protect their identities.

Londoners

Nicholas Shakespeare

Nicholas Shakespeare's books include *The Dancer Upstairs* (1995), which was chosen by the American Libraries Association as the Best Novel of 1997; and *Bruce Chatwin: A life* (1999). He is a former literary editor of the *Daily* and *Sunday Telegraph*, and a Fellow of the Royal Society of Literature. Shakespeare has had a base in Ladbroke Grove since 1984 and it was here that he wrote *Londoners* (1986), described by Michael Moorcock as 'one of the best books on London', from which this extract is taken.

Emma Tennant's latest novel, *The Adventures of Robina*, carries as its subtitle, 'The Memoirs of a Debutante at the Court of Queen Elizabeth II'.

Tall, blonde, her nails full of the pheasant she has just plucked, Emma Tennant stands at her Elgin Crescent window in North Kensington and remembers the day she was presented at Court. A Lenare portrait taken at the time, in 1956, shows her in an afternoon dress, dark gloves, and a choker of pearls. 'Artificial', she says triumphantly.

'That green dress looked like a crushed lettuce leaf by the time we reached the Palace. Everyone had hired Daimlers, and we sat in this queue which edged slowly, slowly forward. It must have taken twenty minutes to get down The Mall, and it was terribly embarrassing because, of course, you felt a twit.'

Bobbing a flustered curtsey before the Queen, who sat 'drumming her fingers like a waxwork' – had she lost an innocence by being shown to the sovereign in this way? Emma Tennant thinks possibly she had.

She replaces the portrait in its brown paper bundle under a drinks table, and goes on to talk about moving house. In Kensington, more people – 68 per cent – own their homes than in any other part of London. (Tower Hamlets, not surprisingly, comes at the bottom of the league with less than three per cent.) Emma Tennant is moving round the corner because she needs the money she will make from buying a smaller house. And because, ironically, the area has become too smart.

'This area used to have the highest density of writers in London. Now it's like the smart Paris suburb of Passy. Full of French and Belgian bankers and heads of BBC departments. Last year, I watched two compete in the parents' egg-and-spoon race. They both held their eggs with their thumbs, which made me suspect that was how they'd got to the top.' She gestures through the window at the communal gardens. 'I'm the bane of the Garden Committee. Twice a year the bell rings, and everyone rushes out to plant crocuses and sweep leaves. It's just like a village, they say. We've got a squirrel and two owls here now,' she adds with mock pride, in mimicry of this inner-city rural fantasy. 'One male that goes too-wit-to-woo. One female that goes goo-wit, goo-wit.'

She turns back into the shambolic, crumbling room and continues excitedly. 'Actually, there's a really bad taste story about the owls. I overheard a neighbour saying, "Isn't it wonderful, we've got the owls back." I told Hilary Bailey, who's lived here for ages in a flat that costs her five pounds a week or something. She said, apparently it isn't the owls at all. It's the call the Notting Hill Gate rapist makes every time he plunges into an au pair's basement.'

Comic, grotesque, outrageous, it is the kind of story that appeals to the author of fantasies like *The Crack* – an apocalyptic tale of what happens when the Thames splits open. 'But I'd never have written my books here had it not been for the communal gardens, and the fact my children could run out and play without me worrying they were wandering into the road. Sadly, you no longer hear the shriek of children. It's complete silence because they're all at Eton.'

Emma Tennant's mid-Victorian Italianate home, like the home she is buying, lies on the Ladbroke Estate. Conceived as a great circus, with villas rising from the fields and quarries west of Notting Hill, it was a speculative development that signally failed. The collapse of the estate in the 1850s made the word 'Ladbroke' synonymous with the risks attached to property – 'a graveyard of buried hopes', according to an 1861 edition of *Building News*.

The houses built for the gentry became rookeries. Whole families lived in a single room, dividing where they slept from where they ate with a curtain down the middle. Then the gentry began moving into the mews houses previously occupied by their servants.

Recently, albeit over a century later than intended, they have started to inhabit the villas in the way originally planned by developers like Cith Blake, Samuel Walker and Thomas Allom. Today, many of the houses around Elgin Crescent have been restored to the status of single homes, and their honeycomb conversions removed. 'The money about,' said one estate agent, 'never ceases to amaze me'.

It takes some doing to amaze an estate agent.

In 1985 the value of property in London went up 19 per cent. Andy, who is a partner in Emma Tennant's local estate agent, Faron Sutaria, reckons the telephone rings, on average, every ten seconds. Last year he only went out to lunch twice: once with a cousin who had come back from abroad, and once with another estate agent. They went next door for half an hour and had a pizza. That, says Andy, is how hard he works.

Andy is an unlikely young man to find in property. A graduate in Russian studies, he decided that the only way to secure himself a job was to advertise. Offering £1,000 for the most interesting job opportunity, and with the catchline 'I Want To Move With *The Times*', he placed an advertisement in that paper. He could not have foreseen the result. The newspaper stole his phrase. More importantly, other newspapers reported the ad.

The London *Evening Standard* ran their story the following day. The headline changed with each edition. 'There were two reasons why it was taken up,' Andy says. 'My offer coincided with the latest record unemployment figures. And no one till then had accepted the idea that a graduate would find it difficult to get a job. After the first few phone calls, I realised I wouldn't have to pay a thing.'

He spent three days at the BBC, being interviewed on various radio programmes as to what had prompted him. Offers of job interviews came in their hundreds. 'I'll give you five grand in cash,' said one insurance executive, 'if you say you are going to join my company. Because of the publicity I'll get.'

Totting it all up, Capital Radio reckoned Andy had earned himself £700,000 worth of international publicity. He had calls from Australia, Vancouver and Switzerland. The most persistent was from a man who said urgently he had to meet him at the Skyline Hotel. 'He wouldn't give a name, just said that he had to meet me. He would be wearing such and such. It was so bizarre, I felt I had to go through with it. Not even then did he tell me what he wanted. Then he called from Canada to arrange lunch. We met in Mayfair. It turned out he wanted me to sell gas stoves to north-east England.'

In the midst of this, Andy met Faron Sutaria, an Indian Parsee who, calling himself the 'Real Estate Agent', had started up his business in a basement flat off Baker Street. Andy was impressed. 'Most estate agents are complete nerds. They don't need any qualifications. Often they are as thick as the bricks they are selling. And they spend most of the time with the purchasers, when they should be acting for the vendors. In America, you pay for both services. You use an agent to both buy and find.'

Each day, Andy shows four or five people round the properties on his books. *Immaculate* is not an adjective he eschews to describe a lavatorially bricked terraced house. Nor is *superb*. But then, what he is offering for £150,000 is the fantasy to make it so.

Most people coming to Andy want to live in the Notting Hill Gate area because of the Central line. It is therefore an ideal location for, say, the bankers and broadcasters so disliked by Emma Tennant. Andy finds it easy to divide the city like this. Mention Bayswater, and to him the word conjures up the first-time flat buyer and Arabs overlooking the park. Mention Barnes, and out come epithets like snob, arty-farty, minor television actors. Mention Richmond, and he tells you, with a dreamy, faraway look in his eye, of wealthy, liberal middle classes with the highest educational standards of any borough in the country.

'As in jobs, everyone upgrades themselves.'. . . 'People don't live in W8 or W2. They live in Kensington or Bayswater. They mention the area because of the connotations that go with it. Also, because some postal codes cover a multitude of sins. W11 includes parts of both Westbourne Grove and Holland Park – overlaying a gulf wider than any you can imagine.

Notting Hill Carnival Poem

Michael Horovitz

Michael Horovitz is a jazz poet, torchbearer-co-ordinator of Poetry Olympics festivals, and editor-publisher of *New Departures* publications. A long-term resident of Notting Hill, he wrote this poem at the first Carnival in 1966 which was essentially a summer festival street-party and revival of the pre-war Notting Hill Fayre.

A pageant of floating foliage
beating conga drums and dustbin lids
with clarion pipes and wild smoke paint
and fancy dress stirs joy
enough to get
policemen even dancing
up the Grove – O *rittum*, the rhythm
joins peace loving light-
and dark-skinned hands
and hearts and heads and bands
in jumping jubilee –
grabbing great branches, a shuffling swaying
triumphal march in glad hurrah – *every-*
body do dis t'ing
– children – all ages
chorusing – 'We all live
in a *yellow* submarine'
– trumpeting tin bam good-time stomp –
a sun-smiling wide-open steelpan-chromatic
neighbourhood party making love not war
– and the television all around
have closed their electronic eyes
knocked out by spontaneous reality
now autumn welcomes you to spring
in Notting Hill,
where universe collides
with universe, and still
nothing gets broken

Growing up with Carnival

Polly Thomas

Polly Thomas was born and raised in West London where she attended Holland Park School throughout much of the 1980s. It was during this period that she developed her love of British-Caribbean culture, and first started to attend Carnival. She made her first trip to the Caribbean aged 17, when she stayed for three months in Jamaica with a friend who was visiting her father. She has since travelled to Jamaica, and Trinidad & Tobago more times than she can remember, often as a researcher and writer of *Rough Guides* to the islands. Here she describes why she loves Carnival.

Ask me the best thing about summer in London, and without a moment's hesitation, I'll say Carnival. Growing up on the periphery of Notting Hill, and attending secondary school at Holland Park, just steps away from the heart of the event, I've never been able to understand those joyless souls who don't love Carnival, who refuse to get impossibly excited about the prospect of sharing their streets with some two million revellers intent on sticking two fingers up to the norm for a couple of days and letting it all hang out in public.

Come Carnival Saturday, when the railway bridges and lamp posts have been transformed into advertising hoardings and an army of entrepreneurs are constructing temporary emporiums along what will be the busiest junctions, there's already a palpable air of anticipation throughout the area. Bars and pre-Carnival parties are packed to the gills, while dedicated Carnivalists are starting early by attending Panorama, the steel band competition held in a local park on Saturday night. By Sunday morning, the music stages are fully functional, the crowd-control barriers and banks of Portaloos are in place and the sound-system operators, having claimed their hotly contested street-corner positions, are warming up their sets, testing the equipment so that the bass bounces and echoes through the high, narrow terraces that spread back from Portobello Road. Huge articulated lorries laden with yet more speakers ease their way through the back streets to the Carnival route, trailing bands of costumed paraders in their wake and passing the swanky, prominently deserted homes of those who prefer to set the alarms and flee for the duration. By early afternoon, the streets are heaving, and Europe's biggest and best street party is in full, inexorable swing.

Territorial, cliquey and occasionally arrogant about our precious home, West Londoners can seem a strange lot, but in Carnival we've always had something to really feel smug about. Because though it's Caribbean in essence, the substance of today's Carnival is a uniquely W11/W10 affair, a phenomenon that stems directly from the evolving tastes and experiences of the local human hotchpotch. It's a hybrid carnival, in which the reggae, garage, blues and salsa played by the sound systems sit happily alongside the steel-band trucks, where buying a suitably glamorous designer outfit to model on the streets is more common than playing mas with a costume band.

Although the mas bands remain the stock image of Carnival, alongside the inevitable black grandmother dancing with a beet-faced policeman, when I started attending as a teenager in the 1980s, the costumes and other Carnival disciplines always felt like a somewhat peripheral part of the event. For me they were more a gorgeous interlude glimpsed as we weaved our way between what really got us excited: the sound systems.

Steel-band trucks held mild appeal in that we could watch our pan-playing schoolmates in action, and the soca floats offered the opportunity to keep on partying after everything else had been shut down (they always keep the music playing as they wind their way home, mostly as a way of getting people out of the area), but those huge columns of speaker boxes were the real face of Carnival for us. Stacked up on the same street corners where we hung out when bunking off school, the sound systems were the place to be – very public arenas in which to show off our carefully planned outfits and dance in the open air to the most popular tunes of the year. There was a lovely feeling of unity, of somehow getting away with something just by being there.

My fondest Carnival memories – jumping up with thousands of others under the Westway where Rapattack and Mastermind systems held sway, or watching an entire streetful of heads bounce to the same beat during the acid-house summer of 1997 – have little in common with the carnivals of the Caribbean, but they do illustrate what makes Notting Hill such a special affair. Some traditionalists feel that London's Carnival, with its emphasis on sound systems and music stages, is a far cry from 'real' Carnival in the Caribbean. It has little connection with the celebration of freedom that was created by white planters but usurped by newly-free Africans after the abolition of slavery, and which, in Trinidad, where it is based around tightly-fought competitions for the best masquerade costume, calypsonian, soca performer or steel band, has become the biggest event of the year. But for most people of my generation, these 'failings' are precisely what keeps us coming back year after year. Rather than sticking to the traditional disciplines of West Indian carnivals, our event has grown and evolved alongside wider society. It reflects the changing passions of Carnival-goers over the decades and accepts almost anything that wants to be a part of it. Brazilian samba bands and traditional Indian drummers fill the streets alongside pumping soca flats and costume paraders, while Glastonbury-style music-stages host everything from World Music crooners to international hip-hop acts which compete for attention with raw ragga. (Only the Royal Navy float, hauled out every year complete with submarine but no music, hasn't really got into the spirit of things.) Carnival has moved with the times, and while the event wouldn't be the same without mas and steel pan, it's vital that it's able to embrace the new as well as the old.

From the beginning, Notting Hill Carnival has been a creation of the area's diverse population, in terms of both race and class, and an offshoot of an underlying bacchanalian spirit set in place by West Indians who settled in Notting Hill during the late 1940s. They set up the clubs and shebeens that first attracted the white middle classes here, eager to prove that they didn't share the xenophobic sentiments of much of the rest of the population. In doing so, they paved the way for the multi cultural Notting Hill of today (becoming less diverse as gentrification reaches every last corner), and laid the foundations both of the area's party spirit, and of its unending creativity – an ethos that said if you want something, get up and create it and be part of it rather than watch from the sidelines.

There's always been plenty of contention as to how Carnival began and it's difficult – and perhaps rather pointless – to try to pin down the exact origins of an event that has developed so organically. However, it is generally agreed that the idea of a festival in Notting Hill came about as a means to unify the community in the aftermath of the 1958 race riots. In the early 1960s, Rhaune Laslett, a dedicated community worker who ran a local play group, began organising an annual procession in the tradition of an English summer fête, with children of all races parading the streets dressed up as folk heroes. This has little to do with Caribbean carnivals, but given the local demographics it wasn't long before the West Indian community became more directly involved. Claudia Jones, a political activist and founder and editor of the seminal *West Indian Gazette*, had staged the first of several pre-Lenten 'Caribbean Carnivals' in 1959. An indoor, cabaret-type evening featuring well-known steel bands and calypsonians, Jones's carnival had many of the elements of the event back home, and by the mid-1960s, when Laslett asked local residents to introduce some more Caribbean elements into the summer street parade, they were able to draw on the network of carnival artists who had performed at Jones's event. In 1965, with just three players on foot, the first mobile steel pan band hit the road and the roots of today's Carnival were planted.

Under the guidance of individuals such as Leslie Palmer, who had grown up in Trinidad, the event continued to grow each summer, and a Carnival Development Committee was formed in 1972. By the early 1970s, it was a decidedly Caribbean affair, with all the Trinidadian carnival traditions firmly in place. However, calypso had never really carried the swing in London; the mixed bunch of party-goers at local black clubs had been dancing to Jamaican rocksteady and ska for years. Jamaican reggae had by now become the music of choice in both the Caribbean and Notting Hill, and Carnival got its first taste of the very Jamaican institution of the sound system in 1974. The event was never quite the same again.

The carnivals of the early 1970s also reflected the wider militancy that set the tone for the era. As the Black Power movement took hold in the Caribbean and the USA, and black people in the UK faced ongoing racism from the police, who made full and brutal use of the SUS laws, Carnival became a focus of black resentment towards the police and vice versa. Disputes were inevitable, and what had become one of the largest outdoor events in the country became marred by the violence which peaked in 1976. Carnival remained a symbol of defiance, described by local restaurant owner Frank Critchlow as a 'victory' rather than a party. By the time I started attending in the 1980s, the problems of the 1970s were on the wane, and though the fun was marred by crowds of opportunist 'steamers', who pushed through the crowds relieving the revellers of their valuables, the party spirit was firmly to the fore again. Notting Hill's bohemian flavour had become decidedly fashionable, and Carnival became everyone's party.

The Notting Hill Carnival Trust, which has organised the event since the late 1980s, brought in the inevitable corporate touch, generating the sponsorship that allowed Carnival to continue, and seeing off annual calls for it to be moved to the more manageable surroundings of Hyde Park or Wormwood Scrubs. Following two murders during last year's revelries, such demands have yet again been raised, but it's impossible to imagine how the event could survive enclosure without sacrificing its spirit.

Even though many former Carnival die-hards now prefer to spend their August bank holiday elsewhere, bemoaning the fact that 'Carnival isn't what it used to be since they imposed the 7pm curfew/changed the route/commercialised the whole thing', the event is still as exciting as it ever was, for me. And judging from the fact that the crowds continue to grow, I'm not alone.

Practicalities

The Notting Hill Carnival takes place each year on the Sunday and Monday of the last bank holiday in August. On the Saturday before the event, the costume gala is staged indoors; venues change each year. From around 7pm on carnival Saturday, steel bands fight to take part in the annual Panorama competition at Horniman's Pleasance, just off Kensal Road. Details of all these events, as well as calypso competitions, can be found at the official Web site (www.nottinghill-carnival.net.uk), which also has lots of useful background, a map of the area and lists of masquerade bands as well as some useful links.

It's also well worth taking a look at one of the many annual carnival guides published just before the event; the best are issued free with

London's *Time Out* listings magazine or *ES*, the *Evening Standard's* Friday colour supplement.

My London
Mustafa Matura

Playwright Mustafa Matura left the Caribbean in 1961 to live and work in London. He is now an established theatre figure in Britain: *The Times* called him 'our finest dramatist of West Indian origin'. His latest play is *The Last Brahmin*. He moved to Notting Hill in 1981 where his greatest source of inspiration is the Portobello Road. The following description was first published in 1993.

I first discovered the West London area of Ladbroke Grove during the 'Swinging Sixties'. At that time it was a vibrant cosmopolitan community attracting those in search of its liberating lifestyles. It was the home of young long-haired hippies parading in their colourful clothes and new-found freedom; a large Caribbean community, adding a spicy flavour to the proceedings; and the annual street Carnival. Others, drawn to its slightly soiled, roguish atmosphere, added to it the hustle and bustle of the antiques and fruit and vegetable market stalls on the Portobello Road, which on Saturdays competed for attention with the visitors' exotic fashions. The whole area was bursting with life.

Coming from and writing about the Caribbean, it is not surprising that the area became (as we say) my *lime*, my watering hole. Why not? Hemingway found his Spain, Joyce his Dublin, Runyon his Bowery. I had found my London.

I have seen Ladbroke Grove pass through many phases since then, some good, some bad: hippy, punk, radical chic, rasta, bourgeois respectability. Like most areas of London, 'the Grove' has had its fair share of notoriety. There were famous murderers, who caused the council to change the name of the place where their crimes were committed; there were shady landlords who knew certain call girls, who knew certain cabinet ministers, who resigned in disgrace in the Sixties, who all went on to have Hollywood movies made about them. As they might say in the Grove, 'I should be so lucky.'

Nowadays, on a good day, having written my fill, I can begin a stroll, walking south along the still hustling and bustling (even more so) Portobello Road market. Fancy, surreal hairdressing salons, object *de* kitchen shops, new, New-Age religious shops stocked with mandalas, crystals and Brazilian witches rub shoulders with honest record shops, all pumping out the latest in-music, next to travel and cookery shops. I could see Jo Kenyatta in his red, gold and green knitted hat and his shiny, third-hand suit, who will shadow-box me while telling me tales of his wayward nephew Brandy, 'who if he doesn't look out, he go' get in bad trouble,' as if I am to deliver that message. Or I could decide between Malaysian or Italian for lunch. These days the Italian pizzeria is in the ascendency, with delicious melted cheeses that are a joy to behold. Then a black mini-skirted silhouette will pass by; following her progress, I will see the latest pictures and pieces being hung at one of the many art and ceramic galleries, containing mostly large daubs for large reception areas, or huge alien-like figures looming in the carefully trained spotlights. I swear, a recent exhibition is of all black painted canvases of different sizes.

On the next corner, I could see Red Reg in his sharp, black leather hat and wind-proofed coat, arranging incense, hats, socks and pictures of Martin Luther King, Malcolm X, Pope John, Caribbean childhood scenes and soft-focus, semi-erotic couples coupling, all of which he sells. I could walk past him and go to Rose, sitting behind her glass-fronted show-case which reflects the glittering baubles inside, and the shimmering party frocks hung above her; and Rose might tell me of her last exotic trip abroad, or one she is planning. How she does it I do not know . . . I just don't go to the right parties, that's all.

Or I could cross Lancaster Road and browse at a shop containing the most beautiful stone, metal and wooden works of art from India, from everyday utilitarian objects to the most intricately carved windows and doors; or similar stuff, in a shop opposite, from Africa. I walk past the betting shop quickly, having once been hooked on numbers; I have a 'there but for the grace of God' attitude to the dazed men I glimpse inside, and move on to the Warwick Castle, a pub that has been preserved in time by the thick layers of nicotine and grime that occasionally peel off, further concussing its unfortunate customers. But it has the distinctive attraction of having two green baize pool tables that attract the finest players from miles around.

Through the smoky haze, I could glimpse Classical in his long overcoat, nursing a half of Guinness, watching the action, checking who to play (meaning, who he can beat) before putting down his token coin. I could see Manny, Indian Tony and Lindsay arguing over whose coin is next while moving their own to the front; then Prang with his booming voice, with the authority of his flowing dreadlocks, would settle matters by shouting, 'Nobody en' playing next, me playing next, dat's my ten pence dere. I put my mark on it an' it's mine. You Manny an' Lindsay an' Tony, too cheat.' And while the shamed trio withdraw in disarray, blaming each other for their own bad reputations, I would slide my coin next to Prang's.

And to prepare for the mammoth battle of skills, wills an' wiles to come, I could wash down the fine lasagne with a pint of lager, not by any means the best, but better bad beer than no pool, I tell myself.

I sometimes win, and sometimes lose, as the wise man said. But during those one (or two or three, or four five six) hour periods that I spend trying to play next, liming, gossiping, marvelling at others' skills, luck, misfortune, blunders, observing the karmatic dimension of the games, I am in a writer's paradise.

People don't just give me ideas for stories; in the Grove they give you their life stories also, and they come in every shape and size, from the acted-out telling to the perfectly timed punch lines; what more could one ask for? It's like being in a real-life, long-running soap opera, which I tell myself I'm only researching in order to write about.

Not true. I became a character in it some time ago, 'de writer feller', the one who prays that the gentrification process that is taking place in the area now does not totally destroy its unique character and characters, and who hopes that somehow, by writing about it, he is preserving it, but now with the added knowledge that the Grove's own vibrant, resilient sense of life will continue to replenish itself, and those that lime there.

Why, yesterday, I swear I saw a young hippy girl, wearing a bright, new afghan coat, with a mirrored bag hanging from her bony shoulders and yellow, flared, velvet trousers flapping at her ankles, striding up the 'Bello'.

It's that kind of area.

A Taste of the Action

Duncan Fallowell

Duncan Fallowell was born in London in 1948 and moved to Notting Hill Gate in 1970, though he has lived in many other parts of the world. He is the author of several travel books and novels, the latest being the soon to be published *A History of Facelifting*. These diary extracts were originally published in the London *Evening Standard* during 1998.

To the Cobden Club for a drink with Vasko, a Serbian. Now that sweet Iris Palmer has taken the fashion victims into the basement, the upstairs room has become one of the dreamiest resorts in town. Something about its theatricality reminds me of St Petersburg: huge, grand, with a dash of barbarism.

Vasko asks if he can tell the Home Office he's my long-term boyfriend in order to obtain asylum, residency, work permit, whatever, in the UK. Actually he lives with an Italian girl on Denmark Hill – where do they find these places? Whenever I've landed on Denmark Hill it's because I'm totally lost. I tell him he'd have better luck in Denmark. 'No – Denmark Hill,' he reiterates. He doesn't get the joke. His English isn't good.

Why not marry the Italian? 'She married already.' Unfortunately, I have to say no too, because I may wish to use the option one day for a genuine love and if I've already shot my bolt an' stuff. . .'Boltons?' Vasko picks up, 'you know someone in Boltons?' No, no, no. He's overheating. It must be the red wine – normally he drinks only vodka. He looks downcast. To mollify him, I say I'll ask the barman.

Kymon is thinking of joining the Royal Navy which is an attractive thing to do but it would be a loss – he's the nicest barman in London, with wonderful eyes and a wicked laugh. I ask 'Do you know any girls who might marry a charming Serbian? They don't have to be ethnically clean.'

Kymon tilts his head and clicks his tongue: 'Sorry, but the only girl I know who wants to get married is a Bosnian. And she wants to get married for the same reason.' Perhaps they could marry each other?' 'What would be the point of that?' wonders Kymon. What indeed.

The Champion pub in Notting Hill Gate was the first gay bar I ever visited – that was in 1967 and I've been popping in occasionally ever since, though it's not my scene and has had an odd series of landlords, some of them homophobic. In Gay Liberation Front days a couple mates of mine were thrown out of it for wearing crinolines. The barmen, with rare exceptions, were morose and the customers generally resentful of the most innocent attempts at communication.

More recently it has become stranded between the traditional gay pub and the new-style bar, with neither the mixed chumminess of the former nor the youthful buzz of the latter. In fact it has a sullen ghastliness all its own, laced with a strong dose of self-disgust. So why go in at all? Because it's *there*, conveniently sited on the Gate for a quick drink and a look, hope pathetically springing eternal.

But now it's overstepped the mark. A blackboard was hung in the Gents several landlords' ago for playful graffiti. Chalked on the blackboard these days is a large message: 'No loitering – anyone found loitering will be asked to leave.' Occasional naughtiness has occurred in there but it was never hopping and surely a certain informality is understandable in the Gents of a gay bar.

I asked the lunchtime barman the reason for this horrid message. Had there been complaints from the public or interference from the police? 'No,' he replied tautly, without looking at me and continuing to stack glasses, 'we put it up ourselves. People were loitering in there and it's against the law and we uphold the law.'

Well, this is the first time I've ever seen such a sign in such a place and if they really *had* to, could it not have been phrased more sweetly or prefaced with 'Sorry, lads, but'? Oh no. They have chosen to reproduce exactly that nasty, life-hating puritan tone we've been fighting all our lives. So after more than thirty years, it's goodbye, Champion.

The Ground Floor Bar has been trying to gayify itself by advertising in the gay press. If it succeeds it might do something to soften the brutal atmosphere of Portobello Road at night – as would the reopening of the Electric Cinema (is that *ever* going to happen?). So I checked it out with Chris, my Polish Bristolian friend who prefers women.

'The music's too loud,' he said, 'and everyone is too far apart.' 'Everyone's too far apart, Chris, because it's not very full, but I like that. Can you see anyone gay?' 'What about that bald chap in the corner?' 'He's about as gay as a baboon's arse.' 'I thought so.' 'No, Chris, that means not very gay at all. There's someone reading over there.' 'Is that gay?' 'Depends what the book is.'

We crane. 'AS Byatt' he says. 'Oh gawd, about as gay as a soggy banana. What, Chris, are you reading these days?' '*In With The Euro, Out With The Pound*. And you?', *Memories and Portraits* by Ivan Bunin.' 'Is he gay?' 'No. He was a Russian of the *ancien régime* who wrote incredibly modern short stories on the subject of love. Ah, I spy two pretty Cockney boys watching football on the telly. I hope they're gay.'

We crane again. 'Don't think so. Oh look!' says Chris. His eyes light up as a young man flaps by in Oxford bags and a very tight shirt. 'Is that one?' he asks. 'Could be.' Tight shirt leans over an occupied table and says something in a fey voice. Chris gives me a knowing glance. 'I believe I've spotted one too,' I confide, 'the butch one down there drinking incognito with a girl. Doesn't fool me.'

Oh – it's closing time. When are the authorities going to kill this absurd 11pm guillotine? It makes a mockery of London's claim to be the world's most happening city and killing it would do more than anything to *humanise* the streets at night. As for the Portobello Road, I don't think we really need a gay bar. Round here everyone mucks in.

A Pashmina Incident

Justine Hardy

Justine Hardy was born in England, trained as a journalist in Australia, and now works between India and London, writing books and making documentaries. She lives in New Delhi and Notting Hill. The following incident was recorded in her most recent book, *Goat* (2000).

Then the idea came if I sold shawls it would be a way of making some of the money that Gautam needed. It would be so simple. I knew I could do it. I had already made my first sale without even trying a few weeks earlier, on a brief trip to London.

It had been cold too in Notting Hill. People on the street had surprised expressions, caught out by the first frost. They scuttled along, looking up at the sky just to check that it really was as bleak as it felt. The beautiful but weary were making their way to a popular café to while away the long hours until another evening's entertainment began.

I was not looking my best. The back of my grey tracksuit resembled the sagging folds of an elephant's bottom. My gym shoes were a memento of an inter-school netball tournament circa 1982. The one redeeming feature of my ensemble was a pashmina shawl. It was the colour of flame-tree flowers and it had been given to me by a houseboat-owner in Kashmir with whom I had stayed years before. I had become immediately attached to it without really knowing anything about pashmina.

As the Notting Hill rain started, I retreated into the folds of my shawl and took refuge in the doorway of a post office. Inside a woman in a tight white jersey was shrieking at a man behind one of the glass serving screens, telling him that he had absolutely no idea about service. He didn't seem to mind, happy, perhaps, just to admire the sharp nipples that the tight white jersey showed off so nicely. Its wearer abandoned her tirade and came towards me.

'Can you believe how rude some people are?' she said in Manhattan Islandese.

I smiled back at her.

'That shawl, I want it. Where did you get it?'

'From Kashmir.'

'Belief.' She pulled one end of the shawl towards her.

'I must have one.'

I looked at her.

'Oh, forget my manners. It's a New York thing. Let me buy it from you.'

I couldn't think of anything to say.

'Come on, how much is it? I have cash, I'll pay you right now.'

'£200.'

The shawl was four years old – £50 a year seemed reasonable.

'Great.'

She tugged more forcefully at the dangling end of the shawl. It fell free, aflame at her feet. She picked it up, twined it around her neck and grabbed my hand, pulling me down the street. We stopped in the rain outside an antique shop with a French mirror in the window (one of those ones that have reflected the image of a thousand courtesans). The American twirled in front of the glass.

'I love it, I love it.' She opened her bag. 'Now, what about a discount?'

'Please, may I have my shawl back?'

I remember holding out my hand.

'Come on,' she wheedled.

'If you would like it I have told you how much it is, otherwise please may I have it back?'

She pushed four £50 notes into my hand and walked away.

Notting Hill in Film

Mark Shivas

Mark Shivas produced the feature films *Moonlighting* (1982) with Jeremy Irons, *A Private Function* (1984) with Michael Palin and Maggie Smith, and *The Witches* (1990) with Anjelica Huston. He has also produced many works for television, most recently, Alan Bennett's *Talking Heads* and *Telling Tales*. Shivas was Head of Television Drama and Head of Films at the BBC for ten years and lives in Notting Hill. Here he relays many of the area's star-studded film appearances.

Notting Hill was close to the Gaumont (1917) and later the BBC (1948) studios in Lime Grove, Shepherd's Bush and then to the BBC Television Studios at White City, so it's no surprise that so much celluloid has run through so many cameras in the area for so many decades. And of course Notting Hill holds such a variety of buildings and streets – squalid and elegant, green and grey – that it's likely there's something being shot there almost every day.

The oldest feature film I can remember where Notting Hill appears is *The Blue Lamp* (1949). The old Paddington Green police station was there, though it vanished later in the path of the Westway. The movie, starring Dirk Bogarde, had police cars, their bells clanging, chased down a very sylvan and unpopulated Ladbroke Grove then passing Penzance Place, Latimer Road and Scrubs Lane.

The Bramley Arms in Bramley Road, now offices, featured in *The Lavender Hill Mob* (1951) and turned up again in *The Squeeze* (1977), *Quadrophenia* (1979) and *Sid and Nancy* (1986), but it wasn't until Notting Hill became world-wide news with the race riots of 1958 that the district was increasingly used for filming.

The producer Michael Relph told me that his film *Sapphire* (1959), a whodunit described by the *Monthly Film Bulletin (MFB)* as being about 'the problem of the negro's position in contemporary society', nearly didn't happen after the various mayors of the Notting Hill boroughs lobbied the boss of the Rank Organisation to get it stopped. Only by dint of Relph and his director Basil Dearden taking no fees did they persuade the Head of Production, Earl St John, to give it the go ahead – the film was shot in streets off Ladbroke Grove.

Colin Mclnnes's novel *Absolute Beginners*, published in 1959, called the area 'Napoli' and described it as 'the residential doss-house of our city. . . one massive slum, crawling with rats and rubbish . . . There are one or two sections that are positively posh; not fashionable, mind you, but quite graded with their big back gardens and that absolute silence which in London is the top sign of a respectable location.' The 1986 film of the book was shot entirely in a studio.

Look Back in Anger (1959) used Kensal Green Cemetery, while three years later Leslie Caron in *The L-Shaped Room* lived in a room at the top of a crumbling house in St Luke's Road with 'a maladjusted negro jazz man (Brock Peters) able to hear everything through the thin partition'. The *MFB* decided the film had 'nothing specific to say about life in a London bed-sitter in 1962'. The hero of Michael Winner's film *West 11* (1963) was Joe Beckett (Alfred Lynch), a rootless young drifter with (again) a dingy Notting Hill bed-sit, living an aimless existence centred on coffee bars, jazz clubs and pubs around Colville Terrace and Powis Square.

Things cheered up with Richard Lester's *A Hard Day's Night* (1964) in which Ringo Starr is pursued by fans down Lancaster Road. Lester's film of *The Knack* (1965) featured another chase, this time through one side of the Portland Arms (now Orsino's restaurant) and out the other, as in a scene shot but eventually dropped from the Beatles' film.

When Assheton Gordon, designer of *The Knack*, started looking for locations for *Blow Up* (1966) he took the director Antonioni to see places as he discovered them. 'He then wrote the script into the locations and I think that is one of the reasons it worked so well.' *Blow Up* became the archetypal Swinging London movie – *Time* magazine produced its famous edition on the topic in the spring of that year – and John Cowan's studio in Princedale Road (now a design consultant's office) was used for David Hemmings's photographic studio and his 'orgy' with the two girls on blue paper. His Rolls Royce convertible passed by Pottery Lane several times.

In 1975 Antonioni returned to Lansdowne Crescent for *The Passenger* with Jack Nicholson. Karel Reisz's film of David Mercer's *Morgan, a Suitable Case for Treatment* (1966) featured David Warner in a gorilla suit on the escalator at Notting Hill tube (shot at night when the station was closed) while Vanessa Redgrave's house was in Campden Hill Square.

Nineteen-sixty-eight and 69 were busy years for filming in the Hill. Kevin Billington's *Interlude* (1968), a love story, with Oskar Werner, was exciting for me because his lover, played by Barbara Ferris, had a flat in the street where I then lived in Holland Park. Billington shot in the Orangery in the Park, in Norland Square and in Addison Avenue, where he later bought a house.

The Italian Job began in Portobello Road; Tom Courtenay starred in *Otley*, Dick Clement's spy spoof; and Elizabeth Taylor played a magnificent whore in Joseph Losey's baroque *Secret Ceremony*, with Mia Farrow, Robert Mitchum and Peggy Ashcroft. Much of this last film was shot against the tiled walls and vaulted ceilings of No.8 Addison Road, designed by Halsey Ricardo in 1905 for the store owner Sir Ernest Debenham.

Most memorably, 1968 saw the making of Nic Roeg and Donald Cammell's *Performance*, though it wasn't released (recut) until 1970. James Fox played a crook on the run; the plot, such as it was, had him overhear a musician mention an address. He turned up on the doorstep in Powis Square to find Mick Jagger with Anita Pallenberg and others, taking drugs by the sackload, living in what the *MFB* primly described as 'voluntary and eccentric retreat'.

John Boorman's *Leo the Last* (1969) perhaps made more use of the area's contrasts than any film before it. Based on a play called *The Prince* by George Tabori, Leo was Marcello Mastroianni, an aristocrat who studied poor slum dwellers through a telescope from the safety of his mansion. The critic Alexander Walker called it 'Mr Deeds Goes to the Ghetto' while the *MFB* wrote: 'The film is not about racial prejudice nor is it the standard liberal treatment of the race issue in Britain. Notting Hill, where it was shot, just happens to be the home of a lot of negroes. It is a film about exploitation of social class and the pressures impinging on slum-dwellers.' Boorman sprayed the houses of Testerton Road (now demolished) just around the corner from Latimer Road tube station a dramatic black, and Mastroianni was seen with Billie Whitelaw and many others in the therapeutic waters of the Kensington Sports Centre in Walmer Road.

One of the most infamous addresses in all of Fifties' England was 10 Rillington Place, being the home of John Christie who had murdered seven women there in the 1940s and early 50s (see p 129). It was also the title of a 1971 film made by the American director Richard Fleischer. So notorious was the address that the little street was expunged from the map, but not before the movie used the house next door for filming. Richard Attenborough gave a memorable performance as Christie.

There were a few films shot around Notting Hill in the Seventies, but the first British feature made by a black director, Horace Ove's *Pressure* (1975) was made around the Harrow Road, and kids who were squatting in houses around Ladbroke Grove had parts in it. *London Kills Me* (1991), Hanif Kureishi's only foray into directing, featured Trellick Tower and was set in the seedier parts of Portobello and North Kensington, with some interior shots on Chepstow Villas (see p 28).

Stephen Frears's gritty *Sammy and Rosie Get Laid* (1987), from a Kureishi script, also took place in and around Ladbroke Grove, and the commune bulldozed at the end was under the Westway at Westbourne Park. The same grubby feel as the two Kureishis comes through again in the Finnish director Aki Kaurismaki's dark 1990 comedy *I Was a Contract Killer*.

The end credits of *Notting Hill* (1999) thank 'everyone in Notting Hill' and indeed more of the area's attractive sides were seen in this film than in any other before it. Portobello market (including a memorable sequence across the four seasons), Richard Curtis's own blue doorway in Westbourne Park Road, the Coronet cinema, Rosemead Gardens (for the night-time visit by Julia Roberts and Hugh Grant) and Stanley Gardens. The restaurant was a card shop in Golborne Road (see p 93) and, of course, the model for Hugh Grant's bookshop was none other than the editor of this book's own Travel Bookshop in Blenheim Crescent.

Thirty years after *Blow Up*, Assheton Gordon returned to Princedale Road to work on the live action version of *101 Dalmatians*. When it came to the recent sequel, the new director clearly didn't realise what the film of *Notting Hill* had done for the renown and expense of the neighbourhood. He considered the environs of Ladbroke Grove not to look quite smart enough for what he was after!

But then, Notting Hill

Nikki Gemmell

Nikki Gemmell has written two novels, *Shiver* (1997) and *Cleave* (1999); a third, *Lovesong*, is being published by Picador later this year. Her work has been internationally critically acclaimed and translated into several languages. She was born in Wollongong, Australia, and now lives in Notting Hill with her husband and son. Here she describes living in England, and moving to Notting Hill.

> *Although he enjoyed his time in London, he admits that he "felt like someone from another planet'. A naturally shy man, by 1970 he had decided to return home. "One day I looked at the man in my local service station and I suddenly realised that if I lived here ten years I wouldn't know that man any better."*
> (Peter Carey, *The Book Collector*)

Arrival

I moved to London because of a man, at the age of 30, and I didn't know what to expect. About the man, or the place. I'd heard that the region of greater London had a population the size of the country I'd left. That Britain's average density was 632 people per square mile, compared to six in Australia, where I was from.

The man had a flat on Fleet Street. One room. It figured.

In those first, glazed days of arrival I began the search for green, and space, and sky.

I found pocket parks and squares tucked within the city but they were reluctant, they wouldn't let me in. I walked around and around those squares' empty green but the gates were locked and the fence iron was spiked and couldn't be scaled and I didn't understand. My new home was a tough nut to crack. It had stone that was harder and sharper and smoother than the honey-grainy sandstone I had left far behind, the new stone was fine and cold to the touch and stained the tips of my fingers black. It had a sky that was low, so low that it hung like the water-bowed ceiling of an old house. And its rain was soft, there was no weight in it, and I wanted wind and push and wet, I wanted rain like at home that drenched clothes in three seconds.

I began dreaming of home too much, of ready smiles and tall skies and flinging sun into my lungs, of *warmth*.

The man said to hang in there, that one day we'd be rich enough to move out, to walk in one of those reluctant parks, imagine that. But I'd read in one of this country's newspapers that this was the land that looked askance at ambition, and boldness, and striving, that took refuge in denigration and sneer.

For 18 months I hung in there, in our one room on Fleet Street. Because of the man, not the city. It refused to enchant me. I walked cobbles and pavements that whispered of old smoke and grit and blood and spit and I wondered, often, at what I'd done. My man, another expat, did not understand this attitude: he'd read the *Spectator* since he was eight, belonged to the PG Wodehouse Society, loved his Scotch and his Savile Row suits and was from Melbourne, a wintry city. This was his life's goal, to be in this land. Whereas I was from Sydney, a warmer place, and the English cold felt as if it had curled up in my bones like mould. Like so many Australians in the UK I hadn't yet learnt how to dress warmly, hadn't learnt the secret of layers.

We had no proper kitchen, no oven, no washing machine and my grandmother couldn't understand the life choice I'd made, the dramatic drop in my standard of living. But the man wouldn't allow me to give up. He taught me to lean far out of the window and twist my neck to catch the sky. To warm my fingers on the hot water bottle before I touched his skin. To look, really look at the history around us. He showed me the Roman walls by the Barbican, and the plaques in Postman's Park, and St Brides, the writers' church with its ancient crypts, and we managed to brew a happiness in our dark, little bedsit.

But still I had that nagging gravitational pull south, it was like the smudge of a storm cloud between us. Home filled my heart. I couldn't find a new home in London. I constantly tasted air that was stained by cars, the cram of exhausts. My lungs had been coddled for most of my life and in this new place my breathing shallowed and my walking slowed and my sleeping ballooned in the tenacious cold. I slept a lot. And my life shrank.

What I was told

'You'll never be invited into an English person's house.'
'They have plastic tubs in the kitchen sink.'
'It's impossible to get a decent shower.'
'They'll only invite you into their homes as you're leaving.'
'Every kitchen has Fairy washing-up liquid. Isn't that hysterical? Fairy.'
'They sunbake on grass. On the one day of sunshine a year.'
'If ever you DO get invited into one of their houses, just remember the magic words *would you like another cup of tea*?'
'Why?'
'Because they actually mean 'Would you go now, please.
They never say what they mean.'

The colour of the city

I'd read that London was a red city, sanguine. From the Great Fire to the bombs of the Blitz, to the phone boxes and mail boxes and buses, red was the colour of the energy of the place. But to me it was a cold, steely grey, an energy that was uptight, unwelcoming, hard. I only saw red when the smartly dressed woman on Regent Street poked me in the head with the spoke of her umbrella, and drew blood, and didn't stop, didn't look at the damage she'd inflicted. The English were meant to have invented manners, weren't they, so why were they so impolite? Why wouldn't they meet my eyes? Or tell me their name when I thrust out my hand and gave them mine.

I wrote to my grandmother that sometimes I didn't understand what I'd done, I didn't know why I was here.

'You're in love', she replied, and left it at that.

What happened at the laundromat

One Monday evening, during the weekly laundromat ritual, the man steered me into a jewellery shop in Covent Garden and bought a ring in the middle of the washing cycle. He later proposed, formally, over the ironing board. He was doing the ironing. I was soaring.

He signed a three-year work contract. He was wedded to this place, I was not. But I was wedded to him. And so I stayed.

Go west young woman

I must have been just about the only person who moved to Notting Hill in the late 1990s without knowing what Notting Hill was. The man's new job was out west and we needed somewhere closer to his office. I favoured Kensington or Chelsea. I'd read about those glossy places as I slavishly pored over English *Vogue* as a teenager in the sticks, dreaming of being a Sloane. But the man liked a flat in some suburb with a Hill in it. He said a film was coming out soon and I would see what he meant. I'd heard of a film about a murderer who put acid in a bath. He said not that one. This one was about a different Notting Hill.

I twigged when the person looking at the flat ahead of us was one of the girls from the All Saints, wanting to buy a gift for her mother. I began to think that maybe I could like this place, suddenly I wanted that flat and this suburb, I wanted to beat the girl from All Saints. We were told we would have to be quick.

The colour of Notting Hill

White, and green.

White, from those lovely rows of stately terraces – the London of Henry James and prams wheeled by nannies in parks, the London, at last, of my imagination. White, from the cherry blossoms in the early spring that floated down to the roads like tissue paper snow. Green, from the awning of the deli on Elgin Crescent that's crammed with goodies (at last, proper food!). Green, from the coolness of the beautiful communal gardens, empty, languid and dank in the heat.

We didn't live in one of those terraces, and we didn't have access to any communal gardens, but we had a little garden of our own, a handkerchief one at the back of our flat. The All Saints girl wasn't interested in the end. Things were looking up. Especially when I began telling people about where we had bought and they began filling me in about this Hill place.

'But it's only a basement flat, and it's tiny, and it's just hanging on by its fingernails to W11. The street's really ugly, it's all bare, with council flats down one side.'

'It doesn't matter. You just wait.'

First impressions

It wasn't the best beginning.

What was all the fuss about Portobello Road? It was meant to be glamorous and chic, but to me it just seemed dirty, messy, scruffy. And then there was the nightmare ride into town during rush hour on the 23 bus. (Why did people in England cough so much, and why didn't they cover their mouths?) And don't get me started on the cram that is *Tesco* on Portobello Road. Or the post office near Ladbroke Grove tube. I hadn't yet learnt how to meekly queue. I was too jittery and impatient for all that.

Home wasn't much better. People used the entrance to our flat as a communal rubbish bin, they just tossed their refuse over the rail. In our back garden, lolly wrappers and empty cigarette packets and a sanitary pad were all thrown over the back fence. Cigarette butts were flicked from a window above us onto our terrace. What was it about the English, and respecting someone's personal space? Maybe it had to do with that ratio of 632 people per square mile compared to six. Maybe that's why they coughed so much. And the post office was always packed. I had a lot to learn.

The husband said we should try to prettify the front area, to dissuade people from using it as their rubbish bin. I bought a plant from the market – it was stolen. I bought a shiny silver rubbish bin – it was stolen. One day we came home and one of our front windows was smashed – the stereo was gone too. And all my favourite CDs, none of the husband's, they didn't want his. We managed to laugh at that.

They didn't steal the damp. It had begun sprouting its insidious spores the week we moved in. We realised the sellers had been canny, scraping the flaking back and painting over it and urging a quick sale before they had to scrape again. Someone told me that Notting Hill was built on mudflats, that there was often dampness and subsidence here. We would have to live with it. We did. We were newly married, and euphoric with it. We could cope.

I much preferred the story of Notting Hill being built on the piggeries. That we lived where they slaughtered the livestock last century and a terrible smell used to emanate from the area. A century later the smell was bliss after the dirty, steely, black-lung taste of Fleet Street. Something was happening to me in Notting Hill, I was uncurling, relaxing, walking taller.

I was loving playing in history in this land.

I was loving the fractious energy of London, the dynamism of being in such a vast metropolis now that I had my sanctuary to return to each night. I felt like I was finally living *in* the world, rather than on the edge of it.

And after two long years of living in England, I was making friends.

The key

'To be fair to the English,' said a Kiwi who'd been in the UK about the same time as me, 'maybe they don't befriend us because they don't think it's worth it. Maybe they think we're just here for six months, or a year at the most, so they can't be bothered. It's only perhaps when they sense that we're making an effort to stay, and like it, that they extend themselves. Maybe that's the key for us – sticking it out.'

'The English will keep you at a distance,' said an American film director, 'until you speak up and give it back to them. Then they know they can't intimidate you and they respect you for it. And after that they're rock solid, loyal friends.'

Rock solid, loyal friends. Suddenly we were making them around Notting Hill. When our flat was flooded because of a dodgy plumber renovating the bathroom above us, we had a daisy chain of neighbours helping us rescue our books. I was bumping into people I knew, again and again, as I walked up the street. I was talking to English people. We were getting invitations to dinners and readings and parties. And we didn't have to take the bus to them or the tube, we could walk.

'It just takes time,' said the husband.

'And Notting Hill. I feel like I'm back in a community again.'

'Yeah, maybe that. And maybe it's just you. Maybe your attitude has changed.'

'Yeah, perhaps.'

What I love about Notting Hill

That I walk up the road to post a letter, and come back with a chair.

That I know the lady at the fruit stall on Portobello Road who sells me mangoes and peaches from all over the road, and calls me darlin', no matter how wet and cold the day has been or how long she's been standing out in it.

That our postman is called Terry, and always stops for a chat, and people back in Australia say incredulously: *you know your postman?*

The cherry blossoms in spring, that walking through them as they fall still makes me smile out loud.

That there used to be a racecourse called the Hippodrome around the rim of the hill, and there's a plaque that tells me that.

That there *is* a hill. I love the dynamism of places that aren't flat.

That I once saw a squirrel in our garden.

That the rubbish in our front entrance doesn't get to me anymore.

That the Nu-Line hardware stores are just up the road, and they always have what I need, and suggest canny things that I didn't even know I need, but do.

That there's a cool cinema within walking distance, right near a great second-hand bookstore, right by a good coffee place.

That the smoothie shop opened.

That pastries on a Saturday morning, from the green-awninged deli, have become a garden ritual.

That the silvery eucalyptus in our backyard, with its startling colour against the English *greens*, is thriving.

That one of my favourite pastimes is sunbaking on a warm weekend, with the ten national newspapers of this land, on a rug in our backyard, *on the grass.*

That I don't know the service station man, but I do know the people in the deli, and the woman in the plate-painting shop, and the vintage clothing store.

That I've started being invited into English people's houses.

And no, I'm not about to leave.

Sources and Further Reading

Ackroyd, Peter, *London: The Biography*, Chatto & Windus 2000

Adams, Eddie (ed.), *Westbourne Grove in Wealth, Work and Welfare*, Gloucester Court Reminiscence Group 2000

Amis, Martin, *The Information*, HarperCollins 1995; *Money*, Cape 1984

Athill, Diana, *Stet*, Granta 2000

Barlay, Nick, *Crumple Zone*, Sceptre 2000

Begbie, Harold, *Broken Earthenware*, Hodder and Stoughton 1909

Chesterton, GK *The Napoleon of Notting Hill*, 1904; *Autobiography*, Hutchinson 1936

Coke, Lady Mary, *Lady Mary Coke Letters and Journals 1756–1774*, Kingsmead Reprints, Bath 1970

Curtis, Richard, *Notting Hill*, Hodder and Stoughton 1999

Da Costa, Rosalind, 'Growing Up in Notting Hill', *Notting Hill Revealed*,

mynottinghill.co.uk 2000

Denny, Barbara, *Notting Hill and Holland Park Past*, Historical Publications Ltd. 1993

Monica Dickens, *An Open Book*, Heinemann 1938

Dirsztay, Patricia, *Church Furnishings: A NADFAS guide*, Routledge & Kegan Paul 1978

Donald, Anabel, *The Glass Ceiling*, Macmillan 1994

Duncan, Andrew, *Taking on the Motorway: North Kensington Amenity Trust 21 Years*, Kensington & Chelsea Community History Group 1992; *Walking London*, New Holland 1997

Ellen, Barbara, 'Still fighting the bad guys', Interview with Caroline Coon, *Observer Review*, 30 July 2000

Gladstone, Florence and Barker, Ashley, *Notting Hill in Bygone Days*, Anne Bingley 1969 (1924)

Gordon, P, *White Law: Racism in the police, courts and prisons*, Pluto Press 1983

Green, Jonathan, *Days in the Life: Voices from the English Underground 1961–1971*, Heinemann 1988/Pimlico 1998

Hardy, Justine, *Goat*, John Murray 2000

Hayter, Alethea, *A Sultry Month*, Faber 1965

Heath-Stubbs, John, *Collected Poems 1943–1987*, Carcanet 1988

The Historic Buildings Board of The Greater London Council, *Survey of London XXXVII: Northern Kensington*, University of London, The Athlone Press 1973

Hodgson, Vere, *Few Eggs and No Oranges*, Persephone Books 1999

Horovitz, Michael, 'Notting Hill Carnival Poem' from *Wordsounds and Sightlines: New and Selected Poems*, Sinclair-Stevenson 1994

James, Henry, *The Wings of the Dove*, 1902

James, PD, *A Taste for Death*, Faber 1986

Jephcott, Pearl, *A Troubled Area: Notes on Notting Hill*, Faber 1964

Jones, Richard, *Walking Haunted London*, New Holland 1999

Keeler, Christine and Thompson, Douglas, *The Truth At Last: My Story*, Sidgwick, 2001

Kennedy, Ludovic, *10 Rillington Place*, Gollancz 1961

Kindersley, Tania, *Goodbye Johnny Thunders*, Hodder Headline 1996

Kureishi, Hanif, *Sammy & Rosie Get Laid*, Faber & Faber 1988

Kurtz, Irma, *Dear London: Notes from the big city*, Fourth Estate 1997

Lancaster, Osbert, *All Done from Memory*, John Murray 1953

Lewis, Wyndham, *Rotting Hill*, Black Sparrow 1951

Logue, Christopher, *Prince Charming*, Faber 1999

Low, Crail and Minto, Lucy (compilers and editors), *Rock & Pop London: The Handbook guide*, Handbook Publishing 1997

Machen, Arthur, *Things Near and Far*, 1923; *Far Off Things*, Secker 1922

MacInnes, Colin, *Absolute Beginners*, Allison & Busby 1959

Mayne, Roger, *Photographs*, Jonathan Cape 2001

Mitchell, Leslie, *Holland House*, Duckworth 1980

Moorcock, Michael, *King of the City*, Scribner 2000

Neville, Richard, *Hippie, Hippie Shake*, Bloomsbury 1995

Oliver, Paul (ed.), *Black Music in Britain*, Open University Press 1990

Phillips, Charlie and Phillips, Trevor, *Notting Hill in the Sixties*, Lawrence & Wishart 1991

Phillips, Mike and Phillips, Trevor, *Windrush: The irresistible rise of multi-racial Britain*, HarperCollins 1998

Raban Jonathan, *Soft City*, Hamish Hamilton 1974

Read, Piers Paul, *A Season in the West*, Secker 1988

Richardson, Anthony, *Nick of Notting Hill – The bearded policeman*, Harrap 1965

Rous, Lady Henrietta (ed.), *The Ossie Clark Diaries*, Bloomsbury 1998

Selvon, Samuel, *The Lonely Londoners*, Alan Wingate 1956/Longman 1985

Seth, Vikram, *An Equal Music*, Orion 1999

Shakespeare, Nicholas, *Londoners*, Sidgwick & Jackson 1986

Shaw, Henry, *Notting Hill Synagogue* 1900–1960

Sherriff, RC, *The Hopkins Manuscript*, Victor Gollancz 1939

Sinclair, Iain, *Lights Out for the Territory*, Granta 1997

Soremekun, Sarah, *Portobello: Its people, its past, its present*

Tennant, Emma, *Burnt Diaries*, Canongate 1999

Vague, Tom, *Entrance to Hipp: An historical and psychogeographical report on Notting Hill*, Vague 29, 1997; *London Psychogeography*, Vague 30, 1998; *The Grove*, unpublished manuscript (ongoing)

Waugh, Teresa, *The Gossips*, Sinclair-Stevenson 1995

Wells HG, *Love and Mr Lewisham*, London 1900

Whetlor, Sharon, *The Story of Notting Dale: From Potteries and Piggeries to present times*, Kensington & Chelsea Community History Group1998

Whetlor, Sharon and Bartlett, Liz, *Portobello, its People, its Past, its Present*, Kensington & Chelsea Community History Group 1996

Copyright Acknowledgements

Extract from *All Done from Memory* by Osbert Lancaster reprinted by permission of John Murray

Extract from *Prince Charming* by Christopher Logue. Published by Faber & Faber. © Christopher Logue 1999

Extract from *Far off Things* by Arthur Machen (Copyright © Estate of Arthur Machen) reproduced by permission of AM Heath & Co Ltd on behalf of Janet Pollock as the Literary Executor of the Estate

Extract from *Absolute Beginners* by Colin MacInnes reprinted by kind permission of Allison & Busby. Copyright © 2000 the Estate of Colin MacInnes

Extract from *Black Music in Britain*, Oliver, Paul (ed.) by Anthony Marks

Extract from *King of the City* by Michael Moorcock reprinted by permission of the author. © Michael Moorcock and Linda Moorcock, 2000

Extract from *Hippie Hippie Shake* by Richard Neville reprinted with permission of Bloomsbury. Copyright © 1995 Richard Neville

Extract from *Windrush* by Mike Phillips and Trevor Phillips reprinted with permission of HarperCollins. © Mike Phillips and Trevor Phillips 1998

Extract from *Soft City* by Jonathan Raban reprinted by permission of the author. Copyright © Jonathan Raban 1974

Extract from *The Lonely Londoners* by Sam Selvon. Copyright © Samuel Selvon 1956

Extract from *Londoners* by Nicholas Shakespeare reprinted with permission of the author. Copyright © Nicholas Shakespeare 1986

Extract from *Lights Out for the Territory* by Iain Sinclair published by Granta. Copyright © 1997 Iain Sinclair

Extract from *Burnt Diaries* by Emma Tennant reprinted with permission from Canongate. Copyright © Emma Tennant 1999

Tom Vague *Entrance to Hipp: An historical and psychogeographical report on Notting Hill*, Vague 29, 1997; *London Psychogeography*, Vague 30, 1998; The Grove, unpublished manuscript (ongoing) Copyright © Tom Vague

Extract from *The Gossips* by Teresa Waugh reprinted with permission of the author. Copyright © Teresa Waugh 1995

Extract from *Love and Mr Lewisham* reprinted with permission of AP Watt Ltd on behalf of the Literary Executors of HG Wells

Extract from *Portobello: Its people, its past, its present* by Sharon Whetlor and Liz Bartlett © 1996 Kensington & Chelsea Community History Group

Index

216
England &co